Asian E
in Am

Asian Refugees in America

Narratives of Escape and Adaptation

ELEANOR HERZ SWENT

Foreword by Judy Yung

McFarland & Company, Inc., Publishers

Jefferson, North Carolina, and London

LIBRARY OF CONGRESS CATALOGUING-IN-PUBLICATION DATA

Swent, Eleanor H. (Eleanor Herz)
    Asian refugees in America : narratives of escape and
adaptation / Eleanor Herz Swent ; foreword by Judy Yung.
        p.   cm.
    Includes bibliographical references and index.

    ISBN 978-0-7864-6339-8
    softcover : 50# alkaline paper ∞

    1. Refugees — United States.   2. Refugees — Asia.
3. Asian Americans.   I. Title.
HV640.4.U54S94   2011
305.9'06914095 — dc23   2011028198

BRITISH LIBRARY CATALOGUING DATA ARE AVAILABLE

© 2011 Eleanor Herz Swent. All rights reserved

No part of this book may be reproduced or transmitted in any form
or by any means, electronic or mechanical, including photocopying
or recording, or by any information storage and retrieval system,
without permission in writing from the publisher.

On the cover: Mr. and Mrs. Chin and H.S. Ting (in black)
from the Oakland Adult Day School ESL class at the Golden
Gate Bridge, San Francisco, California, May 1981 (photograph
by Eleanor Swent); map © 2011 Shutterstock

Manufactured in the United States of America

McFarland & Company, Inc., Publishers
    Box 611, Jefferson, North Carolina 28640
    www.mcfarlandpub.com

To my children, who were fortunate
enough to be born in the U.S.A.

ACKNOWLEDGMENTS

I am indebted most of all to the narrators who entrusted me with their stories, in the hope that they would be faithfully transmitted. If I have failed them in any way, I beg their forgiveness. I owe thanks to Judy Yung, Professor Emerita at the University of California at Santa Cruz, who advised and encouraged this project from the beginning. My fellow teachers at the Chinese Community Center, Ann Baxley, Helen McCully, Mary Soo-Hoo, and Noeline Tam have helped me, and I am ever grateful to the late Ed Shands, principal of the Neighborhood Centers, for enabling me to join his faculty. Colleagues at the Regional Oral History Office at The Bancroft Library, University of California at Berkeley, Laura McCreery and the late Willa K. Baum, gave professional guidance. Helen Chu Buckholtz assisted with the Cambodian interview. My late husband, Langan Swent, inspired me; he was a decorated veteran of World War II, with a deep life-long concern for international understanding and peace, as well as safety in the work place. We first visited China in 1978 with a delegation from the United Nations Association of San Francisco, thanks to Richard Gray, founder of World College West. My children and other friends and colleagues have also encouraged me; I cannot list them all, but I believe they know how grateful I am.

TABLE OF CONTENTS

FOREWORD BY JUDY YUNG

I have known Eleanor "Lee" Swent for over 30 years. As the librarian of the Asian Branch Library in Oakland, California, I used to make bookmobile stops at the Oakland Chinese Community Center, where she taught English as a Second Language (ESL) to recent immigrants. The Vietnam War had just ended, and Oakland was experiencing a large influx of Southeast Asian refugees. As educators and civil servants, we shared the responsibility of helping them learn English and acculturate to American life. I soon discovered that we also shared an interest in recording and preserving the stories of Chinese immigrants. Lee was conducting oral history interviews with recent refugees from China and Southeast Asia while I was doing the same with older Chinese immigrants who had once been detained at the Angel Island Immigration Station. This common interest in oral history as well as our participation in the activities of the Chinese Historical Society of America kept our friendship alive through the years.

How did it come about that a white, middle-class woman who had grown up in the mining town of Lead, South Dakota, and been educated at Wellesley College, would become interested in the lives and stories of Asian refugees? Lee thinks it probably all began with her father, who graduated from Yale University in 1908, at a time when many students from China were attending Yale on Boxer Indemnity scholarships.[1] As a result, her father developed an interest in China, which he passed on to Lee at an early age. Then while attending Wellesley College in the 1940s, Lee's good friend turned out to be Alice C. Sze, the daughter of the Chinese ambassador. She reinforced Lee's interest in Chinese culture and history.

After earning her master's degree in English from Denver University, Marrying Langan Swent, a mining engineer, raising a family of four children, and traveling all over the world, Lee was ready to embark on a teaching career in 1967. To her delight, she was assigned to teach advanced English at the Chinese Community Center in Oakland's Chinatown, where many of the students were recent immigrants form Asian countries. Lee proved to be not only a capable ESL teacher, but also a social worker, friend, and confidante to certain students

1

as well. Lee would help them find work and housing, get driving licenses, and deal with the police. And at times, she even helped nurse the sick and comfort the bereft. Her students began to open up and tell her these horrendous stories of how they had fled war, poverty, and political persecution in their homelands to come to America. She was so moved and shocked by their stories that Lee felt compelled to begin tape-recording them after class with the intention of preserving the stories for posterity and someday getting them published. She was well equipped to do so, having completed two oral history classes at the local junior colleges and participated in an Oakland community history project with Willa Baum, noted oral historian. With their willing cooperation and the guarantee that she would keep their identities secret for fear of political reprisals, Lee was able to interview a total of 40 students, index the taped recordings, and deposit them in the oral history archives at the Bancroft Library.

In 1986, Lee was recruited by Willa Baum to work as a specialist in mining history for the Regional Oral History Office at the Bancroft Library. She left her teaching job and spent the next 20 years conducting oral history interviews with over 100 significant people in California mining history before retiring in 2004. Through the years, she stayed in touch with some of her former students and did not forget her commitment to get their stories published and more widely read. While looking for a publisher, she re-interviewed nine of her former students about details concerning their journeys to America and the outcomes of their lives in America. They were glad to cooperate because, as one of them said, "We want to let people know what we have been through and what we have achieved here."

Although many recollections of Asian immigrants and refugees have been published in recent years, Eleanor Herz Swent's *Asian Refugees in America: Narratives of Escape and Adaptation* offers the less-told stories of Chinese men and women who escaped political persecution during the Cultural Revolution by swimming across the ocean to Macao. It is astonishing to learn that some of them did not even know how to swim. But by tying nylon satchels or inflatable balls to their bodies, they managed to stay afloat. There were known cases of strong swimmers who were able to tow their girlfriends through the cold, shark-infested waters to Hong Kong. "It took six hours and he was very tired, the most tired he had ever been in his life," reported Swent. Others like Lee Chung prepared for two years before making the attempt. The son of a former landowner, he had been denied an education and assigned to labor in the rice fields. He saw no future for himself living under Mao Zedong's Communist regime. "Give me freedom. I am a person," he said as he risked his life and the welfare of his family to swim his way out of China.

The most harrowing stories in this book deal with the hardships of Southeast Asian refugees who escaped Communist rule by boat after the Vietnam War ended. It is to Swent's credit that she was able to record these stories soon after they arrived in America and again two decades later, often with updates of their lives in America during the intervening years. Take the case of Be Thi, whom she first interviewed in 1981. Tears streaming down her face, she told teacher Swent of the agonizing boat trip from Vietnam to Indonesia— 600 people crammed into a small boat, seven days without food, robbed and beaten by Malaysian pirates — and almost being starved to death in a refugee camp, where she and her two young daughters slept under the sky without medicine or cover. But her hardships did not end there. After resettling in Oakland with her husband, she tells Lee in subsequent interviews of having their home burglarized and grocery store robbed by black neighbors, their sewing factory extorted by Vietnamese gangs, and her labor as a housekeeper exploited by white employers. On top of these difficulties, she was constantly worried about her family in Vietnam and about the trouble she was having being accepted as a Vietnamese daughter-in-law by her husband's Chinese family, especially when she had failed three times to bear a son. Life in America became so stressful, that Be Thi tried to commit suicide. But for the sake of her three daughters, she persevered and worked hard so that by the final interview in 2005, Be Thi had repaid the $4,000 loan for her passage to America and earned the love and respect of her children, her in-laws, and her employers.

Through these stories of flight, freedom, and suffering as told to and by Eleanor Swent, we can come to a deeper understanding of the horrors of war, political oppression, and man's inhumanity to man. At the same time, we can begin to appreciate these immigrants' abilities to survive and overcome adversity. Many of them credit luck for their survival and the generous assistance of the U.S. government for their successful resettlement, but listening to their stories carefully, we can denote other factors as well — intelligence, courage, perseverance, religion, family ties, and a strong determination to begin life anew and work hard to achieve the American dream.

Judy Yung is a professor emerita of American studies, University of California, Santa Cruz, and the author of Angel Island: Immigrant Gateway to America.

PREFACE

In the same month that I gave away our high chair, July 1966, Mao Zedong, premier of China, drew a poster with large letters saying "Revolution Is Justified." These two events, one highly personal and one affecting more than a billion people on the other side of the world, intersected a few months later in Oakland, California. When I was no longer a full-time mother, I began to teach English as a Second Language (ESL) to adults. At the same time, Mao's poster had launched the Great Proletarian Cultural Revolution that ravaged China for ten years, propelling landowners, merchants, and scholars to flee, many of them to California, where they had to learn English.

In January 1967 I was assigned to teach in the Chinese Community Center, in the heart of Oakland Chinatown. A two-story concrete block building, drab except for an "Oriental" entry with a red tile roof curved upward at the corners, and a small bamboo garden, it had been built by Chinese-American merchants to house classes for their children to learn Chinese language and culture on weekdays after American school and on Saturdays. Each classroom had blackboards and a padlocked cupboard for supplies, and could comfortably hold 35 desk-chairs, or ten more when crowded. The Oakland Adult School rented the facility for free daytime ESL classes for adult refugees, holding a "white card," and immigrants, with a "green card." A few had little schooling; some were well educated in more than one language. They were a barometer of political oppression: a surge of arrivals from any particular country would soon be followed by news of an uprising there. On registration day applicants lined up around the block, and as the classes were filled, teachers were sometimes offered bribes if they would accept more students. We turned them down, of course, and this was the first lesson for some newcomers to learn.

In 1967 the students included Korean and Japanese wives of American servicemen; Iranian refugees from the recent revolution; Thai ladies keeping house for their college student children; and Portuguese, Polish, Mexican, and Chinese men who left at mid-morning to go to work as dishwashers and busboys in restaurants. Shortly before this, in 1965, the U.S. immigration

ESL students line up on registration day at the Chinese Community Center, Oakland, California, September, 1980.

laws had been changed to define eligibility by hemisphere; this allowed an influx of ethnic Chinese newcomers from Cuba, Latin America, and the Pacific Islands. For them the designation of the classes as English as a Second Language was a misnomer, as they already knew one or more dialects of Chinese, as well as Spanish, Portuguese, or French.

The founders of the Chinese Community Center were loyal to the non–Communist Republic of China, and the school was always closed to celebrate its national day, October 10, or "Double Ten,"[1] 1911. The gymnasium/basketball court/multipurpose room was off-limits to us except when we were honored guests at the Thanksgiving dinner held on the Saturday before the official holiday. This was well attended by the leaders of the Chinese community and teachers from both adult and Chinese schools. Outstanding students, with their parents, from the children's school were introduced and praised. Long, earnest speeches given in Chinese and translated into English extolled freedom and compared the new immigrants to the American Pilgrims. The buffet dinner included chow mien as well as roast turkey.

Americans have traditionally had their historical and cultural roots in Europe, and looking from there toward Asia, spoke of the "Far East" and "the Orient." Now we are shifting to face the Pacific Ocean and a Far West beyond the shores of California.[2] The newcomers from there have crossed a much wider ocean than the Atlantic, geographically and culturally. They differ from most previous immigrants in bringing longer histories and different writing systems, new foods and ways of eating.

Chinese is written with characters, which represent words or ideas, not sounds. Educated Chinese know thousands of written characters, and can communicate in writing with each other, although they may speak languages differing as much as German from English or Italian from Swedish. The spoken languages are tonal, causing extra difficulty for Chinese persons learning English, who listen attentively for rising or falling inflections, and hear them as different words. There are various systems for translating Chinese spoken words into English; for example, the capital city used to be called Peking, and now is Beijing. The province from which most émigrés have come to America used to be called Canton; now it is Guangdong, and the principal city, formerly Canton, is Guangzhou. Their language is commonly called Cantonese. In Vietnam and Cambodia, many Chinese people came from the district of Chaoshan and speak the Teochew or Chiu Chow dialect. Thus the narrator Phuong, in order to find work here in Chinatown, needed to learn not only English, but also a different dialect of Chinese.

The Vietnamese refugees had an initial advantage over the Chinese in learning to read and write English. Vietnam was formerly a French colony, so most Vietnamese had some familiarity with the French language. Under the French colonial rule, until World War II, a classical education consisted

The re-named Shoong Family Chinese Cultural Center, Oakland, 2010, formerly the Chinese Community Center.

of three languages and methods of writing. First was the French language, written with the alphabet familiar to all Europeans. The second was the Vietnamese or national language, written in a system called *quoc ngu,* developed in the 17th century by Father Alexandre de Rhodes, a Roman Catholic scholar and missionary. He transliterated the Vietnamese language into the alphabet, extending it with various diacritical marks. Since the writing closely follows the usage, it is relatively easy to learn. The third language, which Mr. Tran calls "Chinese letter," is no longer emphasized in Vietnamese education. Called *chu nom,* or Southern writing, it dates from the battle of Hanoi. Although they were a vassal state of China, the Vietnamese retained their distinct culture and showed their independence by continuing to write their own language while using Chinese characters.

Naming is a practical system, where families are large and complex. An individual is immediately identified by family and by generation. The family name comes first, as if we said "Washington George." Siblings have a common generational name, helpful in the case of a large family where the oldest siblings might have younger siblings of about the same age as their own children. Persons are commonly referred to by relationship, rather than by a personal name: older brother, younger sister, father's sister, etc. The personal name may be propitious, or attractive, like "flower" or "fortune." The idea of naming a child for another person is appalling and never done.

As a bride, I had lived for seven years in Mexico, and although safe and

Typical old house in Oakland Chinatown, 2010.

well cared for, I had also known the distress of feeling mute and incompetent in a strange culture, which gave me a special empathy with the newcomers. As I came to know my students, both in the adult school and in the ESL program for refugees and immigrants at the campuses of the Peralta Community College, I knew that their stories of fear and flight were important historically and should be preserved. Beginning in 1970, and continuing to 2004, I conducted interviews. At first I asked some of the students to stay after class and speak with a tape recorder. In time, some of them came to my home on a weekend or in the evening and brought companions to recount experiences that they considered especially significant. On some occasions, I went to their homes and recorded the stories of their friends or relatives. One man who realized he was making history had documented on flattened C-ration cartons the details of his escape from Vietnam; he was particularly grateful to have it preserved for posterity. Some, like Louisa and Ruth, came to me and wanted to express and explain their happiness in a new culture. The interviews were one or two hours long, and the subjects were given the transcripts to approve. Two women requested changes, which were made.

All of the refugees were eager to share their experiences, to tell how and why they came to America, often at great risk. Some still feared reprisal for themselves or families still in China or Vietnam and did not want their names to be used; others willingly told me their stories while I took notes, but were reluctant to have them recorded on tape. When I told them that the tapes

Morning Tai Chi and Chi Gong (traditional exercises) in Oakland Chinatown, 2010.

would be deposited in the archives at the University of California–Berkeley, a few were frightened; they had heard that there were Communists there. Most of them accepted my assurance that they would not be endangered, and so their interviews are available for research there at the Bancroft Library. Some of the interviews led to years of friendship as we continued to meet and document their experiences.

The first narrators came from China during the terrible years of the Great Proletarian Cultural Revolution when schools were closed and scholars and merchants were forced to "learn from the masses," as Mao exhorted them, by working in the fields as peasants. Lee Chung, who says, "Give me a freedom. I am a person," was one of hundreds who swam for hours in the ocean to escape from this oppression. Later newcomers came from Vietnam and Cambodia; many had been refugees once or even twice before: fleeing from China when the Japanese invaded during what we call World War II, known to them as the Sino-Japanese War; from North to South Vietnam after the partition of 1954[3]; and now to America, arriving stripped of status, without work, nationality, or language, but still sane and dignified. In 1975, the Pacific Bell Telephone directory for Oakland listed no residents named Huynh, Nguyen, or Tran. In 2003 the directory showed more than 150 Huynh listings; and one and a half pages of seven columns each, about a thousand listings, for Nguyen, A to Yung; over five hundred Trans, from An to Xe.

Mr. Tran, formerly a high-ranking army officer in Vietnam, briskly introduces himself: "I am descended from General Tran who defeated Kublai Khan at the Battle of Hanoi in 1220." My mind reels; I can only think of the Samuel Coleridge poem, "In Xanadu did Kubla Khan a stately pleasure dome decree." Mr. Tran continues, jumping over more than seven centuries, "Since then we do a special kind of martial exercise in my town." He pauses and quietly comes to the present: "But now, since 1954, we cannot do that exercise anymore. My brother had the genealogy book, but unfortunately we cannot bring it along. It is since a long time and thousands, thousands of names. It is a kind of precious heritage." By preserving their recollections now, the newcomers begin to restore and repair that precious heritage. They want their stories known, by their children and also by their new American neighbors, even though in some cases they ruled out attaching their real names or photos.

These various recollections imply crucial questions: Separated from your country, your work, and the language you speak, how do you define yourself? How could anyone dare to leave his native land? Where does one find the strength to endure? How do you tell your children what your life has been like? One of the heaviest burdens of the newcomers, as for many European immigrants before them, and indeed for any American parents, is to convince their descendants that freedom must not be taken for granted, and that forebears should not be forgotten. As these remarkable new Americans learn different words and customs, they also enlarge our national vision, enriching our culture while assuring us that human dignity can rise above terrible circumstances. Mr. Dang, who left Vietnam in a boat, says, "I think my self [*and he says it in two words: my self*] is very valuable."

1

NEWCOMERS FROM CHINA

Swimmers

I Come from China by Swimming

"I come from China by swimming," says Joe Chow, and he is not joking; he is earnest and repeats, "I come from China by swimming, but I cannot swim." This is 1970, and Joe is learning English as a Second Language in the adult school in Chinatown, Oakland, California. The old men in the class are narrow-shouldered, wearing faded dark blue cotton[1]; they sit in the back seats, never looking into the eyes of the teacher, writing slowly with pencils held upright like brushes.[2] Tired from working late at night in restaurants or as janitors, they practice dutifully the patterns of a strange language — not "I to school come" but "I come to school." A few younger ones, like Joe, wearing new nylon jogging suits, have broad shoulders and sit at the front of the room, tense and eager to learn, trying a variation, "I come to school by bus," "I come to school by car," and "I come by swimming."

Others in the class help to piece together Joe's story: he is one of the hundreds, perhaps even thousands, of young people who swam to Hong Kong and Macao during the "Great Proletarian Cultural Revolution," beginning in 1966 and lasting for a decade, when schools in China were closed and families of teachers and landowners were persecuted. Henry Leong says that of his high school class in the Sze Yup Districts of Guangdong Province, 50 percent attempted this escape, and he thinks 50 percent of those succeeded. If they managed to avoid the village patrol of informers and police, armed with guns and dogs, then they had to swim through shark-infested waters. If they arrived first at Macao, the swimmers fell into a well-established system of cruel shakedowns before they could find sanctuary in Hong Kong.

Most of the swimmers, like Joe, did not really know how to swim. They tied something to their bodies for buoyancy: not a genuine life vest, which would attract suspicion, but commonly a rig of a nylon jacket or satchel and some kind of inflatable ball. No one will ever know how many swimmers

13

drowned because of misplaced confidence in these makeshift contrivances. Most of the swimmers kept their plans a secret to prevent reprisal against their families. Wing Lee's family had two bicycles, which made them relatively affluent; he had to abandon one in his escape attempt, and the other was confiscated by authorities as punishment for his defection.

Lena's parents took her with them and escaped in a small boat, but her brother had to swim; it took him eighteen hours, and his legs were swollen like this: she holds out her hands to indicate a diameter of more than a foot. She knew a girl who was in the water for more than two days and nights, was nearly dead when she finally reached shore, and had to be hospitalized for a week.

Philip, now an assistant cook at one of the best waterfront restaurants, was an exception: a good swimmer. Every morning he practices tai chi, a traditional Chinese exercise; he says he is also good at kung fu. Because of his exceptional ability, he towed his girlfriend. It took six hours, and he was very tired, the most tired he had ever been in his life. Still, he feels he was lucky; the girlfriend married him. One of his friends towed a girl who ran off with someone else once they reached Hong Kong.

Paul is now a busboy at a fashionable restaurant. The starched white collar of his uniform almost covers an ugly scar on his neck. He and three schoolmates swam from China together, planning for a time when the moon was dark and the tides ebbing. They went in the summer when the water is warm. He couldn't see the sharks when they came, and he was the only one of the four to make it to freedom.

Bill planned his escape for two years, never telling his family, so they could not be implicated. He traveled with two others, walking for eight days from his village to the shore. They carried balls of rice mixed with oil and sugar, and ate nothing for the first two days, so they had enough for the entire journey. Once they were chased by a soldier who had a gun but no dog. One day while hiding in bushes, they heard terrible screams from a young girl who was caught by a soldier and dogs. He thinks she was killed; he dreams of this at night and hears her screams again. He is a good swimmer, so he swam the distance, about four miles, in four hours with no aid. Using a rope, he towed a friend who was a nonswimmer and held a basketball. They chose an August night when the water was warm, and they saw no sharks, but when they reached the shore there were oyster beds, which cut his feet. The friend wore tennis shoes and ran off, leaving Bill to stumble on bleeding feet the final half mile. He says, "If I know he do that, I cut the rope in the middle of swimming."

In Berkeley, relatives and friends gather at the home of Alice, a graduate of Sarah Lawrence, wife of a post-doctoral fellow, and mother of a month-old baby. The house is redolent of pig's feet and ginger, traditional Chinese dish for nursing mothers, which her cousin Kenny is cooking for her, although she seems somewhat dubious of its value. Kenny's father and uncles graduated from Yale and Harvard Medical School, returned to China, and were oppressed as "followers of the capitalist road." Kenny, faced with a bleak future, left China before finishing high school. He and his girlfriend, later his wife, swam together, twice. The first time, they were with a group of classmates and were captured by the police. She was freed after a long interrogation, and he was sentenced to hard labor for two months. They tried again to escape, the two of them alone, and succeeded. They share an apartment in San Francisco with two young men who also swam. Kenny has just completed cook's training under a program for refugees; he is very thin, but he says he has gained 20 pounds since he arrived.

In Hong Kong, an American-educated Chinese businessman scoffs at the swimmers. He calls them renegades who can't accept discipline or abide by laws, and who cause trouble on the mainland and in the Crown Colony; he says that is why the Chinese authorities have allowed so many of them to escape. The swimmers all say they escaped to find freedom and education. There are stories within these stories: a swimmer betrayed by a girl after he tows her to Hong Kong; a mother punished for her son's defection by forfeiting their bicycle and being told he is dead; a father who lives alone in America for 60 years, sending money to his wife in China; a kind stranger in Macao who buys slippers for a barefoot boy. Wing Lee runs for six hours from a villager, and later thinks it wasn't necessary: "They could stop us, but maybe they don't because they don't want to hurt their conscience." Lee Chung is exasperated by a girl in Hong Kong who chooses not to finish school when it is available. It is hard to imagine the courage or the desperation that impels someone to wade into the ocean on a dark night, clutching two basketballs.

To Take Care the Old Man

Wing Lee has a Confucian[3] motivation for swimming: his father escaped from China 19 years before, and his mother tells the son it is his duty to join his father and take care of him as he grows old. Six months after he arrived in the United States, he wrote this essay in the ESL class; his English is imperfect, but the idea is clear:

My Family's Brief Summary

I have five members in my family. There are my father, mother, one sister, one brother, and me. From the physical appearance. Here the difference between us. My sister and brother had taller stature like my mother's. I had the short stature like my father's. But I am very regret because under restraint by the circumstance we separated in two parts. My father and I in United States. The rest of my family in China. So I hope someday the whole world can unify together like one family, the people expect to anywhere they can do at any time.

He is interviewed in 1978 at the community college, where he studies data processing. He is about five feet three inches tall, slender, with an angular face, and very stiff short hair. There is a dark mole on one cheekbone. At first he trembles with nervousness, but gradually this passes, and he becomes fluent, even using occasional expressive gestures. "I trust you," he says, and he wants to tell his story, but not to use his real name. His father, hidden in a boat, left China just before the Great Leap Forward, in August, 1957.[4] He left his wife, a daughter almost four; Wing Lee, two; and a baby still unborn. Eventually he made his way to Oakland, where his brother had a grocery store, of which he is now part owner. For 18 years the family in China received monthly checks and letters from him. They lived in a large two-story house made of yellow earth, tamped and molded into blocks. They had their own vegetable garden. When Wing Lee was ten, they began applying for him to join his father, but the application was denied each time. After waiting nearly ten years, his mother told him, "We must reach our goal, to take care the old man." His story:

I left my house at two A.M. on August 6, 1975. I tried to sleep before that, and I was in bed, but I cannot sleep. I said goodbye to my mother, just took her hand. She didn't go to bed, just stay up by the altar, praying. I can't see if she is crying because we don't have the light because we don't want other people to see. We have electric light, but don't want anyone to see. The village doesn't have police, just militia, the people of the village. I took a bag like a flight bag, with two basketballs, some food, and some medicine. Just some medicine against the snake, and some balls of fried rice, and some peanuts.

[*First he and his three trusted friends went to the temple to pray for a few minutes, burning incense and "spirit money."[5]*] It is just ordinary paper, but it is to supplicate God to defend us. My mother bought it, but that's illegal, because the Chinese government right now destroyed all the temples, but at that time, the temple was still not destroyed. We prayed to the God called Gun Yam [*Guan Yin, goddess of mercy*], just for a few minutes.

Then we rode our bicycles on the freeway about one and one half-hours to the mountains. This is the freeway from Canton to Macao; it is the yellow soil, and on the two sides has trees, very beautiful. This is forbidden land; it is forbidden to go there. And we went far away [*far apart*], and if the first one have trouble, the last one would withdraw. I had seen this highway just one time, when we went to analyze the situation. Many villages by the road, and a militia station; they carry a gun and cross-examine people. We wear sport shirt and pants, and not shoes, only slippers, so we look just like farm boys, and they don't stop us. And on top of the bag, it has several bunches of bok choy [*green vegetables*] and a very old apron on top, too. So I think I have fooled them. If they stop me and look at the two basketballs, I will go to jail. So then we got through the forbidden land, and to the mountain, and rode up a very steep slant. We go up the mountain and down the hill, and by the side has pretty big forests. We sneak into the forest and throw away the bicycle. That hurt a lot, sure, because very valuable. We didn't get any tired then because when we think about Hong Kong, very exciting. And we can't sleep because a lot of big mosquitoes. So until night we left the forest and get to another mountain. We just stay in the forest all day, and then after about 20 minutes, we crossed a big terrain, no people live there, just patrols go by on motorcycles, carry guns and have German dogs. That's the first big dangerous. And we saw not a lot of them, but several, and we just stay down flat, and the dogs don't notice us, and we are very careful so the flashlights don't see us. And after we crossed this terrain, we got into another mountain, and in there has a lot of bush. We crossed many mountains; I can't remember how many, up and down. At first we went up to the highest mountain, to look at where is Macao, and we see a brilliant area, and then we have the hope and the direction.

Then on the second day we just hid in the bushes. We had water because the mountain has many creeks. We were not worried about animals because we had knives, and in those mountains there are no tigers. A small animal, like a fox, we can deal with. We thought we had enough food because we planned at first three days, but on this second day we lost the direction. And we walk all the second night, up to north instead of south, until morning. It is all wasted. It is very hard to go up and down the mountains, and we must go like a cow hitting the head to make a way in the bush. Very, very hard.

The third day we stay in the bush, and then suddenly it had a shower, a pretty big storm. We used a plastic raincoat to cover the head. Then a woman, about 40 years old, came out from a village to take care the cow, and she saw us. We try to talk to her, say, "Aunt, if you help us we will give you ten dollars." We had ten dollars. But she just ran back to the village and shouting, "Escapees!" Then we ran all afternoon, about six hours, until five o'clock, to get far from that village. And after, when I am in Hong Kong, I think about that, and those people saw us; they could stop us, but maybe they don't because they don't want to hurt their conscience.

Then we came to where we saw the water, but we cannot get to the edge of the water, because there are police, and now all day we had no food. And we waited until about ten o'clock at night and very carefully got down to the water. We left our clothes, only wore our briefs. We had a plastic bag with new clothes inside. When we bought it, they told us it is waterproof, but when we got to Macao and open it, the clothes inside are wet. But it is strong plastic, and it also can be used to float the body. We have some nylon net to hold together the two basketballs, and we lie on that, so the balls float the body in the water, and also we row with the hands. We swim all night, about six hours or more, until we know it is getting to be morning, and we already saw Macao. It is not far; if we walk, we can get there in about 20 minutes, but then the tide changed, and the water is very strong against us, and we are very tired and hungry, and the water is very cold, and we have no power to go against the water.

We stopped at a small rock island. We were very cold and hungry. Until the morning, we just crawled up on the rock. Then when the sun came out, we hid in the gap of the rocks. Just we caught some fish, and some raw oysters that we could break and eat. We can see China is very close, so we hide in the gap of the rock. And Macao is close, but China is closer. I still have ten dollars, and I ask the one who is the strongest to swim back to the village in China and bring us some food, but he won't do that. And I don't really want him to do that; just I ask him to because I am so hungry. And we see many boats went by, and we call to them and ask them to take us, but they won't. I don't know why they refuse to help us.

Then at night we didn't have any power to go to Macao, so we just went back to the Chinese side, and walked along the edge of the water about 20 minutes, and suddenly we heard the German dog barking and the soldiers fast chased to us. We can still see them in the moonlight, and the dog chased to us, and I with the other guy ran fastly to the water, and the other two guys just let down and let the dogs bite to them, so they were caught. But I found out from someone in Hong Kong that they are alive. They just were in jail for months, and it is not really in jail; just they point a gun at you and make you hard labor, and if you try to stop, they kick you. So this time we went again to Macao, and because this is the delta, here, the tide doesn't have much effect. I don't know how to explain, but we got to Macao in three hours, at 5:50 in the morning.

And by now we are very tired and very hungry. In that part of Macao, the people don't need to work. They just stay home and open the door at night, and they can make a lot of money. They let us in, and they cook food and give it to us and give us dry clothes to put on, and then they say we have to give $2,000, or they will inform to the government. But my friend's brother knows some gangs in Macao, so we send him a letter, and he came to Macao and asked one of the head of those gang to talk to this resident. And then he said, "Okay, forget about the $2,000; just give whatever you want." So we gave him $300 for each. And he will give us 10 days to pay it. When I got to Hong Kong I wrote to my father, and he sent the money.

Then I went by secret boat to Hong Kong. I am not afraid of that because it is a very valuable boat; it is about $100,000, and I know that this man will not do something dangerous because he will not want to lose his boat. And he is very careful. We are inside the boat, in a place with a little window, and they arrange that if there is anything wrong, they will ring a bell, and we go out the window into the water. So we get to Hong Kong okay, and we go to a small gulf where no policemen, and they tell us where to go to get the bus, and we go to a hotel and meet our relatives, and we are safe. In Hong Kong I go to the government office and tell them I escaped from China, and they give me resident I.D. I write to my father, and in three months I can come to the United States. Even in Hong Kong I am safe, but I must be careful, because if I am disorderly, they will send me back to China.

I think they have discriminated against my family in China at first, but now it is finished. They took away the bicycle, and that was important. We had two bicycles, and now they don't have any. They also fined them more than $100. And they took my letters and didn't deliver them. I wrote to my mother and asked her to send my China I.D. card and my diploma that I graduated from high school, and she sent them to me. I think she didn't know for about a month if I was alive or not. And they took away my pay for the work I did. Before I leave — it is August — a few days later it will be payday. Every half year is payday, and I worked almost all the half year. And this half year, all my working points were confiscated, and they didn't give my pay to my family. I graduated from high school in the town. I stayed there during the week and went to my home for the weekend. Then after I graduated, I had to go back to the village and work on the farm. I like to work on the farm; since I was a little boy I liked it, but I want to continue my education.

If I work as hard in the U.S. as I work in China, I could earn $100 a day. In China I work eight, ten hours a day, I must carry very heavy, two hundred pounds, and my pay is 72 cents a day. And one pound of pork is $3.50. Every year they give me a clothes ticket to buy cloth, and then I must take the cloth to a tailor to make the clothes. And there is no allotment for the oil. The farmer must grow his own peanuts and take to the factory for the oil. One hundred pounds peanuts will get 26 or 28 pounds of oil. And the old people who can't work anymore cannot grow the peanut, have no oil, must buy at a very high price. Several villages together are a production brigade, and each village is a production team. Everyone in the village must work for the production team, to grow the rice. And everyone has also a small plantation to grow the vegetables and the peanuts. Before liberation [*in 1949*], my family were very, very poor.[6] I think better now. And the punishment for the crime is according to the status of your family. If you are very poor, just ordinary person, you will be punished lightly, but if before, your family very rich or important, you must be very punished. So I think the Chinese government doesn't plan well, to send everyone to the farm when they finish high school, because to modernize the country, they need people to have education, and after two or three years on the farm, you forget to study. I don't want to defame the Chinese nation; it is a very rich country, but the people doesn't have enough food, and they need to modernize.

So now I am very happy here, and I help my father and my uncle in the grocery store, and I also study very hard. Last semester my grades were four A's and one B. So I hope I can finish the university and study business. I have a lot of respect for my mother. She is a very good mother. Her health is not strong; she is only about 44, but in China that is an old woman because she has to work so hard. But I think she has a very strong character. My father and I get along pretty well. I'm glad I came to help him. I don't know if there's any chance for the rest of my family to come. The Chinese government say they want to reune the families, but I think because my father did that, and because I did that, they will not let them come.

I Am a Person

Richard, another swimmer, has succeeded in America. In 2003 he is the owner of a butcher shop, and his two daughters are university graduates. His English is good, and he speaks with confidence, giving out his business card and his cell phone number. All this is the result of prodigious effort. Twenty-five years earlier, his name was Lee Chung. Although he was a top student, he had been denied schooling in China during the Great Proletarian Cultural Revolution (1966–1976) because his father, an educated landowner, was declared "bad" and out of favor with the officials. Lee Chung left school at 13, and was sent at 15 to work in the rice fields. After studying the Chinese classics at home, he decided, "Give me a freedom. I am a person." Beginning at 16, he trained for his escape for two years by secretly swimming two or three hours every night after midnight. The actual swim seems to have been not too hard for him, except for a severe cut on his leg that took three months to heal. Lee Chung was interviewed first in June 1979, and again 25 years later, when he had changed his name to Richard. This is what Lee Chung recorded on June 22, 1979:

I was born in 1954 in Guangdong, Chung San, Lung Du. My family lived in Lung Du a long time. I have three brothers and one sister, and a father — he was a farmer — and my mother, too. I was the youngest. My sister lives in China, and two brothers live in China, and one brother swam from China to Hong Kong, the same than me. I came earlier; then he came a half year later. My oldest brother studied 12 years; then he is a teacher. My brother after the older brother, he is an engineer. He studied 16 years.

My father worked as a farmer in Lung Du, just everybody all together. We had a private vegetable garden at our house. My father was an important man in the village, I think. In 1966, he was good, but when the time was 1967 and 1968, he was very bad. Now I have a letter from my brother, and he told me that now my father is good again. I am very glad to know that. I know my father is a very good man. He didn't hit a little kid. I knew my father

Richard at his butcher shop, with "lucky bamboo" plants on the meat counter, 2004.

didn't hit me. He didn't hit my brothers and sisters. He didn't loud ask another person. He's a very good man, I know. I heard my mother say, my father had very good. He can sing, he can write, he's very good exercise, too.[7] My father was a bigger man, I think almost six feet. In China, that's very big! And I guess he was almost 200 pounds.

Lung Du was a small village, I think about 40,000.[8] The Japanese didn't come to my village, because it is too small. My father owned a big house, and we grew rice, vegetables, and also fruit. My father did the farm work, and the people together. There were two harvests of rice, in summer and fall, and in spring we harvested vegetables. I didn't ask my mother about [*life before 1949*], because I was afraid to ask my mother. I was afraid to ask my father, too. My house was next to the neighbor's houses. Behind the houses was a very small lake, a pond, very good! Sometimes we had ducks. We had a well; every house had one in the front yard, and also in the back yard. Before 1962 we didn't have electric light. After 1962, every family had electric light, because there was a paper factory near my village, so we got electricity. My mother didn't know what is an electric iron; she just know the iron with the fire inside. She washed my clothes by hand, in the house.

Every house had a toilet, too, a big one, not the same kind you have here. It was also in the back yard. Our house had a front yard, and here's the door. Here's the living room; it had a second floor. Then a bedroom and a hall, and beyond that, another bedroom, and this also had a second floor. The first bedroom is for the father and mother; the second bedroom is for the children. I slept downstairs. Upstairs, over the living, is also to put the books and some other clothes and anything. Not food; extra food is in the kitchen. Behind the bedroom is the kitchen. Maybe it has an upstairs, maybe not. The hall, to go from my mother's bedroom to the kitchen, is outside my bedroom. The hall has no roof; it is open. The hall from the living room to my mother's bedroom has a ceiling. In my bedroom, you can shut the door and sleep. It has a window, too. In my house, it had steps to go upstairs. Sometimes the houses have ladders. In the kitchen, my mother burned rice straw for the fire, and leaves from the trees, from the lichees and the plum trees. Then the back yard has also the ducks, the chickens, the pigs. The toilet is by the place for the pigs or the ducks. Every week, this is cleaned. My mother did that. At home, my mother did everything. My mother said, "A boy outside takes care of everything, but at home, everything is the mother." So my sister, before she got married, she did with my mother, wash the dishes and cook the dinner. Sometimes I helped to carry the water. And my job was to carry the night soil from the toilet to the place to fertilize the vegetables. This was my job.

I was seven years in school, until 13 years. In my class at school, there were 35 in one room, boys or girls together. Each class had two sections, A or B. Not because you were smart or not smart, just if you get good grades.[9] If you get good grades, you are A. If you not, then you are B. I study six years, and six years I was in A. The teacher decided the group, according to the schoolwork.

They told me at the school that I cannot go to school anymore because my father died. [*As the son of a landowner, he was ostracized by the Communists.*] Maybe someone hate my father. When I quit the school, I start to study by myself. I study by myself, and my brother taught me at summer time and vacation. He taught me so I can read anything in books in China. I had to work as a farmer from 15 years. So I study by myself two years at home. I feel very, very bad. I have a question, so I ask my mother, why? Why I quit school? Why at 15 years I ought to work? So my mother said, you didn't luck. In 1967, they tell me I cannot go to school; other children go to school; every day they learn Chairman Mao's thought. I studied at home, but not Chairman Mao's thought, because I already studied that. I read another book, every kind. I had a lot of books at home. My mother knew how to read a little.[10] I know how to read any kind of Chinese book, like "The Romance of Three Kingdoms," and "The Water Margin," and "The Monkey." That's a very good kind of book in China.

When I was 15, I cannot study any more, so I knew I must to work. I went to the village office and said, "I plan to work." Then the man said, "All right; you can." Also he told me what kind of work to do. I cut rice, and also

I transplanted rice seedlings. I brought the rice cutter from my house. Every-one has one; it is a big curved knife, with an edge like a saw; it has teeth. I cut the rice and tied it to dry in the sun. I carried it on the shoulder to the place. Before, there was no machine, but now there is a machine to do. We hit the rice in a big bowl, put the stems in there, and beat it to get the seeds. For two years I did this, once in summer and also in fall. In spring and winter, another kind of work. In spring, do the vegetables, and in winter, all kinds of work. There is very good fruit in my village: bananas, and also the plums, and also the lichee. In Lung Du there were several kinds of lichee; it's a very good fruit. Inside it is white, and also has a heart. We can get them here, but very seldom. Not in cans, because China doesn't have the machines to do it. You can buy them dried, but it is not very good. I read the newspaper, said this year can buy some in England or America, but not very much, just a little. Maybe two years more, we can buy in England or America. Just in China south can buy this fruit. China middle and China north don't have. And this little place can do this; another place cannot; just Lung Du. There is another very good kind, red with two green lines. It looks very good and tastes very good, too. I didn't eat that fruit; I just read a book about it.

During the Cultural Revolution, the elementary school, below junior high, was open in my village. After junior high it was closed up. The students went to school, but not to study: to hit, to fight, and to do anything, but not study.[11] My third brother went around the country then, to Kwangchow, Nanjing, Beijing, Shanghai, and also Soochow, Hangchow. I wanted to go to those places too, but I never went. I sometimes went to Guangzhou. Maybe three or four times I went to visit my uncle. I have two uncles and one auntie in Guangzhou: my mother's brothers and sister. I went in a boat, by riding a bicycle, and by boat; another person riding a bicycle, and I sit down behind, to go to the boat. My brothers each had a bicycle, and my sister had one, and I had one. My friend riding his bicycle took me to my brother's house on the day that I left. After I left, they took my bicycle away from my mother's house. When I swim to Macao, the oldest man in the village took my bicy-cle.

So I plan to swim, at about 16 years. Usually I work, finish, and at home I always study. So I think, give me a freedom. I am a person. Not in jail. So I plan to swim. I to my brother said, "I thought of swimming. Do you agree with me?" And he said, "Very good! I help you!" He lived with my older brother; my sister got married; my second brother got work, not at home. Just me at home with my mother. My brother lived at Chi Hai, very near Macao. So everything I prepare. I talk my mother, "Give me a freedom." So I swim at night. At twelve o'clock I riding a bicycle to the river, swim two or three hours, and then I went home to sleep. Sixteen years old, I plan to swim. Eighteen years old, I swim. So I swim from China to Macao, in February,

very cold. I just riding a bicycle go to my brother's home. Then at night, I
walk a short time, and swim, about three and a half hours, because my brother
lived very near the ocean. Two persons swim. I and my cousin.

The place is a little place of the Pacific Ocean, between Hong Kong and
Macao. The wave is very big; just hurr, hurr, hurr. February 28th and May
first, that's very high tide, so that's very good. The moon was dark at the
28th. No moon, very dark. See Macao, is big light; see China, is very dark.
At night time, eight o'clock, the dogs work on the bridges, so before eight
o'clock I came to the ocean. Don't have the dog; don't have the police. No
sharks. A lot of rain. In Macao's ocean is a stone, very big stone. This wave
pushed me over the stone that cut my leg a long time. Three months it cut.
I had the ball inside of a ball tied to my body. I used a bag tied to my body,
and swim to Macao. I wore just short pants, no shoes, and I had a dry coat
in the bag, to put on my body. I had about 50 Hong Kong dollars, and a
little gold. In Macao, I have a dry coat, so I put it on my body so I walk in
Macao street. So I guess it is about eleven or twelve o'clock. In Macao, it's a
good time. Everyone in the street! I wave my hand to every car. I put my wet
clothes in a bag, so he didn't know I swim from China. He looks at my leg,
don't wearing the shoes, you know, so he said, "You swim from China?" I said
yes. So he buy a slipper, give me and my cousin, so he take me to my cousin's
brother. So my cousin's brother give him some money, said, "Thank you."
He's a very good man. So I and my cousin is lucky, have a good man take
care me and my cousin.

I lived in Macao seven days; all the days it rained. My cousin's father
lived in Hong Kong, and he went to Macao to visit me and my cousin. I
knew it was very dangerous. Then came to Hong Kong in the bottom of a
boat, have a long time, about 12 hours. The boat is used to carry men from
Macao to Hong Kong. It's very good. We pay one thousand dollars. My uncle
helped me pay because I and my cousin grew up together.

After I left, the policemen didn't bother my brother, just bother my
mother. Some men said, "Your boy swim to Hong Kong; he died." So I write
a letter to my mother and say I was successful. A long time, they ask her,
"Why did he swim?" My mother said, "I don't know. He's my boy, but it's
not me." Before I swim, I told her, "You don't need to work. I can do anything." So I came to Hong Kong, and my brother and me, we tell her, "You
don't have to work because I send money. Because at 55, you can retire." So
in 1973 I came to Hong Kong, so she already retired.

I got a job in a sewing factory. I was a cutter for a long time, six years,
but sometimes I do the steam iron because the boss said, "You can help me
take care of the men." So I take care of 12 men working at the factory a long
time. I studied ABC in evening classes, seven to nine. Because in China I
knew China word; I didn't know English, so I studied first ABC in Hong

Kong.[12] I have a girlfriend in Hong Kong; we worked together at the sewing factory. She was 17 years old. I don't plan to get married; she is just a friend. So I ask her, "You can study, and why didn't you go to school to study?" And she said, "It is too hard." And I said, "Why! I like to study, and I can't, and you say it's too hard!"

My godfather would take care of me, my mother told me. My godfather is a good man at China. My mother knew my godfather for a long time. He was my mother's neighbor. So he came to U.S. He lived in America for 60 years. In 1945, the Japanese stopped the war, and my godfather came to China for one year. He spent a year in Lung Du, and then came back to America. My godmother stayed in China until 1962, when she went to Hong Kong. I was born in 1954, so I knew my godmother. She had just one daughter; she is retired now. She came to America about 30 years ago and lived with her father a long time. My godfather didn't have another wife here, never. He did a long time a butcher and a grocery. My godmother came here in 1973, before my godfather died, and she lived with her daughter. My godfather went to Hong Kong then, and died in Hong Kong in 1975 about 90 years old.

I came in October 1978. My godfather's nephew brought me. Because I swim from China, I can do. I have a white card, not a green card.[13] When I came here, for four months I didn't have a job, but in April I got the job to do the butcher. It's a grocery store, also have a meat counter. The boss teaches me, and also the boss said, "You think how to do this." So now I can do everything: round steak, filet mignon, top sirloin, T-bone steak, rib steak, sirloin tip, short ribs, hamburger meat, and neck bones and chops, everything can. I get $600 a month, and I work eight hours every day. I walking from school at 12 o'clock, eat lunch, and work from one o'clock until nine. If I live in here one year, then I can go to junior college and not have to pay.

My boss was born in Toi San. I can understand him; I speak Cantonese, and I can understand Toi San, and also I can say Mandarin, and the language of my small village. It is not Toi San; it is very special, and other people cannot understand it. It is just one village language. Someone said the language of Lung Du is almost like English! The people of Lung Du are not Hakka; they are Han.[14] The people are not different from other Chinese, just the language. Maybe the language came from a long time ago, when the people moved to Lung Du. And every night I do my exercise, tong long. I read the book; my tong long teacher has the book. The man made it just three hundred years ago, in Shantung. Then the businessmen came to South China and brought tong long, and the men liked it. It has the way to fight long and to fight short, and tong long can get more power. Kung fu is more than a thousand years, and tong long is just three hundred years old. The old teacher in Shantung put every better thing from kung fu, in tong long. Tong long is all the better things.

TWENTY-FOUR YEARS LATER, AUGUST 2003
At Richard's butcher shop, a man at the counter didn't speak English, and directed me to a woman at the rear. Her English was scant, but she said Richard was out on a delivery. He came in then and first introduced the woman as his "mate" for 20 years, then changed it to "wife." Richard is heavier now; his English is fluent, and he speaks with confidence. The boy who swam from China is now a solid entrepreneur giving out his business card and cell phone number, pleased that his story will be told in a book. He works every day from eight to seven, but he can take time to talk some Wednesday morning after eleven when business is relatively slow.

OCTOBER 2004
Lee Chung, now Richard, recorded another interview 25 years after the first, in the office area at the back of the butcher shop, where there was a small stove and a package of oatmeal on the counter. He spoke carefully and clearly, with no self-pity, as he told of his physical pains and the burdens of business. Only at the end, when he says he had no chance to study, he blinked back tears.

Right now, at this shop, is the sole owner myself. The building is a rental. I do have three employees and then me and my wife. Most is retail and part of the restaurant business, like meat cutting. Some restaurant don't have the equipment for cutting, and then they give it to me to finish the job for them. They buy the meat from me, and then — like pork chops — use the power band saw to cut it. The shop is open seven days a week. I worked seven days a week more than 25 years. When I start my own business, I rent a meat counter, and then I start the business, a meat counter over there in the grocery shop for like three years, and then my partner said, "Why don't you come with me and try Chinatown, to start the business over there." And then, "Why not?" More than 20 years. Never close; we close one day, Chinese New Year. And then a long period, only I took one week vacation, went to China to visit my mother.

I do have my older daughter and my younger daughter, and both graduated from college this year. The older one studied in UCLA for business in accounting for four years and then took one year for business Master's degree in USC. The young one graduated this year from UC–Berkeley. And then both have a job started in September. They do both live at home. At home, they do always speak Chinese, Cantonese. My wife came in 1979, one year later than me. Her father lived here before. Her father immigrated her come here. I had another friend studied at the Chinese Community Center. Over there then we went some days together, to play together, and we feel we talk very well, and do things together. I think we got married one year later, in 1980. Her father and mother live together with my brother-in-law and live very close.

Richard's shop, 2010, now the New Hop Lung Market, in Oakland Chinatown.

My mother died in 1992, in China, but she came here when I immigrated and then became a citizen, and I immigrated her to come here to take a look. I said, "Come here, and if you like it, you stay here. If you don't like it, come back to China; it doesn't matter." So she came and lived here two years. She got internal cancer. She found out here, in Merritt Hospital. So she died in China. My older brother came in 1998, and my older sister came also that year. I applied immigration for them.

Right now, everything is okay, but I do have one time, very bad on my back, because I carried too heavy. At that time I lay down in the hospital for nine days. I even cannot get up. I lay down all day, all night. Nine days. I had not surgery; I almost went for surgery, but then my friend said try a chiropractor. And after that, I got better and better when I see the chiropractor, every time. At that period, for two years, cannot work. Very very painful. The muscles shrink because my spinal bones are twisted. Touched the nerve, and then the nerve is getting ... the bone is hit the nerve. And then all the muscle is shrink. Acupuncture did not work at all. Because the bone is twisted. They had to slowly, slowly, slowly move it back to normal. But right now everything is back to normal. Everything is normal now.

That year, my daughter was just born, the same year. My wife worked for waitress in a restaurant. Those years my brother-in-law helped me a lot. On that time, only the Medi-Cal and Medicare I do have. At that period, they got all the money I have. Very hard. That's a very down moment for me.

Two years. After that, my godsister found another person to hire me. She said, "For helping Richard a little bit. Let Richard do something." Do light work over there, might be service for the customer, and then little by little my back was more strong, and then okay. For a couple of years, and after that, my back went back to normal.

It used a lot of time to build the business. Like license. I came to this shop in 1986. At first I do have another partner, until 1995, and then my wife and me decide because my partner didn't like to continue the business, and so we bought the whole business. Yes, kind of the business start is very headache, you know. You have to go through everything. My brother-in-law, he's very good in business. He could speak English. He came here longer than me; then he went to business college here and found a job to do computers. He helped me a lot. For architecture, for license, for getting the contract, talk to the builder, and then inspectors. Because Oakland is more difficult; the health inspector and the building inspector is completely different. That is more work for them. Well, I had the experience for six years. For the new-comer, that is a big problem.

Yes, I do have my insurance. Too expensive here. For health insurance, I have to pay my age, for the benefits, it is almost $1,200 a month. And my daughter right now has insurance for her company and it is almost $1,000 a month. And also right now the big concern is the insurance, the business: workers' compensation, and then the liability. That is very expensive. When I see the bill come, I got a big headache. Like last year, the liability is $1,700 a year. And then the company said, "We don't carry that kind of business no more." And then I have to find another company for the liability, and then another company, the cheapest is $5,790 a year. No control! I have to pay more $4,000 a year for the liability. The worker's comp every year goes up: last year, $5,700; this year, $6,200. Every year they jump. When you get salary paid more, the insurance is more. The rent goes up every year, but it depends on the Consumer Index count. That is more reasonable. Not like insurance, when they jump like 20 percent, 30 percent, even 400 percent. The Consumer Price Index, each year, like in 2002, it's only 1.8 percent, and this year, it's 2.5 percent. That's more reasonable. Yes, some part of that you have to raise a little bit, but you cannot catch up, because the whole area, you know, it's not the same. Some stores don't have to pay rent; they can lower down the price, and then they get more business. Some, like me, have to pay rent and have to pay everything. If you get a higher price, the customers go away, and then you have to just keep the same level. I think more than about 20 butcher shops in Chinatown. But they do have meat, grocery, or produce. But only me has only the meat business; that's a lot of competition. I sell mostly pork, beef, chicken. I don't deal with the company that has ducks. Only the pig, the market hogs, they do kill and then split in half. Then the beef they do quarters, like front quarter, hind quarter. And also you know, because of mad cow disease, they pay more than 60 dollars to inspect each cow, each one, to keep safe for the customers.

My girls don't work in the job here. Might be helping me for the paperwork. The girl is not for the meat business. Also, they do a lot of community work. The older one for the police department for three or four years, over there in Chinatown, for the detectives, as a volunteer, and the young one four years in Muir Hospital in Walnut Creek, for a volunteer. I tell them to do more helping for another people. They both do a lot.

I'm beginning here at seven-thirty, and get out, it depends on, sometimes the early is six o'clock, and the later might be eight or nine; it depends. But mostly is six-thirty or seven o'clock. We close the shop at six. I have to do some paperwork. The store opens at eight-thirty. I have to come earlier because the delivery men, they come very early in the morning. When all the orders are received, I do have time to cook a little bit and eat here and drink a cup of coffee. Oatmeal! My daughter said, "Why don't you eat oatmeal in the morning for your breakfast?" And I said, "Okay." She bought for me. Eat lunch here. Right now my children went home, and we eat dinner at home. I've gained more than forty-five pounds. Right now my weight is 155 pounds. Right now, at night I don't do that very exercise anymore. I take a walk. No more tong long. Too tired, and getting older. Always hurt. Right now I take a walk after dinner. Well, after 30 years, my health is not so good right now. High blood pressure, high cholesterol. That's getting older. No one can without it.

My mother passed away. I went back to China to do everything. I met with the family over there and then talked about my mom passed away, we do remember, and then bought a place for her to lay down. A lot of change over there. Right now, much better than before. At least the people, they don't hungry over there. They do have meat, and they might be not so good for speech, but they do have no more empty stomach. That's better. Much better than before. My brothers all went out, and then the old house is sold already. I do have my older brother in Chi Hai, and my second older brother came here already, and then my sister. I do have another brother, two years older than me, in Hong Kong. He decided not come, because in Hong Kong, very good.

Most of the time I watch TV at home. Any kind of sport I like to watch on TV. Like football, basketball, baseball, tennis, golf. Every kind. Sometimes weekends we do play mah jong with my friends at my house for fun for a couple of rounds; that's all. Sometimes play mah jong for fun; that's okay. We start at eight o'clock, and we end at eleven-thirty. For a good time. I don't like to gamble at all, for my whole life. I haven't been in Reno for more than 10 years. For Chinese New Year my wife said, "Why don't we go one time over there?" Okay. We do go over there for one time. Most I talk to a lot of people, don't gamble, because all the money goes to the dealer's pockets, not you.

I'm tired right now. Not like before. The age is older, and everything is not like before. Too tired right now. If I retire, might do some work, some take-it-easy work, might be a part-time job. Right now the two daughters graduated and found a good job, and my heavy part is already done. Let the young men do it. They both do have a boyfriend. They both are very good gentlemen. And also very good study at school. They both is very good honor student for all four years. That's why I tell them, "I don't have opportunity to study. Right here, you have all kinds of opportunity, so you have to do good." When they were young, I did tell them about China and how I swam. And I sent them to a Christian school because it was safe and clean and they have good education.

AUGUST 2005

At mid-day, four butchers in white coats were busy with many customers. The first butcher in line didn't speak English, and he hurried to get another fellow who was proud of his fluent English; he talked loudly, showing off for his fellow workers. "Richard make too much money so he retired; now he travel all over, Australia, China, Hong Kong, all around. He and his wife, travel all around. He work very, very hard, never take a day off; now he retire." He prattled on, making his point, proud of his fluency, proud of Richard's success. Years ago, Lee Chung had said, "Give me freedom; I am a person." Now he says he is tired and feels old, but he is admired and respected by his fellow workers, he has earned "too much money," and his daughters are well educated. He must feel that his efforts have been worthwhile.

Rosanna

Rosanna is a second-generation swimmer; her father and two brothers escaped from China before she did, all by swimming. As an ESL student in February 1985, she was 32 years old, thin, wearing glasses and stylish Hong Kong clothing. She smiled easily and spoke fairly good English as she recounted her story:

Rosanna's parents are both Chinese, but her mother was born in Japan, where her grandfather had a business. Later he returned to China, which he said was a big mistake. Rosanna's mother graduated from university in China as a doctor and practiced throughout her life, with little disturbance from the Communists, but with little pay. She had the same salary from 1949 on, whereas her classmates who went to Hong Kong or Taiwan became wealthy. Rosanna's father also graduated from university, and he had a business in

Guangzhou. For the first years after liberation, things went well, but then everything went down, down, so in 1959 or 1960, he walked for four hours "over the mountain" and then swam for one hour around Shenzhen, to escape to Hong Kong. In Hong Kong he owned a delivery van company but is now retired. He managed somehow to return to Guangzhou from time to time to visit and to plan for Rosanna and her two brothers to escape, one by one. Ten years ago, her older brother escaped by swimming, followed in two years by her younger brother. Five years ago, in 1979, she escaped. When her first brother escaped, it was extremely dangerous, but by the time she left, it wasn't quite so bad. The mother died of a heart attack three months after Rosanna escaped, but she was fully in accord with Rosanna's leaving.

In Guangzhou, Rosanna worked as a nurse taking care of babies. For a time after graduating from high school she was sent to the countryside and had to work carrying burdens on a shoulder pole. That was terrible, and she cried all the time as she worked. She trained for the escape by going with friends to a lake near Guangzhou, ostensibly for picnics, and swimming for three hours at a time. She escaped with two young men, one of whom had swum once before to Macao, been caught by the police, and shipped back; consequently, he knew the route and its hazards, and he was their guide. They left in October, when the water was still warm, and they chose a night with no moon. First they went by bus to the coast, and since they didn't have travel passes, when they came to a checkpoint, they had to get out of the bus before the checkpoint, make a wide circuit walking around the town, and catch the bus again beyond. She had a life vest of some sort, and a backpack with a little food and water. They swam for six hours, from about 10 P.M. until about 4 A.M. The points of extreme danger were the departure from Guangdong and the arrival at Macao. To go from Macao to Hong Kong, they were hidden under the floor of a passenger ferry; they had to pay a lot of money for this passage. The father had traveled to Macao and made the arrangements. When they arrived in Hong Kong, they waited until three A.M., when it was totally dark and there were no police around. Then a taxi driver called her father, arranged to meet in central Hong Kong, and put the three of them in the trunk; this was the most uncomfortable time of all. When she met her father, she says she cried a lot.

A TELEPHONE MESSAGE, OCTOBER 2, 1988

Hi — how are you? This is Rosanna. I'm going to say goodbye for you. Oh! Because my husband find a job — *[long pause, sigh]* — that's a grocery store in Los Angeles. So we will going to move there. But anyway I remember you; I miss you very much. You are so nice for me. At the first time I came to the United States you teach me a lot of things, and you are so nice. You got a lot of help for me. Thank you very much. Thank you. Bye-bye.

Vocabulary Lessons

Dorothy Loo wants to know the English word for the scar on the shoulder that comes from carrying heavy loads on a shoulder pole. Told that there is no such word, she is amazed; it is inconceivable that Americans don't need this term. Another day, she wants to know the word to use when your feet are very cold, but your torso is warm. Again, she is told there is no English word, and she seems doubtful; perhaps she thinks that the teacher just has a very limited vocabulary.

Several students want to know the word for tree bark. Oddly, for them this word belongs in the basic vocabulary. They need to speak of famine, a defining experience in their lives, when people are so hungry they eat the bark of trees.

Annie Chung works the late night shift at a cookie factory, packaging cookies. She usually finishes the work assigned to her before the shift ends, and then she asks her supervisor for more work. She wants to know what he means when he says, "Oh, brother!" I am reluctant to tell her that he is expressing his dismay that she raises the bar for other workers.

A refugee from Odessa, a well-educated engineer, gets a job as laborer in a warehouse. Even though he is overqualified, he is happy because "nobody screams." When he managed a factory in the USSR, everyone in the production chain "screamed" at subordinates to fill the assigned quotas.

Millie asks the meaning of this answer to a request: "I don't see why not." She can't tell if it means yes or no.

Ching Ping laughs and says that her daughter's first words in English were "Hurry up." Evidently there isn't a Chinese equivalent.

A discussion of soup: English, Spanish, and Chinese have different concepts. Miss Chan has trouble understanding "chicken-rice soup." The word that translates as "soup" in Chinese means a clear broth, and a different word means rice porridge; it seems it is impossible in Chinese to say "chicken-rice soup." In Spanish, the word for soup includes what we call "casseroles," so Mrs. Gonzales needs to learn that macaroni and cheese is not soup.

Kenny Wu works in a grocery store out of Chinatown and wants to know what he should say when he gives change to a customer. He has noticed that the checkout clerk in the American market says, "Here you are," and sometimes, "There you are," or, "There you go." None of it makes sense to Kenny.

Daughters

Chairman Mao Zedong is quoted as saying, "Women hold up half the sky," to promote their emancipation. The horrible practice of foot-binding was outlawed in 1911, and currently, when families are limited and there is a surplus of boys, girls in China are becoming valuable. Traditionally, the need prevailed to have a son to inherit property and to tend the parents' graves after their death. My American-born Chinese friend is the third daughter in her family, and the Chinese name given to her means "Little Brother Coming." This could have made her feel second-rate, but it did not. When her little brother was born, she and her propitious name were given all the credit, and she felt esteemed.

These three women wanted to tell their stories of lives straddling cultures: Ruth was born when infant girls were not even named; Louisa was temporarily abandoned when the family faced starvation; Fong was used as a pawn to bring her family to America.

Seldom Flower

JANUARY 1977

The class enrollment includes students from the following countries: Burma, Cambodia, China (including PRC, Hong Kong, and Taiwan), Colombia, Guatemala, Greece, Korea, Malaysia, Mexico, Peru, Philippines, Russia, Spain, United States, and Vietnam. The most advanced is Ruth, 41 years old, with bright eyes behind glasses.

When Ruth was born, the fifth daughter in an important military family, her father's failure to sire a son was a crisis not only for the immediate relatives but also for domestic staff and dependent army units. Daughters could not inherit, and unless the father had a son, all his property would pass to a distant male relative, leaving his children and the entire retinue impoverished. After the birth of three daughters to her son's first wife, the frantic grandmother found another wife for him, a girl from a poor family, forced into the marriage against her will.[15] When she bore two girls, the second one was not even named. She was given one more chance before a third wife would be acquired, and fortunately, her third child was a son, so she was retained, and bore two more sons. Her position in the family was now secure, but she had to endure continued harassment by the enraged first wife. In time the grandfather pitied the fifth daughter and named her "Seldom Flower." A more poetic name would be "Rare Blossom."

She is interviewed in her Oakland apartment, where there is no furniture. The living room is empty except for five pairs of shoes on a mat by the door. The kitchen has no table or chairs. As she tells her story, "good" can mean variously virtuous, prosperous, or happy; "poor" can mean lacking in goods, unfortunate, or unhappy. She uses the word "patient" as a verb, which is apt, for the women of her family have had to exercise patience with a vigor that needs expression as a verb, rather than an adjective. After what her mother went through, her hesitancy about getting married is no surprise. In class, she often says, "It can't be helped," or, "I

trust in God," and she uses two hand gestures—one a faint waving, as if to push
something away, the other of hands clasped in prayer. Rejected as a girl, she found
dignity in adopting Christianity and a new name. Here is her story told in 1979:

    I was born in 1936, in the south of China, near Canton. My family lived
in the capitol city, but my mother had to go back to the little country, which
belongs to my old family,[16] for the daughter or the son to be born. It is our
custom, an important custom. So my family is a good family, also famous
because long ago, our family is from the north of China, and my ancestor is
a famous man, a soldier, very good and could fight very well, and then because
of war, moved in the south of China. But when my father was very little, my
family was very poor, poor. My grandmother also ate the poppy—it is very
bad. China fought the war with England and gave Hong Kong to England
because of this, the poppy.[17] So my grandmother must eat the opium, smoke
opium. She couldn't stop. So my father, when he was a little boy, he said, "I
must go out and study the good." So when Chiang Kai-shek opened the
famous school, Whampoa [*Military Academy*],[18] my father went there and
studied. And then when he became better, my family was very good.

    But in China, the son is important, so when my father married my first
mother [*his first wife*], he got three daughters, no son. In that time my father
was very rich, so a far uncle said, "Your property belongs to my son." So my
grandma was very worried because she had no grandson. At once, she finds
a girl in the country to be my mother, only 17 years old, and very poor. Her
mother is dead, so her father wants her to marry my father, because he is a
famous man. So my mother's father tells her, "If you don't want to marry,
then get out." So my mother is very worried, and she just wants to die. So
then she must serve my first mother and work very hard. So my mother was
very poor. So my mother always cry, cry, cry.

    My first mother took all the money, to help her brothers, to make a house
for her own family. Then she told my father, "The money is lost!" Then she
said my mother took it. But my mother is very good, and my grandma is very
good. My grandma said, "Don't make trouble; that's okay. The family is good;
that's enough." When my mother cry, cry, my grandma say, "That's okay, the
family is good." Just like that.

    When my older sister was born, my grandmother was very good to her,
because she is the first daughter of my mother. I am the second daughter, and
when I was born, all the soldiers and leaders of the soldiers sent a lot of
presents and said, "It is a son!" And all my family just cry, cry. My mother,
my grandma, when she heard daughter, she said, "I don't like it! I don't give
a name for her!" Cry, cry, cry, because no son. They will hate our family, and
all my father's property will go to the far brother. But later, my grandfather
said, "You all don't like the granddaughter, you don't give a name for her, so
then I will give her one." So my grandfather gave the name to me. My name

means "Seldom Flower"; seldom means the opposite of plenty. And when I was little, I was always crying; I don't know why. Cry. Because my mother, you know, she is also crying, so it is not good.

And so my grandma wanted to find some good girl for my father to be a wife, the third one. But in that time, I was just one year old, my mother had a baby in the stomach, so my father just waited. If it's a boy, okay. If a girl, then my grandmother will find another wife for my father. Then my brother is born; then my family is happy, very happy. My grandmother very loves my brother. My mother is better, too, and my father is good to my mother.

But my first mother just calls my mother by her first name. In China, to call the name is very impolite, you know, just like a slave. And my mother told me about that, always she told me about that, and said, "Don't forget it!" Because every night my first mother went to the top of the house and asked God to kill my mother. She used all the methods — sometimes she wrote my mother's name and birthday on something and burned it and asked Buddha to kill my mother. And sometimes she cut a branch of the tree and said something to kill my mother. And when my first sister was born, my first mother used the oil of the goose to fry the vegetables for my mother to eat, because for the new mother to eat the oil of the goose is big trouble. So my mother always told us that and said, "Don't forget it!" But when I was older, my brother and my sister also told our mother, "Forget it, don't remember that. Let it go!" My first mother and my mother always lived together. But my mother just patient, patient, always patient. So she always ask my brothers and sisters, "You must patient. It is good." So my mother always ask me to patient everything. So when I marry, now, in our own family, I patient.

I was born in 1936 and my brother in 1937. Then the Japanese came to Guangzhou, and my mother and father went to the north of Guangdong to fight the Japanese.[19] My auntie, my father's sister, led the rest of us, and servants, to Hong Kong, and we went to the best school, because our family is special. Then, when I just studied kindergarten, the war began, and I left Hong Kong and followed my mother and father. The people in the country were very poor, but we had plenty of food because the army gave my family enough food. And the little country had a school, just a little house, to study with all the girls and boys together. It was a very good time, I think. It is very fun. When our servants made us walk a long way, on the hill, then the airplanes came, then I heard the noise, "Woo! Woo!" Then we all had to lie down under the trees. Very fun, but also very afraid.

After the war, Seldom Flower went again to Hong Kong, became a Christian, and changed her name to Ruth. She attended university in Taiwan and returned to Hong Kong as a teacher. A classmate whose brother-in-law was looking for a wife approached her about marriage.

I don't think about marry. I very afraid; I don't know why. Then after a

long time, I feel that's okay. Then I began to walk with him. Just walking in
the park. And after that, went near the sea to eat seafood. Then I went to
meet his mother and father. Very simple, the family. His mother is very good.
Not rich. Very clean, very neat, everything do very good. All things they
need, they have, but not rich. My mother says, "If you like it, that's okay.
Although poor, poor, just a vegetable seller, poor is not important. Just if you
want to marry, you must find a man with no wife. That's important; poor is
not important." So I lived with my husband, and he had a good job, in a jewelry shop near the Star Ferry. We lived in Kowloon, and then I taught in the
school. Every year I had a baby, three boys. But boy or girl, that's okay.

*A few years later, Ruth and her husband were managing a motel in Texas,
and it may be that this is somewhat similar to the life she knew in the busy family
compound of her childhood, where she can be happy again.*

Different from All the Others

*Louisa dresses well and speaks quite colloquial English; she lives in a pleasant
suburb removed from Chinatown and is married to an American-born Chinese
who drops her off at school on his way to work. She lingered after class one day
and wanted to tell me about her life; she feels singled out for good fortune. On
the evening before her wedding, when her mother instructed her about marriage,
it was not about sex but about starvation. When Louisa was born, the Japanese
had occupied southern China for seven years, and there was a famine; she was
abandoned but survived, marking her as special. Her father wanted her to attend
school, and now she has a successful and happy arranged marriage to a considerate
husband. Her husband's father had starved as a Japanese prisoner of war, and
later the family had suffered from racial discrimination in California. Her loneliness has been alleviated by helpful in-laws and neighbors. She has traveled
widely, and in Europe she bought a rug that isn't needed now in a carpeted home.
She celebrates holidays in a blend of cultures. Her daughter tries to be sympathetic,
but only her father-in-law, who also knew hunger, can really understand how
deeply it hurts to see food wasted. Louisa tells her story:*

I was born in 1944 in Guangzhou. My mother got married at 15, had to
take care of a big house, do all the chores at home, a very hard life. And then
the war, she had to bake Chinese cakes and try to sell them, and the Japanese
soldier came and dumped all the Chinese cake and kick her and stamp on all
the Chinese cake. Very bad, so my mother had a lot of trouble.

When I got married, I asked her to tell me about some things, and then
she told me something. I didn't know anything about it before. My family has
three brothers, and including me, seven sisters. I am number four sister. My

mother, when I was born, put me out on the street so maybe somebody would pick me up, because we didn't have enough to eat — it was a very big family, aunts, uncles, great grandmother. But maybe she didn't put me out long enough, because after a while, she just came back and got me. When I got married, I was young, and didn't know anything about all this, and she wanted me to understand the situation, you know. She suffered a lot. The problem is, too many girls, you know. Every time my mother had a girl, my father was very discouraged; he said, "Another baby girl!" He thought girls brought him bad luck. But he never beat me. He was very nice to me and to my mother. He never hit me. Because I was different from all the others. I am quiet, you know, and don't make trouble at school, and so he very spoiled me.

We moved to a village near Kowloon when I was little. We had chickens and ducks, and we planted sweet potatoes and vegetables. I had to help my grandma dig the dirt and do all this stuff for the vegetables. We had enough for our family and sometimes gave some to our friends. I enjoyed it. And I finished elementary school, and then I had to take care of the family. After school I had to wash the clothes, feed the chickens, and help my mother take care of the youngest brother and sister, help with the cooking. I washed all the diapers and everything before I went to school in the morning. So then about two o'clock, after school, I do all the things, too. After supper, I can study and do homework. I helped my mother a lot. I washed the clothes by hand. I got the water from the well in two buckets with a bamboo pole. We had plenty of water. I went there and got a little can and got a string and dipped way down in the well and got the water and put it in the bucket and filled it up and took it home, with the pole on my shoulder. We didn't have toilets; they still don't have. Just used portable toilets. We put it in a big place, and the ladies come in the morning and take it to the fields to fertilize the vegetables. Just like Germany. They do it in Germany, the same thing. When we went to visit the German village, they do the same thing. It's better than the chemical fertilizer that they make now.

I went to one year of English school in Hong Kong. I traveled back and forth on the bus and ferry. My mother said, "Girls don't need education. Just after eighteen years, get married anyway; don't have to go to school." My mother is a little bit old-fashioned, not like my father. My father said the children should have education. But so many — I have too many brothers and sisters. I had to wash all the clothes and iron all the school uniforms. We had an iron that you put water in to make steam. It was electric. We had electricity, electric light, no refrigerator, no television, just a small radio. Usually I started ironing at nine o'clock in the morning, and at twelve o'clock we had lunch, and after I finished washing the clothes, I ironed again until two o'clock. And after that I was so tired, you know. Especially the white uniforms, you had to starch them. My family is doing a lot better now. They have television at home.

My husband's family was very poor; they lived in a boat, very poor, so my father-in-law joined the U.S. Navy; they hired lots of Chinese people just for cooking and cleaning. And his ship was captured by the Japanese, and he didn't have anything to eat. That's why he's very particular about the food; you have to clean it up, you know; don't leave anything, because he got very hungry. Then after the war, they let him go. I don't want to talk about it, because he got very hungry.

Then they came to San Francisco, and they lived in San Francisco, but too many people, so they sold the house and move over here to the East Bay. People threw the rock and break the window, every day, and so they were scared. They bought the property and built the house there, but after all this trouble, they sold the house. My husband went to high school here, and after graduation, he joined the Air Force. After nine years, he decided to go to Hong Kong to get married. So my mother-in-law flew to Hong Kong first, and a relative introduced me. And I didn't know him at all, you know, so my mother said, "Well, after you meet him, if you think you don't want to get married, it's okay. I don't force you to marry him, because you don't know him. You just know him from the relatives; you don't know him at all, and after you get married, and you're way far overseas, nobody can help you."

So they set a date, and what restaurant we go to, and after that, we sit together and have supper. And I didn't talk to him, and he didn't talk to me. We don't know each other; we don't know what to talk about. I just look at him, and he's all right. He was 29, and I was 17. So I'm very lucky. And we see each other, and about a week later, he asked me to marry him, and we set the date after that, and then we had a party at the restaurant and invite all the relatives. We had a big wedding; it cost a lot of money. He'd been saving for a long, long time, you know. And he gave me money to buy a wardrobe and all the stuff, and the Chinese cakes to give to my friends. And after we got married, we just had one week; we lived in my sister-in-law's house. And he had to go back because his leave is up; he only had about a month leave. After he left, I moved back to my mom's and helped her with the housework. That was in 1961. And after a year, I came over here.

My father-in-law speaks a little English, but my mother-in-law was 40-some years old when she came here, and she said, "I'm too old to learn." Everybody encouraged her to try to learn, but she says she's too old to learn. My sister-in-law is just like me, so if my mother-in-law has an appointment or something, we had to take her there and translate, interpret for her. I did it a couple of times before she died.

When I first came here, I stayed with my in-laws for a couple of days, and then went to Tacoma, Washington, with my husband. We lived in a very old trailer, only one bedroom, because we don't want to buy. I was sick all the time, I didn't get used to the weather, wet all the time, always raining, little tiny rain. Drizzle. Now I have rheumatism from carrying the buckets of water, and every time with the weather I feel terrible in my shoulders. I had that problem since I was young. And my mother put something on it to ease the pain a little bit. And when I told the doctor here, the doctor said, "Well, there's nothing we can do." I take some medicine for it.

So after we were in Tacoma for a couple of months, we transferred to Vandenberg. There weren't any Chinese people, only black people and American people. My husband had to translate all the time. The children were all born in Vandenberg Air Force Base. We could see missile launches day and night, like a fire ball in the sky. We lived there for six years in a big trailer, two bedrooms. I went to night school. After my husband came back and we had supper, I washed the dishes, and he took care of the baby. He had to drive me to the school and afterwards pick me up. And I went to night school, and to citizenship class, you know. He helped me a lot, helping me to learn, to get my citizenship. He did lots of things; he helped me to write and took care of the baby, feed the baby, very helpful. He did a lot of things for me. Sometimes I felt very bad because nobody talked to me, and I stayed home all the time by myself to take care of the three kids. You know, sometimes I cried a little bit.

It's different from Hong Kong. It's very quiet, and nobody talked to me. The neighbors were very nice to me. They helped me a lot. Because the first baby had colic, and she always threw up, very bad for me to take care of her. She was very tiny, and I didn't know what to do. I had to feed her every couple of hours, and then she always threw up. The doctor told me I didn't have enough milk for a baby, so I gave them bottles. And I didn't know how to make formula, so my husband taught me. I learned a lot from my husband, you know. In Hong Kong we just used old rags for diapers, not buy them, you know.

And then my husband had to go to Thailand, so I lived with my mother-in-law about a year and a half. He said, "You better live with the mother-in-law so she can take care of you and the kids." She taught me about cooking and told me how to take care of the baby. And the youngest daughter-in-law [*sister-in-law*] taught me how to drive.

Then we moved to Illinois for a year, and I didn't like it. So cold, and we didn't have much furniture. So about a year later, we moved to Germany. We stayed in Germany for four years. I enjoyed Germany, better than Illinois. We lived in base housing. Every summer we took a vacation and saw all these things. We've been to Switzerland and Berchtesgaden and Wiesbaden. And we saw all these famous castles, like Disneyland, and we went to Holland and France and Italy. In the winter there was snow, and we had to take turns to shovel the snow every morning. I wrote to my mother, and she said, "Oh, you are lucky! You can see all these kinds of things." I sent pictures and souvenirs. We got a big rug, too. But our house now has rugs all over, so we don't need it. We just laid it aside.

Our daughter studies very hard. She got straight A's a couple of years. Sometimes I talk to her about China, and she says, "So cruel!" I tell her, "Well, what can you do when it's wartime and you have nothing to eat?" I tell her, "Don't waste the food." It's very important, you know. And every time my father-in-law comes over and we eat together, he says, "Don't waste the food! Eat all!" When you have a party, you get together, usually you cannot eat all the food, you plan more food, so if we cannot finish everybody takes a little bit home. On Father's Day, we cooked a big roast, a prime rib roast, and we had a couple of pieces left. Then we cooked them another time and ate them. Sometimes the children waste food — they cannot eat it — and you cannot tell the children. Because it's a problem, you know.

When my mother-in-law died, they had a ceremony in the church of Jesus Christ. They joined this church a couple of years ago. Before, the religion is Buddhist. We go to visit the grave every week, take flowers, don't take food like Chinese. My father-in-law goes with us, and the children go, too. And on Memorial Day we all go together, and after that we visit in the house. Then we play mah jong [*a traditional game played with ivory tiles at a table*]. Four play, and the others watch and talk, and the children play. We have a good time. Now all the sad part is gone, is past. Now we look for the future.

I Don't Mind Hard If I'm Happy

DECEMBER, 1984

Fong stops on her way from a house-cleaning job to her swing shift at the pencil factory. She drives her own car and looks stylish — a shaped blow-dry hair-cut, a little makeup, well-fitted pants and a pretty sweater. She has saved enough money to buy either a new townhouse near the lake, not too far from Chinatown, or a small house out in an older residential section of the city.

This is a huge change from the young woman who entered ESL class in the fall of 1982: Birthdate, 1952. Birthplace, China. Speaks the Toi San[Tai Shan] dialect. Nine years of schooling. Address, a private house in Chinatown. She refused to check either Miss or Mrs. on the registration card. Her emergency contact is her grandfather, with a telephone number different from hers. Handwriting very poor, spoken English fluent. In the classroom, there are windows in the walls at the rear and to my right. Fong sat to the far left in the front and with eyes averted, looking into the windowless corner. She was taller than other women in the class, and she refused to converse with her classmates, although a number of them were also from Toi San [Tai Shan]. At first she spoke very little, but then she began to ask frequent questions, almost as if she and I were the only ones in the class. If I couldn't satisfy her, she said, "Never mind, my family will explain it to me."

DECEMBER 2, 1982

Fong asked after class today for help to find a job as a housekeeper or babysitter for an American. She told me about her life; as she spoke, with no change of expression, tears rolled down her face, but she seemed not to be bothered by them and made no attempt to hide them nor to wipe them away. Her father and mother were 16 when they were married, and her father is now 60, her mother perhaps a year older. She has two brothers older than she, and two younger. She is the only daughter and feels herself much loved. They lived in a village in the Toi San district [Tai Shan] of Guangdong, and her father taught school for 30 years in a larger town. When she was 13, she went to the same school as a boarder, going home every other weekend. Her father was a very good teacher, she says, and also a Christian. A number of the students in the ESL class were classmates or neighbors of hers in China, but she won't speak to them nor they to her because of "something that happened." When the Cultural Revolution began in 1966, and most schools in China were closed, she was about 14. The students attacked her father, breaking five of his teeth. Twice he was put in jail. Their house was ransacked, and books and Christian Bibles were burned. After that, Fong couldn't go to school, and she and her brothers worked in the rice fields. It was very hard work, but "I don't mind hard," she said, "if I'm happy. I like to work hard." Her grandmother's sister had a son who came to the United States as a boy of 15 or so; he is the grandfather of her husband. Her father-in-law and her husband were both born here. Maybe the mother-in-law, also born here, is her collateral relative; once she calls her "my cousin." Fong's marriage was arranged by mail through relatives. The grandfather telephones to her and has offered her money when she was desperate, but she can't call him, nor can he befriend her openly, because it would anger the mother-in-law, who is his daughter, or possibly niece, and whose good will he also needs.

Fong came here at the age of 28, happy to escape from the rice fields to life in America. She lives with her husband's parents, siblings, and their children. From the day she arrived, the family spoke only English to her, and they, especially the children in the family, help her with her English. She has learned to use a vacuum and can wash windows and mop floors. She goes to school and to work at will; no one cares what she does. She buys her own clothes, and she has plenty to eat. Her husband, who is about her age, has refused to have anything to do with her. "If he is an old man, I don't marry him, but he's a young man, and I like him. You know, I'm Chinese, and a Chinese wife likes the husband, but the husband doesn't like the wife. So I don't mind he doesn't like me. I just like him anyway." She went back to China last summer to visit for three weeks because she was so homesick, and enjoyed that, but she doesn't like China and thinks America and all Americans are "good." She writes occasionally to her parents but tells them only good things and nothing about her troubles. She went to church twice here and would like to go more often because she likes it, but she needs to sew on Sundays to get money. She is one of the most skillful workers at the sewing factory, usually asked to make the sample for other seamstresses to copy.

Fong isn't exactly enslaved but is certainly unhappy. In two years she has learned to speak English quite well. Last year she went through a job training program, and for a while she had a factory job making pencils at $7.50 an hour, swing shift. She rode to work with a coworker. Her husband didn't care that she went out every night to work. But then business was slow, the factory laid people off, and the sewing factories were not working either. She was clearly in crisis and wanted me to find her a job where she can live in, with someone American, not Chinese, because she didn't want to talk about her life, and American people are better to work for. I found a job for her, doing housework two days a week for one of my neighbors, Mrs. S. From the beginning it wasn't propitious. Fong was distressed and more sullen than usual, and Mrs. S. was suspicious of her, worried that she was a Communist. I tried to explain to Mrs. S. that Fong had ample reason to loathe Communists, but she remained leery.

FEBRUARY 14, 1983

Fong told me on a Monday that she was thrown out by her mother-in-law and had found an apartment alone on the edge of Chinatown. She came to class early and begged me to try again to find a live-in job for her. She was visibly distraught and left class early, but I called and learned that she went to her house-cleaning job that afternoon. The next evening she called me, sobbing, and said she wanted to kill herself. I brought her to my home; she would only stay one night, and she seemed in better spirits when she left. I worry that she isn't getting enough to eat, or enough sleep. She told me that she watches TV all night.

February 11, Friday, was a school holiday in honor of both Abraham Lincoln and the Chinese New Year, the beginning of the Year of the Boar. I was given several oranges, "lucky candies"—toffees wrapped in red and gold foil with good luck characters on them—a bag of candied coconut, and a box of Del Monte dried prunes.[20] Chinatown is bustling, people buying sweets, shooting firecrackers. I was concerned about Fong being alone and gloomy. I called her Saturday evening, and she sounded as if she either had a bad cold or was crying. She said she was not sad; Mr. Yee and his wife had taken her out for supper. He is a former student, an elderly gentleman whose wife, I'm told, was violated by Japanese soldiers during the occupation of Guangdong and has never been well since. They have good-looking unmarried sons, and I suspect him of using English classes as a vehicle for locating nice young Chinese girlfriends for them. Fong is probably ineligible, so taking her out may have been an act of simple kindness. On Sunday, I went again to her apartment, a dingy studio in a rundown building. She has a few pots and pans, a TV, and an electric blanket. In the kitchen was a 50-pound bag of rice. I had brought some packets of dried soup, some oranges, aspirin, Vitamin C and multi-vitamin tablets. She said her boss at the sewing factory had also given her oranges, so she isn't entirely friendless. I made soup for her, and when I left, she seemed fairly cheerful.

The job with Mrs. S. ended unhappily. Something that her teenage daughter treasured was found broken in the garbage. Fong had evidently broken it while she was vacuuming and then denied it when confronted. The daughter was extremely angry and said, with great feeling, "I don't like her, and I don't want her ever to come in my room again." Mrs. S. stressed that she values honesty above all else. Another job was found for Fong, one day a week, working for a woman whose husband was terminally ill. Fong is touched by the wife's devotion to her husband and works for her happily and faithfully. When she was called back to the pencil factory, she kept this job as well.

FALL 1984

Fong has applied for U.S. citizenship, and is studying some tapes to prepare for the test. Once she is a citizen, she can get a divorce without being deported, and will send for her parents. Five years of her life are sacrificed in this plan.

2005

Someone tells me that Fong now has an American boyfriend, and manages a successful restaurant near, but not in, Chinatown.

Fathers

These three men fled from the Communist regime in China: Ken came by way of Cuba, Jack went first to Taiwan, and Mr. Tang came here directly. They all have helpful connections here; probably they once had substantial family prestige. Only Jack, a teacher all his life, well educated and prosperous, eagerly tells his story. Ken, understandably, may still fear reprisal against his family and tells only sketchy details of his background.

Fleeing from War Over and Over

Ken, a man in his late 30s, is a diligent student, but tired and distracted much of the time. His wife is ill, so he shoulders most of the care of their young son. He writes well and easily, and speaks and writes Spanish as well as Chinese. His father, who presumably was either a landowner or an intellectual, in danger

*from the Communists, fled from war-torn China to Spain, to work in a restaurant;
then from war-torn Spain he went to Cuba, where his family joined him, and
where he still lives. Ken came here from Cuba as an immigrant; he is employed
at a market owned by an "uncle." I see him in the morning walking hand-in-
hand with his little boy to Lincoln School. They are sober, walking slowly and
not talking. Getting an American education is a serious matter for both of them.*

Double Glory

*His Chinese name means "Double Glory," but he likes to be called Jack. He
is a ping-pong champion, although he doesn't mention it in his interview; perhaps
he thinks it is too frivolous for a serious life story. He stands tall and straight,
dresses in suit and tie, and carries an attaché case. When it is cold, he wears a
fur hat. He was born in Wuhan, a huge and important city in the Yangtze River
flood basin of central China, not long after the Republican Revolution, and he
has been straddling cultures ever since. He began his studies at an old-fashioned
school, learning to compose the "eight-legged essay," which for hundreds of years
was the criterion for the Imperial civil service. He read traditional stories to his
grandmother and mother, who could not read. He says his mother "bought" a
young servant girl. She may have been enslaved, or perhaps this is a poor translation. His mother's feet were partially bound in the old tradition, but his sisters',
he says, were "free." He married a fellow teacher in the modern fashion and rose
to become an official in the ministry of education in the Kuomintang government,
fleeing from Nanjing to Hong Kong, to Chongqing, to Guangzhou, and finally
to Taiwan in 1949. Jack recalls how exciting it was to be part of a new society in
which women were educated and young couples could go boating together, fall in
love, and have a modern marriage. Although he does not confess to any religion,
he worries that his father, who lost all his sons to war and/or exile, may be in an
untended grave. Interviewed in 1979, Jack begins with a Confucian instruction:*

In Chinese thinking, there are five things which are very important. The
first one is *tien*, heaven: because it has the sun, gives light and heat, and the
moon, and thunder, rain, snow, wind; all come from heaven. The second, *di*,
is earth: the ground grows all the plants, flowers, all animals, to make food.
The third one, *juin*, is king: now, the president, the leader, rules you, he gives
you your job. The fourth is parents, *ching*: because they give you life. And
the fifth one is the teacher, *shi*. They teach you; they shape you. In China,
the name for *teacher* means "born before you." The teacher is born before
you; he has experience; he has education, so he can teach you. The student
must learn how to live, and the name for *student* means "learn to be born."
In China, they used to write these five words and put them in a high place

in the house, on the wall, and pray to it. Every house, almost every house, but I don't think so, now.

There cannot be a bad teacher. If you were a bad man, you cannot be a teacher. In Taiwan, also in China, if you have some bad behavior, you cannot be a teacher anymore. Bad parents? In Chinese custom, your parents — if your parents were bad, you could say something like advice; you could make some advice against them. But I think parents who are bad to their children must be sick, because normal parents make sacrifice for their children. For instance, my wife and I worked more than 40 years. We earned a lot of money, but we used this for my children. I sent them to the United States for study. I have six children; I sent five to the United States.

I was born in Wu Chang, the capital of the province of Hupeh. There are three cities: one is Wu chang; another is Hankou; another is Hanyang; so we put them together, Wuhan.[21] I was born close to Hankou, in Wuchang. I hear that the Chinese government has built a bridge across the Yangtze River, between Wuchang and Hanyang. There is also the Han Sui River, which comes into the Yangtze from the north. The cities are divided by the rivers. There were no bridges, only ferries. Hanyang has a mountain beside the river, and Wuchang has a mountain beside the river. It was one mountain, but in the old times, the Yangtze River cut it. This mountain is called Snake, and this one is called Turtle. The bridge goes from the Snake to the Turtle. The place which is called the Yangtze River gorges is located in another place, in the province of Szechuan. Very, very beautiful. Wonderful! Very beautiful. I was on the boat, in that place, just to see the two sides. Hankou is the "little Shanghai" of Hupeh. The famous cities are Shanghai, Guangzhou, Beijing, and Hankou.

I had two sisters and two brothers; I am just in the middle. My father had just one wife. My grandmother lived with us; my grandfather was dead when I was very young. My father worked for the government, to collect the taxes. When I left the mainland of China, I was 37 years old, and my father was 64. I don't know if he is still alive now. When I was a boy, sometimes he left from home to his office, which is far away from home, and he stayed away for several months, in Hankou. It is much bigger, and the tax collection is more important.

When I was a boy, there was no automobile, almost no bicycle, so it was a long distance walking. We crossed the river by boat. Sometimes we had a car with one wheel, and a man pulled it, when I was a boy. We had servants. My mother bought a young girl, and an older servant was a male. My grandmother, and not the servant, fed me. My father had a good education, but my mother didn't. My sisters just finished elementary school. When I was young, I saw many women with bound feet, very small, very small. My mother's feet were not so small, bound, but not so much, bound just a little. And my sisters' were free.

When the Manchu occupied the mainland, the Han people could not get good jobs in the government, but when my father was 30 or 40 years old, the Republic of China was built. He told me something about my family, about my grandmother, grandfather, but not about the government. I played with my brothers and sisters and schoolmates. Sometimes I read stories for my grandmother or my mother because they couldn't read. Those stories were written like a song, something like a poem.

For 10 years, I went to an old-fashioned traditional school where we studied to write the eight-legged essay for the old examinations; then the school changed. I graduated from the elementary school, middle school, and the normal school and the University of Wuchang. I didn't go in the army, just received the training, because China has a lot of soldiers. I worked for the government. I was a teacher, then a principal of an elementary school, then an officer in the ministry of education. When the Japanese troops marched into Nanjing, the central government moved from there to Hankou, so there was a chance, and I passed the examination in Chinese language, history, geography, mathematics: all that I learned in school. I studied English, but we just learned it in class.

In my family, we all went to the public schools, not Christian schools. I didn't know any foreigners. The traditional education in China, we don't believe in God; we believe in the real. If you are well-educated, you don't believe in Buddha or any kind of God. You must know what is right, what is wrong, to distinguish. Yes, this is tao. You must follow the tao, not superstition.

My older brother went to military school. He got sick during the war and is dead. My second brother was killed by the Japanese bombs in the war when he was fighting. My sisters were alive when I left mainland China; my mother was dead. Perhaps my father went to the village with my sister. She lives in Wuchang, but not in the city. I could not keep the connection with them. Because I was an officer in the Kuomintang government, some people said if I wrote a letter to my father, he would be punished by the Communists; otherwise, I would go back.

I taught students 11 or 12 years old, both boys and girls, and then I was the principal at the same school. My wife was a teacher, and we taught at the same school. Her mother was well educated, and she was a teacher, too; this was unusual. All the teachers ate together, played together after school. We took picnics and went boating. I was 24 or 25 years old; my wife was the same. When we wanted to get married, she asked her mother, because her father was dead. I didn't ask. We had a modern-style wedding; we went to the restaurant; we just invited many friends and relatives to eat, about 10 or 12 people around each table. In old times, I should pay her family some money, but I didn't. We lived with my father for just a short time, and then the war began. My mother died when I was a student. After we were married, my wife taught school, and after the babies were born. We had a hard time because of the war: not hungry, but the food was very poor. I left Wuchang first for Hong Kong, because the government sent me. We fought the Japanese from 1937 for eight years, and I went to Hong Kong the first time in 1938, until 1941. I had three children in Hong Kong, one son and two daughters. But the Japanese came to Hong Kong, and I ran to Chongqing. It took three months from Hong Kong to Chongqing, and the sister got sick. When I arrived in Chongqing, I brought her to a hospital, but they couldn't save her life; too late, something in her stomach. She was very little. The third and fourth were born in Chongqing. We stayed there until we got the victory, and then we returned to Nanjing. My youngest son, the dentist, was born in Nanjing. And when the Communists came, we escaped to Wuhan, and then we went to Guangzhou, Hong Kong, Taiwan. The youngest one was born in Taiwan. We have two daughters and four sons. My wife and children were with me everywhere. They were with me in Chongqing, Wuhan, Kwangchow. We traveled by truck, train. I sent my wife and children to go before, so I can run away easily.

Sometimes I had to climb to the top of the train because all the transportation was for the army, and I couldn't get a seat. I remember one very interesting thing. When I left Nanjing, the Communists were coming, and I had to leave, in 1949. I had to leave, but there was no transportation. I saw many people on the top of the train, so I also climbed on. About four persons used two blankets to occupy a little area on top of the train. I put my baggage beside them. It was evening, and the train will be starting. We bought some Chinese cake to eat. I had prepared a special food box with milk, sugar, and a hot water pot. But they haven't, so I invited them to share my milk, my sugar, my hot water. When we finished, the train started, and they said to me, "Oh, the train is starting. The wind will be very sharp! You may lie down on our blanket." So I laid myself down. Just when I lay down, the train passed under a bridge! Yes! The railing of the bridge was before my eyes! I was frightened! Many people were killed! Oh! Many people who sat on their baggage were killed! When the train stopped at the next station, we could see many people under the bridge, very dim. Oh! I just lay down, only one minute! Couldn't see — very fast! I was lucky! Wonderful, yes!

We had enough food then, because some friend helped me, because he had land in the country, so he had rice. When the time came to go to Taiwan, I made a decision to go. I was in Guangzhou at that time. We knew from the news that the Communists took the city. Because I was working for the government, I followed the government. I sent my wife and children first, they went by boat. I went with them, and then I returned to Guangzhou, and then to Chongqing. I saw Mao Zedong in Chongqing. He had come to Chongqing with Chiang Kai-shek; they had a meeting. He visited the ministry of education, so I saw him, once. He was a tall man, fat. Mao can write poems, Chinese poems, but the people liked Zhou En-lai much better. Mao changed China; he changed some things good, but some things not so well.

When we went to Taiwan, we had no relatives or friends. The ministry of education helped me to get a house. My family lived in that house, and then I returned to Guangzhou and Chongqing. I was alone, so I could get out easily. Later, in Taiwan, I built my house, and it had four bedrooms, so we lived together with my son after he was married. I wish someday I could go to the Mainland. I would like to see it now. My wife's brothers and sisters are there, but we don't know where they are, because we have been separated for 30 years. We didn't try to get news, even indirectly, because we worked for the Kuomintang, and it would be dangerous for them.

We have three children here, and three in Taiwan: half and half. My youngest daughter graduated from UC–Berkeley, and works for Safeway, not in the store, in the office. She bought a four-unit apartment beside the lake, but she had trouble. A black woman didn't pay the rent, and the court called and made her something, and she lied! She had some friend to go to prove for her, and lied! So my youngest daughter moved, and is going to sell the apartment. Too much trouble! Now she lives with her older sister, who is married to a doctor. My youngest son, the dentist, is here now, and he isn't married.

The weather here is very nice, and we have a lot of fruit. In Taiwan, we bought apples from the United States, very expensive, about two dollars each. I have heard, "An apple a day keeps the doctor away," so I almost have an apple every day. I buy a box of apples, 80 apples, in the market, and share with my daughters.

All my children can speak English, not so well as the oldest daughter, but they have all studied here except the third, who works for the bank. He didn't study here, but all the others did. And all my grandchildren can speak English as well as Chinese.

I don't worry so much about my children losing Chinese ideas, because I think everything is going to change, but if it is very good, you must keep it. The young people can't treat their parents so kind, like the old times. The Chinese doctrine, you must treat the other one like your brother, but the society has changed too. In Taiwan, people love money best, only money. Not so good. I think American people are polite, just like the old China. They say, "Good morning," even if they are not acquainted. In China history, if you are a general or a captain, if the enemy is coming, you should fight until you die. You can't run away; you cannot abandon the city. Never! In Chinese world, if it is not righteousness, you would die. If you can do the wrong thing, you would rather die. Something unfair, or wrong, you can't do. Old time, older doctrine.

An Obedient Son

Some years after he was a student, when I see Mr. Tang on the street and inquire about his family, he says, "My children are all grown up, and they are all obedient." It surprises me that with a probable English vocabulary of only a few hundred words, he has needed to learn the word "obedient." Filial obedience is a fundamental Confucian concept still influential in Chinese culture, and he expressed the satisfaction all parents feel when children follow the path laid out for them. As students, Mr. and Mrs. Tang did not stand out in any way: in their mid–40s, drab, shy, thin and stooped. They lived near the school, above a row of shops, crowded with their children into one or two rooms. They both left class early to go to work, he to wash dishes in a restaurant, and she to a sewing factory. In February, Mrs. Tang, clearly distressed, came to me before class and begged for help. She showed me a letter addressed to their son, a student at the University of California at Berkeley, saying that he was no longer allowed to attend classes because he had not paid tuition for the winter quarter. In fact, he had paid the tuition, in cash; they have no bank or checking account. I could visualize the family together at the table, counting out the bills and coins from their wages, accumulated on the last possible day. The son had gone to the university registration office early in the morning. The door was still locked, but there was a mail slot and he pushed the bulging envelope through. He had no receipt, and someone must have stolen the money, but nothing could be proved. Fortunately, I knew a friend in the office of the Dean of the University who believed me when I assured her that the story was true. She verified that the boy had a superior record, and arranged for discretionary funds to be applied. Mrs. Tang was profoundly grateful; I was ashamed. This was not justice, but influence: the way it works in most of the world, but in America I wished it to be different.

2

NEWCOMERS FROM VIETNAM

In the fall of 1974, a Chippewa Indian named Adam Nordwall flew to Rome and, wearing a feathered war bonnet and carrying a spear, bounded down the steps of the plane, planted his spear in the tarmac, and announced that he was taking possession of Italy in the name of the Native American people, just as Columbus had claimed North America, "by right of discovery." This stunt demonstrated the irony of European "discovery" and conquest of a land long occupied by Adam Nordwall's ancestors, who probably came to America from Southeast Asia. The evidence for this theory is found in suggestions of lotus flowers in Central American carvings, some similar words in languages, and the ways in which some Native Americans traditionally looped their hair and carried their babies on their hips. There is also a temporary birthmark, the "Mongolian spot," that many newborn Native American and Asian babies have at the base of the spine, and that soon fades away.

The Vietnamese from ancient times sailed the world and were famed for navigation and hydraulic engineering, but they were not often expatriates. The Red River valley of North Vietnam, through an intricate system of dikes and levees, provided food for a large population; survival both of populace and governments depended on stable maintenance of this irrigation system over generations. The rich Mekong River delta of the south provided abundant food for a smaller population. Until recently, when the economy was destroyed by wars, Vietnam was the third largest exporter of rice in the world. Unlike the southern Chinese, who for centuries had sent energetic young men to Southeast Asia, Africa, and the Americas, few Vietnamese wanted to leave their beautiful country. Although Vietnam was dominated by China for a thousand years, and absorbed much of Chinese culture, it stubbornly resisted full integration into China.[1]

Mr. Tran, a former officer in the Vietnamese army, although he is small and slender, has an indisputable air of authority as he introduces himself, saying, "I am descended from the general who defeated Kublai Khan at the Battle of Hanoi in 1220, and since then we do a special kind of martial exercise in my town. But now we cannot do it anymore." No American, possibly excepting the Pueblo people of the Southwest, can fully appreciate the sadness of this broken tradition.

In Thailand, their neighbor country to the west, people say that when there is a market, the Thai farmer will get up at sunrise to be the first one there. The Chinese farmer will be up an hour before sunrise, to beat him. But the Vietnamese farmer will have gotten up still earlier, and will always be the first to market. They brought this same enterprising spirit with them to their newest home.

3

THE FIRST WAVE, 1975

My Future Could Be Bright

In 1974, the first Vietnamese enrolled as an ESL student for a few weeks. He was a young man wanting to upgrade his English skills before attending a university in Texas. Here are three of his compositions, written in pencil on workbook paper:

NOVEMBER 18, 1974

I am D. S. Van, I came from Vietnam 2 days ago. On aboard, I looked out the window of a plane. I saw San Francisco is very big. When I set my foot on San Francisco I felt cold.... I'm sad because I miss my home, and I'm happy because of my future could be bright.

NOVEMBER 20, 1974

I am D. S. Van, was born in Saigon South Vietnam on June 10th, 1955. When I had lived in Saigon, I wished that I can go to the United States of America to attend at university.

JANUARY 6, 1975

Dear Mrs. Swent,

I will only study this school a week later, because I will have to present at college before Jan. 12th to register. Thank you very much about your educations. Last Christmas and new year, I went to Lake Tahoe. I like it very much. That was the first time I've seen snow, but I was very cold because my shoes were wet.... It's still one month and a half to be Vietnamese new year. This time I'll be in Texas alone. I think I'll be sad and homesick. Thanks again. Sincerely yours, Van S. D.

Four months later, in May 1975, thousands of refugees from Southeast Asia followed him, all hoping for bright futures.

On the Way to Find the Freedom

[*The author of this primary document asked me to copy and publish it. It was dated May 7, 1975, and written with ball-point pen on the backs of flattened C-ration cartons*]

At approximately 2400 hours P.M. on April 29, 1975, the ship HQ 502, her name is Thi Nai, departed from the military navy port with technical of the ship very badly. One engine working. A few hours by a medivac happened at Vietnamese Navy HQ main gate. And got confused with a lot of people and vehicles were jam traffic. They are senior officers serving in ARVN [*Army of the Republic of Vietnam*]. Some people cooperated by the USA system. Some Vietnamese Catholic, almost from North Vietnamese by birth, just passing at Nha Be logistical support base. We picked up the commander of the Vietnamese Navy fleet at about 4 o'clock A.M. After got through Nha Be, some noise come from the south by 122 mm. rocket and 105 mm. howitzer. Continuous the noise. A fire mushroom appeared by the Communist rocket to hit Nha Be gas pool.

On the morning of May 1st, 1975, we got to Con Son prisoner islands, about 10 o'clock A.M. here was the rendezvous place for all Vietnamese Navy vessels under way. Found out the USN Seventh Fleet waited for us.[1] At about 10 o'clock A.M. an unknown target aircraft flied over the ship. Immediately all groups of anti-aircraft was ready which wouldn't fly back.

In the same day about 1300, an ARVN Dogbird L19 appeared and flew around the ship. The copilot jumped out from the plane suddenly, with the float which was given by the main pilot. Right away a frogman jumped down over sea for rescue. A few minutes after that, main pilot jumped out from the airplane. During fly by itself for a few seconds then dropped down in the ocean. We haven't seen main pilot any more. After that incident occurred for freedom, 2 other UHIB helicopters safe landed on the ship. They came from Can Tho airbase, was Departed while the Saigon broadcast announce the RVN government was surrounded. On May 3, 1975, a rear anchor was dropped oversea. Occurred by some sabotager. At about midnight an image body jumped out oversea from the tail of the ship. Few people saw him and recognized he were an ARVN officer, Major Tuan. He left his family in Saigon who wouldn't like alone.

From day to day, people on board got problems as water and foods. Each person just received a quarter of water and 3 spoons of rice for a day. On May 4, 1975, a DE U.S. Destroyer ship has given supply to us so people had no problem about waters and foods. A pregnant lady going to give a child was sended to USN ship also. However each meal combat individual were issued for 2 persons. People on ship had not enough meal to eat. But loudspeak said:

> Ship company has some foods for sale, as
> $1 for 7 pack of instant noodle
> $1 for 5 cans of sardine
> $1 for 4 meals of C ration

(The C-ration, we received a supply from the U.S. Navy ship. It was supposed to be delivered to all the people on the ship. But some corruption. They tried to sneak out or they hide it, then they sell it again. They didn't give enough to the people, so the people are still hungry, and they sell it.)

Make bowels movement, that was a big problem. Two toilets on ship only. Many people stand up long line, waited about 2 or 3 hours for your turn. On May 7, 1975, a minor burned was on ship because a woman used gasoline for cooking rices. Some seamans used CO_2 stopped fire immediately.

Same day, these USN ships supplied to us the 3rd time. This late one, USN ship gave to us an USA flag and the Vietnam flag was changed for the USA flag at 12 hours A.M. During all people stand up sharp and the national anthem was sang by the Vietnameses. Some people cries, no longer Vietnam but Vietnam stay in their hearts all time.

At 1600 hours P.M. we got in Subic Bay. People got ashore after checked out baggages by U.S. Marines. Then they got aboard another cargo civilian ship, Green Wave. At 2400 P.M. the same day, the Green Wave got under way to Guam. She brought 4,300 persons aboard. On cargo ship we felt better and more comfortable as foods and medical cares. However, that was unfortunately people. People got wet and cool while it was rain at night several times.

Presented on the Green Wave ship we recognized former president's advisor, ARVN Colonel, District Chief, and Province Chief. As in my consideration the medivac occurred while RVN was surrounded by the Communists. And approximately included the following:

> 50% all brands of ARVN officers with their families
> 10% politicians
> 20% American workers
> 10% people like to be free

A Man Who Escaped Twice

Mr. D. did not want his name known, nor would he consent to have his voice recorded, but in April 1983 he was eager to have me write down his story. He was a student in the ESL class for refugees at Laney College, and he brought with him to the interview a Laney classmate and his older brother Mark, who speaks English well and acted as interpreter when needed. They greeted me in Vietnamese style, taking my hand in both of theirs, bowing slightly, and calling me "Ma'am." All three of them had left Vietnam as "boat people" who risked their lives after the initial exodus in 1975; this was Mr. D's second escape.

Mr. D. is small and very bright-eyed. He comes from a Chinese family and thinks his parents moved to Vietnam in 1918. His father had a restaurant in Saigon, and they lived in Saigon proper, not in the Chinese district, Cholon. He went to Vietnamese school for five years, reads and writes Vietnamese, and speaks it fluently. He speaks Cantonese Chinese very well, but he can't write Chinese. [*Mark interrupts to say that Mr. D. speaks Chinese better than Vietnamese.*] He helped his father in the restaurant and is a very good cook. He is married and has seven children, who are now between 12 and 21 years of age. In 1975, when he left, the oldest was 12 and the youngest about four. He joined the army as a reconnaissance scout who went out into the villages, spotted the Viet Cong, and sent information back to the Vietnamese army forces, who could then attack. He had no contact with American military personnel.

In May 1975, when the Communists took over the government, he somehow found himself on a ship offshore, was picked up and rescued by an American ship, taken to Guam, and from there he was flown to Ft. Chaffee, Arkansas, where he stayed for three months but didn't learn any English. There was no communication with his family, and they didn't know where he was or that he was alive. He was one of 1,600 Vietnamese who petitioned ICEM, International Committee for External Migration, to go back to Vietnam. They were flown from Ft. Chaffee to Camp Pendleton, where they stayed for two weeks, and then were flown back to Guam. From Guam they took a Vietnamese merchant vessel to Saigon and Danang.

Immediately when they got off the ship all the returnees were taken to "re-education camp" at some place that was very far, 900 miles, from Saigon, in one of the "new economic zones." Fifty men slept in each tent. They had water to drink, which they got from the mountains, and every morning received a handful of red potatoes to eat. They were given a shovel, and they worked every day under the hot sun for 12 hours or more, shoveling and farming, growing red potatoes and vegetables. In the evening they were given political lectures, but they didn't pay attention. During this time, he suffered greatly with malaria, which he has not had since he came back to the United States.

At the end of a year, he was able to notify his family that he was there. They had never known that he was in America, nor whether he was alive. His wife was allowed to visit him once every three months in the camp, but it was very hard for her, and it was a long and expensive trip by train, so she seldom came, and he didn't see his children at all. At the end of six years, only one hundred people were left in the camp; he was one of the last released. One morning they gave him one hundred dong [*Vietnamese currency*] and told him he could take the train to Saigon. Three months later, a friend told him he could get passage on a large ship that was leaving, so he left, without discussing it with his wife, presumably for her protection. He did not have to pay a lot of money. The ship had over one hundred people on it, and it took them just three days to get to Palau Bidong. They were not attacked by pirates, who only attack small ships without guns, so presumably his ship was armed. He stayed for three months in the refugee camp at Palau Bidong, again under the auspices of ICEM, who then flew him to the refugee camp in the Philippines, where he stayed for another three months and studied ESL for two months; this was his first contact with English. Then he was sponsored by the International Institute, flown to Oakland, and met by the International Institute people, who took care of him and got him into the ESL program for refugees. Two years later, he writes quite well, and seems to understand a lot. Asked if he plans to go back yet again to Vietnam, he laughed and said no, that he wants to bring his wife and seven children here. They have asked him not to send packages anymore because it made it hard for them.[2] In five years, he hopes to have a job as a cook in a restaurant, and meanwhile, he will do anything, any kind of hard work. He is 41 years old now, and he feels confident and ready to build a new life.

Mark makes it clear that he himself is Vietnamese and not ethnic Chinese. He is 28, speaks fluent English, and has curly hair [*a permanent?*]. His wife has a beauty parlor in Danang, and he says she has a good business. She kept two sons with her, and he came here with two sons. He and the two boys live in West Oakland by themselves and are not in contact with the Vietnamese community. He knows how to drive a truck, has been in Los Angeles, has worked as a carpet cleaner, but can't find a job at the moment. Mark spoke earnestly of what a beautiful country Vietnam had been. People lived a very good life there; they had food; people had cars and trucks and nice furniture, with plenty of jobs for everyone. There were no problems and no worries until 1975 when the Communists took over, but from then on, the North Vietnamese came, and they were wild people, just like animals. In North Vietnam they had been very poor, and they over-ran South Vietnam, destroying the former pleasant happy life. They took his truck away from him; he could still drive it, but it belonged to the State, not to him. He didn't seem aware that there had been a war before 1975, and he dimly recalled learning in school of the partition of 1954. His resentment was directed at the decline after 1975; the North Vietnamese told them that they would be good to them, but instead, life changed for the worse.

He left Danang, in central Vietnam, in a small boat with fifteen people. They did not have to pay much money, only had to buy gas for the boat.

They didn't have permission to go, so they didn't bribe any officials. They took no property with them, he said, not like some people. He didn't actually say "like the wealthy Chinese," but he glanced at Mr. D. and said that many people, like the Chinese, were able to bribe officials and take a lot of gold and diamonds with them, but in his case, he just left. Those like him weren't able to buy their way out, and when they escaped, they either made it or died. He went to Hainan and then to the south coast of Guangdong, where he saw people who are very, very poor and have a hard life; until then, he had evidently thought that all Chinese were wealthy. After spending a while in a refugee camp in Hong Kong he came to the United States.

Both Mark and Mr. D. emphasized that they are grateful to be here; they will do any kind of work, no matter how hard; the important thing is freedom, and so long as they have that nothing else matters. They were thoroughly disillusioned by the false promises of Communism.

I called Mark's apartment a few days later to thank him for his help with the interview. One of the sons answered the telephone, speaking very good English. He took my name and number, very politely, and called me "Ma'am."

Miss Tran

SEPTEMBER 15, 1975

Miss Tran, 22 years old, animated and apparently happy, composes a sentence using the conditional tense: "If I had not left Saigon, I would be sadder than now." She lives with an American family somehow related to her; they also own an apartment building where her father and brother live by themselves.

SEPTEMBER 20, 1975

Mrs. Chim, an old Chinese lady, stays after class to tell me she is worried about Miss Tran, who has told her that in her room she has a handful [*she gestures to show how much*] of gold, and she spells it out, "g-o-l-d," to be sure I understand. Mrs. Chim, older and wiser, is afraid Miss Tran will be robbed, or taken advantage of by some young man who will tell her he loves her, but only wants her gold.[3] She urges me to advise Miss Tran to rent a safe deposit box for six dollars.

SEPTEMBER 22, 1975

I present a lesson about going to the bank and renting a safe deposit box for valuables. It is well received, and many of the students say they will do this. Miss Tran doesn't commit herself.

OCTOBER 20, 1975

Yesterday while Miss Tran's father and brother were out shopping, they were robbed of a new sofa that cost $200, a stereo set, a cassette tape recorder, and a portable radio brought from Saigon and worth over $100. The owner told them not to report it to the police, just to forget it. Today they are buying new locks for the apartment. I wrote on the blackboard, "You lock the barn after the horse is stolen," and everyone responded to this obviously universal concept. Miguel Sanchez says that in Cuba they say, "You throw the machete after the snake has slithered past." Mr. Lok says that in China they say, "You close the pen after the sheep has escaped."

Miss Tran wonders why the landlord did not want to report the robbery. I don't like any of the possible answers: he colluded with the robbers; he fears reprisal if the robbery is reported; the police will do nothing, and it's not worth the effort of reporting. I can think of an example of the conditional tense: "If there were no robbers, I would be happier."

Hot Tap Water

JUNE 2, 1976

Mr. Nguyen asks if the tap water is safe to drink. He notices that it has something in it like white powder that goes away after a while. When he washes dishes in the running hot water, they get clean, and the grease comes off even without soap. This is fine, but he wonders if it is good to drink, because of this mysterious substance. After some discussion, I conclude that it is the steam in the hot tap water that makes it look milky. I suppose he has not washed dishes before.

The Captain and the Songbird

A romantic story, perhaps a plot for an operetta: a music-loving captain in the South Vietnamese army, serving in a provincial post, buys a songbird to keep in his quarters, falls in love with the daughter of the songbird seller, and they marry. But— the captain's father does not like the girl. Two years later, a refugee for a second time, in a strange country, cooped up in a small apartment with a daughter-in-law he despises, the old man weeps. In time, he is somewhat consoled by his grandsons, but he never reconciles with his daughter-in-law.

The former captain, now a student, takes particular delight in learning new idioms. After his son is born, he reports, with eyes twinkling, "My baby keeps me

on my toes." The baby's name means "only chief" and he will have a good destiny.
He stops crying when they play Vietnamese music for him. The captain was born
in North Vietnam, and when the country was partitioned in 1954 he and his
father, a government official, went as refugees to South Vietnam, leaving the cap-
tain's mother behind. The father took a second wife, and they had a daughter. In
1975, when the South Vietnamese government fell, the captain was at certain risk
of losing his life if captured, so he had official permission to leave, taking with
him his wife, his 70-year-old father, and his half-sister's three-year-old son, Vu.
The family pattern repeats: a little boy taken from his mother, and a flight to a
strange home. Interviewed in February, 1977, the captain says:

In my country there are many kinds of song birds, and they sing very
well. I met my wife; she went to see her father. He went to the forest to get
song birds to sell them. I went to his house to buy some birds. I bought them,
and I nursed them in a cage. I lived in Saigon, but I worked in the provincial
close to Saigon.

I am a Buddhist, and my wife is Catholic. Her family is Catholic. Her
country is the country of Ho Chi Minh: Ha Ting in the north of the middle
of Vietnam, in the mountains. My wife studied English in high school in
Vietnam. The mother of my wife died a long time [*ago*]. My wife goes to
church every Sunday. My wife wants to baptize the baby, but I don't want.
My father told me, let my baby grow up, and he will choice religion. My
father always told me, Buddhist is the same Catholic; they both are good. We
think the good is up to each person, and if we think good, that's good. We
don't need the picture to hang on the wall. Her father was happy when we
got married. My father was not happy; he didn't like her. Different way of
living. My father always told me that he doesn't like her.

My father and mother were separated when I was three years old. My
friend's mother told me my father fought with my mother and my mother
doesn't like. My mother left him. Sometimes she came to see me. When I
came to Saigon, in 1954, I knew my mother was in Hanoi. I don't know if
she is alive now. My father's second wife stayed in Saigon. Many people who
lived in Saigon had to go to the country to work. I don't know if she is alive
or not. I don't know about my sister, if she is alive. My wife had a cousin
lived in New York, and her cousin received a letter from Saigon, so we know
her father died.

I feel close to my sister, and when I was in Saigon, if I have money, I
give her money to pay for tuition. My father didn't have money. Every month
I had to give money to my father and his daughter. In my country there were
no social security. Before the war, I was a teacher. I went to the university
for three years, and I taught math in night school. In my country there are
not many jobs. I taught for the purpose of money. In my country I wanted
to study data processing, but I have no money, and in the university there are

no data processing subjects. Now I am studying data processing at Laney College. I signed up in advanced algebra, and my teacher told me I don't need this, and he told me to take calculus on differential equations, and I am taking calculus to review.

We knew that the Communists will take over my country. Everybody know this about 15 days before. Because I was a police officer, so I knew that. I have some friends in the Vietnam navy and they told me that the United States will let the Communists take over my country. At that time I always turned on the radio to listen to BBC and ABC from the United States. On the day the Communists took over Saigon, I didn't dare to go to my house because I knew there are some Communists at the area of my house. A week or two weeks before the Communists took over Vietnam, some soldiers and some policemen were killed by the Communists, so I didn't dare to go to my house. I told my wife to go to the house and take my father and Vu to the harbor, and I stayed in the house of my cousin.

Vu's mother, my sister, went to work. I took two suitcases. We had to wait for a boat, and on April 29 we had to sleep at the harbor, on the pavement. We bought some bread and some noodles. Vu was three years old; my father was 70. At the harbor, there were rockets. I was not afraid because I was a soldier, but my wife and father were afraid. Vu didn't know what is afraid. At that time he was too young to know how.

We got on a boat carrying petrol, a tanker. About 200 people were on it. It was easy to get on the ship. I kept my ID card. At that time we wanted to go to the international sea, and when we got to the international sea, we met the Vietnamese navy, and we transferred to the ship. We had no food for two days, and we have only three cans of milk, and I had to let the three cans of milk to my father and Vu. We had water to drink but no food. On the Vietnamese ship they had food, and on the way to the Philippines the American navy gave us food and water. I got off the Vietnamese ship at Subic harbor there, and then we got on board on the big ship. In Subic Bay we saw my wife's aunt, my wife's mother's sister. She is in Stockton now. From Subic Bay we went to Guam, and we stayed a month in Guam. I think it was a good time because we were very happy that we escaped the Communists.

His wife recently received a letter telling her that her father has gone to stay with her mother. Since her mother has been dead for years, she knows that her father has died. They are still afraid to write to the sister, whose little boy is here.

My wife and baby and my father and Vu are all well. Now my father is happy because of my son. I think he is better now. On the day, he plays with my son. He speaks to my wife, but he doesn't like her. When we go to Stockton to visit my wife's family, he is happy to see them. We went to Stockton to celebrate Tet [*lunar New Year*]. My wife took some special food, and we ate together. We talk about Vietnam a lot, and we know the people live in Vietnam are very sad now. And we really know they don't have enough food and medicine. Sometimes Vu is a bad boy and makes my baby cry, so I use chopsticks to spank him on the back side. In the Vietnamese custom, the children have to obey their parents.

Wartime Bride

She has beautifully manicured hands and well-styled hair, wears eye make-up, and some elegant jewelry; she looks as if she has always been pampered and carefree. When she comes to my house with her husband to be interviewed, I hope to learn the secret of surviving so gracefully the horrors she recounts in her family history. His English is excellent, much better than hers, but she freely interrupts and prompts him, and frequently they talk in alternate snatches, showing a comfortable, gentle relationship. When he tells of meeting her, he says thoughtfully, "This was the beginning of our family life."

In December of 1984, she begins her story of violence and loss by giggling and saying, "I can't speak." The giggling is from distress, not amusement. When asked how many brothers and sisters she has, she first counts herself among the sisters. Her husband explains why it was easier in Vietnam to have large families: "We don't have things like life insurance, insurance on everything. When you go to school, you don't have to pay anything. And if you get sick, the public hospital does a better job than the private hospital. And taxes, ordinary people like us, we don't have anything to pay. Really."

Her story begins in central Vietnam. Hue, where she was born, was the old royal capitol city, and her Christian family was possibly associated with the imperial court or at least with the French colonial regime. In 1959, five years after Vietnam was partitioned, her family moved to Quang Ngai because her father was in the militia. He died shortly after that.

I was born in the center, in Hue. I have a father and mother; I have eight — four brothers and four sisters. I am one. So I have three sisters and four brothers. In Vietnam, it is a medium-sized family. Some families have 20, 24, 15 children. Do I want 20? Oh, no! Four is enough here! When he gets a paycheck, he gives it to me. I don't know about tax. My family are Christians. I have uncles who are priests, and two sisters [*nuns*]. On my father's side I have one, and on my mother's side I have one. And my great-grandfather, they cut his head off because he was a Christian. My mother told me this.

She met her husband when he was working for the U.S. embassy inspecting elections, and she took her mother to vote. He called on her mother a few times and then began to court her. Three months later, they were married, evidently in great style. The wedding cost, according to him, 100,000 piastres; she says it was even more than that, and they were given lots of gold, jewelry, and beautiful clothes.

We lived with my mother one month, and then we went to Saigon to visit relatives, for New Year's, because we marry [*for a honeymoon*]. Tet is the new year, and that year was the Year of the Monkey, Mau Thun.

They celebrated the lunar New Year [January 21] of 1968 with a big party at his aunt's house in Saigon. Then, leaving their possessions with the aunt, they went by bus to visit other relatives in another town. That night the Communists launched the surprise attack on Saigon, known in America as the "Tet offensive," and all of their beautiful things were destroyed in the bombings.[4] They had to stay in Saigon for two months, in great distress, and finally were able to get transportation back to Quang Ngai when the airports were usable. When she got off the plane, she was told that her mother and three siblings had been killed in the bombing there. As she tells about it now, she literally wrings her hands. Her mother had a beautiful and very expensive jade necklace of more than forty beads. In Buddhist thought, life bears four burdens: birth, sickness, old age, and death; therefore, multiples of four are unlucky. After the mother's death, other members of the family tried to sell the necklace, but no one wanted to buy it. Her sister owns it but doesn't wear it.

Alternating, words rushing out, they tell of her next experiences. He lived in the embassy compound, and they only saw each other for lunch and dinner. On several nights when she was alone with the babies, bombs exploded just on the other side of the wall of their little house. Fortunately, he had arranged a sort of bunker, which saved their lives. She had no help from the government and, oddly, insists that her children were not troubled.

We lived in Quang Ngai one year, and when my husband go to Navy, I must go to Saigon. I had my own house; it was very small. I had two children then; one year, one child. Now they are eight, six, four, three. I was almost hit by rocket three times, and I didn't have anything from welfare. But the children don't understand; they are too little.

He was sent to the United States for duty as a liaison supply officer and arranged with his U.S. counterpart in Saigon to rescue his family, if necessary. In spring, 1975, she was notified that she was to be evacuated.

They told me, I just have five minutes to pack. And they told me, don't bring too heavy, and don't tell anything; don't talk about it. So I didn't say goodbye to anyone. I couldn't bring souvenirs, anything. I had to leave everything. We went on a plane to Guam for ten days, and then to Florida. That time, the airplane dropped down in Travis airport, and I told them, "Let me get off here," but they didn't hear me. I said, "I have my husband who lives here," and they told me they can't do that. So I stayed in camp in Florida for three weeks, an air force base. The children were 16 months, 2 years, 4, and

6, and they were sick that time, really, really sick, from the change of weather. It was hot in day and very cold in night. I wasn't sick, but I get tired. Very very tired.

She shows a snapshot recently received of a sister's wedding in Vietnam. All of the people are gauntly thin. In contrast to her own expensive wedding, this one was a poverty-level affair: only one pig and twenty chickens were served. She now has a filing job in an office, and he is a civilian employee at a navy base. They have some security together for the first time in their lives. There is no dream of returning to Vietnam.

He says, "Right now, what we are trying to do is completely settle our family in this new land."

A Tale of Two Keys

Somewhere near the Saigon airport, on May 1, 1975, a motorcycle was left, with the key hidden near by. Also somewhere in the city, there was a well-furnished, carefully locked house; that key is now in Oakland, California, along with a bankbook for an inaccessible account. These details are recalled by a gentleman, Mr. Tran, who sits with his brother, one year older, at the rear of the classroom. Their superior education—they know Chinese, Vietnamese, French, and English—and their qualities of good character are of little practical help to them here and now. The younger one worked for 12 years for an American firm and is more confident of his English, so he speaks for both of them, generally saying "we," almost never "I," and pointing out that they have been refugees again and again. They were interviewed on February 5, 1977.

You know, the war happened for a long time for us. We are refugees many times. Now for my brother, the third time. He was a stationmaster in China, in Yunnan. You remember there is one railroad from North Vietnam to China, Yunnan District. My brother left Yunnan because of the Japanese war with China. He left all belongings in Yunnan to go back to Hanoi. From Hanoi to South, and Saigon to here. So you remember now this is third time he is refugee.

In my family, my mother had five children, three sons and two daughters. My brother is older; I am the second. My father died when I was seven years old. My mother took a small business to support our family. So after we finish elementary school, we must go to work to help our mother. Very difficult in our life. The life in Hanoi very difficult to find a job, so we must do everything we can to help our mother.

I was born in the center of Hanoi. When we were young we went to the French school. Because this French school belonged to the Chinese and French men. So I could speak Chinese for a long time; I speak only, but I cannot read or write, but French I can read and write. When I was young, we lived together with my family in Hanoi, but when I was 20, we lived together with my brother. We lived separately from my family. We rented a house; we take care ourselves, everything. Because I can say to you, it is a hard life for us a long time, when we were young, because we belong to the poor family, so everything we must make for ourselves; we have not the same as the rich man.

I think I was 17 years old when I stopped school. I could not continue my school because the tuition is very expensive. My brother and I, we would like to study hard, but we cannot pay the tuition. When I was old enough to go to work, I remember first I worked with the Bank of China. I worked at daytime, and at night we opened one course to teach French to Chinese. So we earn a little money to help my mother. And after that, I had seven years experience in the French hotel and restaurant. I was manager of the hotel restaurant. There are two hundred rooms; I take care about it. I know very well about the French food. It was a good job. After my brother left the job in China because the war between Japan and China, he was an accountant for a French firm. This was a big company, I think the same as Safeway here. So when the Communists came to North Vietnam we must leave from Hanoi to South Vietnam.

The first time I came to South Vietnam, the same, same as the United States; I didn't know the way; I had to find the way, everything. I didn't know anyone in Saigon. We had to find a place by ourselves. But we had some money to find a house to rent. So we must find a job. My mother took a small business, I think as a salesman of some kind. My brother found a job in a Chinese firm as accountant, and I found a job in American firm, 20 years. My sister did everything in the family and helped my mother. When she married, she lived with her husband, and my brother and I lived with my mother. After my mother died, my brother and I, two persons, lived together. You know, for Vietnamese custom, when my mother is still alive, she takes care of everything as chief of the family. When my mother dies, my brother takes care everything. I have a picture of my mother I brought from Saigon, in a small frame. I celebrate her anniversary every year; I remember the date she died; we must celebrate.[5] And my father, too. I don't have a picture of my father. We are not Christian, not Buddhist; we are Confucius men; we stay home. For example, when I would like to celebrate my mother's anniversary, we celebrate at home. For my grandmother, we celebrate at home, not in the church, not in the pagoda. We buy a flower and some food to memorize [commemorate].

When we left Hanoi [in 1954], we took some old belongings, but very difficult. We took a big ship from the American Navy for evacuation of the population.[6] The war was stopped so the population could leave. When we left Saigon [*in 1975*], we just had two hours to leave. My sister worked with American delegation between two governments so she can make a list for us to come here. I worked for American firm, but private company, so they have no plane for personnel to go to United States. This firm belong to private company, and not belong to government. I think there are many many friends work for same company who cannot go to United States. I was workshop repair supervisor. I was working for this firm for a long time, about 12 years.

We know for one or two weeks, at that time I remember the situation very dangerous for us, so we prepare everything, but we don't know what day we can go, because my sister doesn't know what day either. So I remember that day on Friday, she came back to our home; we must go at 12 o'clock. At 10 I know, for only 2 hours. I cannot go to bank. I had some money in the bank, but I had no time to pick up money in the bank, so I left all. I had my own house in South Vietnam; it belonged to us, my brother and I. We bought our house there, but we left everything belonging to us, all furniture. I can bring only some clothes, the small suitcase. I can't bring anything. All belongings I left. I could bring only one small radio. I had a big television, electric fan, sewing machine; everything I left. We had not a big house, a small garden, three bedrooms, kitchen, furniture. When we left Saigon, you know the situation very dangerous, so when we left we cannot speak to the neighborhood, to any person. We went from our house to the airport. My sister and brother-in-law took a taxi with their two children, and my brother and I took the motor bicycle. When we came to the airport, we left the motorcycle at the airport. The key of the motorcycle I left in the airport; I put the key in a spot.

The house key I brought to here. I locked the front door of my house, but what became of my house and the furniture, I don't know. I left many things, souvenirs I brought from Hanoi to South Vietnam; I left the whole thing in South Vietnam. Even I had some money in the bank, and the book I brought to here. But when I came in the United States, I had about two hundred Vietnamese dollars, but I could not change them. In my suitcase, I brought only clothes and small papers; for example, identification card. That means we have no everything belonging to us. Even for the way, we don't understand. But now I came here, we would like to learn better to rebuild our life. We would like to live here for good.

Not Any Peaceful Day

Richmond, California, is a tough bayside industrial town north of Oakland, where this woman pediatrician has her office. She sees her fellow refugees from a professional as well as a personal viewpoint and distinguishes between those like

*her who left by plane just before the Communist takeover in 1975, and those who
fled by boat after that. She lived in the United States once before, in the 1960s,
when she had graduated from medical school in Paris and served her medical res-
idency in New York and Washington, D.C., while her husband, a graduate of the
London School of Economics, earned his Ph.D. at Cornell. When they returned
to Vietnam, he was president of a bank and she was a professor in medical school
and director of social service. They knew their status made them vulnerable, so
they took an opportunity to escape by plane on April 27, 1975. Interviewed three
years later, she says:*

In my lifetime, I don't think that we had any peaceful day in Vietnam.
The war is about 30 years, the same. Our plane was one of the last to leave
the airport. So we were very lucky. My brother, who is a judge, preferred to
stay, and he was put in what they call a "re-education camp," and he died a
few months ago. All our friends who could not get out are now in concen-
tration camps. We had a few things with us, a small bag in which we had
money and certain papers. We left behind all our belongings; all were confiscated by the government. They have passed a law after we left, that we are
traitors, and all properties belonging to the people who left Vietnam will be
confiscated, and my husband's bank also is nationalized.

You must understand that the Vietnamese here are quite young, and the
majority have no health problems at all. I have found that some of the Vietnamese do like the cold; they have found that it is very healthy, that you work
better in the colder climate. But they do complain. One of the reasons is that
they are not used to wearing warm clothes, warm underwear. The Vietnamese
like to live outdoors, and they always like to have all the doors and windows
open all day long. And they don't like to be confined in the room with the
heat on. So it's not a question of cold, but maybe the question of confinement,
or the question of having to wear wool, warm clothing.

I think the Vietnamese recognize that they have to have birth control,
now, one way or another, but at the same time, you don't expect them to have
small families because traditionally, they all like to have large families. But I
think it will change because many of these families have been telling me that
they don't want to have more than two or three. So it's going to change, the
way of thinking. There is no help here, and the wife has to do everything.

The young men, the young children, especially the new refugees, they
are different from the first group of refugees. Because the boat cases are the
volunteer refugees, they just risked their life. The other refugees, the first
group, belonged to the families of American friends, or they happened to be
there when the plane left; by chance, they were there. But the second group
really risked their lives, no question about it. Because the sea was very rough,
they had to leave without any food, without clothing, with nothing, because
if they got caught, they risked life.

The Vietnamese are emotionally healthy, very stable; they are survivors. The Vietnamese are always surrounded by their family, who give them protection since a small age. They are never by themselves. At the same time they respect law easily. On the whole they are not violent, which makes them very good citizens. There is a lot of authority from the father and mother; there is no permissiveness. This is one thing that we feel, that the problem of violence and delinquency is much less in Vietnam.

4

LOOKING BACK, YEARS LATER

I Don't Think Our Generation
Would Belong Anywhere

JUNE 1975

Dzung and Binh, in their mid–20s and newly wed, wear fatigue jackets issued by the Red Cross; the olive drab color makes them look sallow. At her throat is a glimpse of a fine pearl necklace. In class, they are serious and solicitous of each other. She uses her own family [last] name. They speak English with French accent and intonation, and he makes, and maintains, eye contact when he speaks. After class, they run to cross Broadway on a yellow light. She is ahead of him, looking back over her shoulder, laughing and holding out her hand as he races to catch up. Her name means "beauty"; his, "peace."

JANUARY 1977

A year and a half after arriving here, he works at a pharmaceutical warehouse, stocking shelves and making deliveries; she is a student at a community college. They are comfortable with each other, frequently speaking in chorus, and interrupting or correcting each other without hesitation. They use some French terms, like "note" for "grade," and "embassade" for "embassy." Like many of the Vietnamese refugees, they were born in North Vietnam and were uprooted when the country was partitioned in 1954 and non–Communists moved to South Vietnam. They were young children at the time of that first exodus; when they left Vietnam on April 24, 1975, 21 years later, they had been married four months. He was a pharmacist, 28 years old, and she was an attorney, 24 years old. They tried for two weeks to make arrangements to leave Vietnam, and in the event, they left on 15 minutes' notice, taking only one change of clothes, their wedding photo album, and their college transcripts, and boarding a crowded American ship. For a month, they were shuttled about in great confusion: told they would go first to Vung Tau, but they did not stop there; told they would go from Subic to Guam, but instead they went to Wake; told they would go to Arkansas, but they went to California. After weeks of uncertainty, they arrived at Camp Pendle-

68

ton in Southern California, and his cousin, who is married to an American and had lived here for several years, sponsored them so they could come to Oakland. They enrolled immediately in the adult school, on June 3, 1975, and later transferred to the community college, entered a job training program, and settled into a small apartment. He begins to tell their story, recorded in January 1977:

We planned for about two weeks to leave Vietnam, when South Vietnam lost a lot of city, at the beginning of April, 1975. We read from the American magazine, like *Newsweek*, that the U.S. Senate had permitted to accept about 130,000 Vietnamese, about one month before the last of April, but I didn't think we had the chance to leave Vietnam because we were not working with American companies or American government. We couldn't apply because the Vietnamese government didn't want the Vietnamese to leave.

She continues with the account, speaking hesitantly in a low voice:

My father had a friend who was an American, so he promised that he would get a permit for our family to go out, but it is not very sure about that, and at about the middle of April, he had to leave Vietnam, because at that time, the U.S. government ordered that all Americans to leave Vietnam. So he said to my father that the permit was in the U.S. *embassade* in Vietnam, but then my father couldn't go into the *embassade* to get the permit, because at that time, a lot of people to make line at the *embassade*, and the GI's didn't allow the Vietnamese to go into the *embassade*, so we had to find any way to go out. And my sister-in-law, she worked in a company, and in that company, a man said that if anybody want to leave Vietnam, could get a permit, but we had to have two thousand dollars per person, but we didn't have enough dollars because my father wanted that all the family to go out; it included ten persons. Because we ask if we can give them gold or anything else instead of dollars because we couldn't get at one time 20,000 dollars. But they didn't accept it because he said that even the gold the price maybe change. At that time, one bar of gold have the value of one hundred dollars, but the price changed every day, so he said maybe tomorrow it would be two bars of gold, and they didn't want that because it's so hard for them to bring the gold out if they have a lot of gold. So they didn't do that, so my husband and I tried to find the dollars. He had an aunt who worked in an American company, so we hoped that maybe she could find any American to exchange for us, so he came to her house, and she said that she had the paper, the permit to leave, because she worked for the U.S. company. That company would allow all of its employees to leave, so she said to both of us that if we wanted, we could leave with her, but she didn't promise to us that we could leave or not because we didn't have our name on that paper. So she said that maybe tomorrow or some day later. So we came home, but about 15 minutes later his mother came and told us that his aunt will leave now, so if we want, we have to go to her house and go with her, so we had to leave immediately.

So we came to a place a few miles far from Saigon on the highway, and fortunately there were two gates which were guarded by the Vietnamese soldiers, so we gave them money, so at the last moment we could go to the ship at the dock. On that paper they had about 20 persons, but at the last moment, one family didn't come on time, so they had only 12 or 13 persons at that moment, so they just counted the number of persons, and it was less than the number on the paper, so they let us to go on out. They just called the name, so because we didn't have the name on that paper, so she told us to go first, and she said, "That is that man," but when we were on the ship, we looked at that name, and it is the name of an old person, about 60 years old!

The curfew began at that time also. We just packed a few things because before that we just packed our clothes because we just think to move in Saigon, in case that the Viet Cong will locate in Saigon, so we just move from one place to another place in Saigon. But we didn't think that we will go *out*. We pack the kind of thing that you go camping. Just two pairs of clothes. That means one on our person and one in that bag. We just bring the film of our marriage and also our birth certificate and the photocopy of our degree. We got on an American ship, and we had to wait until one o'clock the next day to go on the ship, and six o'clock in the morning the ship left.

We were very afraid. On the sea, we had some miles that belong to the Vietnamese government, and outside of those miles, it is international. Until that we passed the Vietnamese territory, during the time that we were still in Vietnam territory, the captain told us that we make no noise, and when they came near the place that they had the Vietnamese navy ships, they told all of us to go down to the inside where they stack the merchandise so that the Vietnamese naval ship would think that they ship just packed merchandise of the U.S. government, so they didn't check the ship, but if they knew that they had some Vietnamese on that ship, they would come to check all that ship. We had food. We slept on the deck. They just have sheet only. But we don't care about that because at that moment what we want is just leave Vietnam, so we don't care about the convenient or not.

We were on the ship about three days and we came to Subic Bay [Philippine Islands] for about four days. When we came to Subic Bay, we felt more comfortable, because at that time we knew that the Americans would accept us, but during the time on the ship, we didn't know yet, so we just had a kind of uncomfortable feeling. We just stayed with his own family on the ship; we didn't talk to other people, because we didn't know the other people. And some were friendly, but some were not, so we didn't like to get trouble with the other people, so we just stayed by ourselves.

After that we went to Wake Island by plane. They separated us at Wake Island, because at that time we had to fill all the application forms, and they wanted that the person have from one family. We had to explain very hard to them, what is our relationship, because they are confused about our last name. How can that his last name different from mine, and from his aunt? We had our certificate of marriage, so we can prove that we are husband and wife, no trouble with us, but if to explain that she is his aunt, it is very hard to prove that his father is the brother of his aunt.

We were on Wake Island about one week, and then we came to Camp Pendleton. From Subic Bay, they told us that we would go to Guam, but before we came on the plane, they told us that we would go to Wake Island because Guam was full. And at Wake Island, they told that people could choose to go to Arkansas, or Florida, or California. And most of people wanted to go to California because they heard that it was warm —

He interrupts her: Warm, the very important thing, warm!

She continues: The weather is good, so I think all the people wanted to go to California, so it is that the camp at California was full so if you wanted to go to California, you had to wait maybe a couple of weeks. Right now there is only one place to go, in Arkansas, but because we are only two, we didn't care because any place is the same to us — so we choose Arkansas, but when we land at Honolulu, they announce that the plane will go to California, and we didn't believe that we stay in Camp Pendleton; we just thought that maybe we land there to get some more oil or anything. So when we came to the airport in San Diego, they just told us to go to the bus to go to the camp, so we were very surprised because we thought that we go to Arkansas! My grandfather went to Ft. Smith, in Pennsylvania, and from there he went to France. He left later than us, at the last day, April 30. We left April 24, very early.

From Subic Bay, we wrote a letter to his cousin here, and also to my aunt in France, so we just wrote a letter to any relatives that we had, and when we were in Camp Pendleton, his cousin came there to visit us, and asked if we wanted, they would sponsor us to get us out. Before that, we had applied at the Lutheran Church for them to find a sponsor for us, but then his cousin came, so his cousin sponsored us. The Lutherans supplied the ticket for us to go by plane to Oakland. We started school right away.

First, when we came here, we think that we have to live by ourselves, to find a job, to get money to live. We didn't — we cannot believe that the U.S. government had the program like the welfare and anything to help the refugees, so it just surprised us. We were just afraid that they would turn us back to Vietnam.

He speaks: We lived only three weeks in Camp Pendleton. Some of them lived there about six months. We lived in a tent; a lot of people, 16 or 20 persons, lived in the tent. We used folding beds. It was very cold there, although it was summer. I met my friend who studied with me in Vietnam, at Camp Pendleton, and both of us lived with his family, about 14 or 12 persons. I think only two families in the tent. Because the other family included the parents, his parents and her parents, and their brother and sister and their children, so they were a big family, about 12 or 14, and the two of us, 16. All day we made the line to go to eat. Because very long line. We stood in line all day, like breakfast, lunch, and dinner. I think my wife was discouraged because she didn't like the food or too much of time to make a line, but I was good.

Adjusting to American ways was not difficult, she says:

The first thing we had to learn, that Americans meet us, they ask, "How are you?," and he has to say, "Fine," I think, because if he said that he is tired, he has to explain all the things why he is tired. Even in Vietnam we learned about that, when people say, "How are you?" you have to say, "Fine," or, "Very well." And they say, "Good" to any food that we cook, even if they didn't taste it. Just we put the food, and "Oh, it's good!" They didn't like that food, but the first thing they said was "It's good."

Binh wasn't surprised: We saw American movies, and read some American books or something, so American customs didn't surprise us. Usually I say I am fine. Except if I am very sick, I will say, "Very sick." But if I am tired a little bit, I don't want to say I am tired. All of the people at work are white, and some of them are Spanish. They are very friendly. I think someday I need to speak, or read the book, almost like the Americans. Now I have plan to study English first. We have the plan like that, because you need to have a degree here. It is easier for her to get a good job. I don't need a degree now, because the salary now is good. If they fire me, maybe I will go to school. When we came, at that time, we didn't have a plan to stay here. We had a plan to go to France, but after that, we changed. I think I was familiar with the city; I didn't want to move again. At that time, my French was better than English. Now I think it is the same. The time here has been very fast. I think very long time first six months, when we didn't have a job, we didn't have a house.

Dzung: The first month, our sponsor provided the food for us, but after that my husband went to Richmond to lay bricks, and then did some house painting, so we got money like that. And also for two months after that, we got food stamps, so we just had to find money to pay our rent only, but not for the food. And then in September, he went to the CETA [Comprehensive Employment Training Act] program, so we had enough money. Sometimes we were worried, but when he went to the CETA program, after that I went, too, so we were not worried. That is why I had to go to work at that time. Because we planned that I work, and maybe during that time he can have a chance to find a good job. And maybe we are lucky; he got his job by himself.

Binh explains: By accident. I think at Christmas of 1975, I went to Highland Hospital to work as a volunteer, to get some experience, and few weeks after that, the chief of pharmacists there invited me to go to a party of the Northern California Hospital Pharmacists. They just elected a new president, their association. And at the party I met the manager of Drug Service, Inc. and I told him that I was finding a job, and he told me the company had an open job. I drive four hours a day, and other hours I am filling orders from the pharmacy. I like driving more, because I have to pull out items many, many times a day, and when I am tired, I don't like to do that.

Dzung has not adopted the American custom of using her husband's last name.

I still use the Vietnamese way of my name. Because now if we change, we have to change all our papers. If we have a baby, we have to wait until that baby is the 21st year old.

Binh accepts differences: But I think maybe we will change after we become a citizen, American citizen, maybe at that time change. We aren't immigrants; we are a special case. We don't want to have children now. We want only one, or maximum two. I have only one brother. She has two brothers and one sister. I think we want to bring up our children a little differently from American parents. Let me see — I can't tell right now. Vietnamese parents have another way to tell their children, and the American parents have another way, not the better way, but a different way.

Dzung maintains her religious practice, and hopes to continue her career.

I practice my religion at home. Incense I buy in Chinatown, candles and things like that. The picture of his grandfather I got from his cousin, and the statue of the goddess I could buy in Chinatown. And the book, like the Bible, because I had some friend in Canada, because they lived over there a long time before, and now in Canada they have like a Buddhist organization, so they brought all those books. I got it from Canada. I read it only on the first day of the lunar month. Not on the 15th, because I don't have time, so I just read on the first only. It depends on the book how long I read. If a book is thick, I have about one hour; the other times, just a half hour only. It's just a different kind of Holy Bible. Every day I just read one page, one holy lesson, like that, so that one, I read every day, but the whole book just on the first only because it takes a long time. I do this every day in the morning. My mother had the book also. She read about 10 days per month. Sometimes she went to the pagoda to do that. Sometimes I went with her; the important days I went with her, but not usually, but she went frequently. My father didn't go; he's like my husband. I think most of Vietnamese men are not good in religion. Our religion is Vietnamese, not Buddhist, not Catholic. Because we have private sponsor, the Lutheran Church did not try to tell us about Christianity.

I am studying. In the first semester, I studied English, economic, history of law, and psychology. I got A in English, and A in economics, too. In Vietnam, I studied macro-economics, but here they have the economics from the USA so it's a little different. When I got A here in economics, I didn't believe it; it very surprised me, because in the first two midterms, I got a good note, but at the third one it's a little bit lower, so I think it will get me not an A, but at the last one I did better. For my course, I had to write a paper.

At college, everybody is very nice, very friendly. In the spring semester, he will go to Laney College in the evening, just one night a week. I will finish at Merritt in three more semesters, to get the AA degree. I plan to study legal assistant. I think that I can find a job as legal assistant, and maybe later if I am familiar with the field, and have more experience, maybe I will return to my career. If not, I will just work as legal assistant. In Vietnam, when I got married, I still worked at my father's office as a probationary attorney. We lived in my parents' home. I knew a little about cooking. My mother had a different idea. She said that a girl needed to know about cooking and take care of the house, because if, she said that now we are rich so we had servants, but even that you have servants, you need to know so to order them to do anything, so if we didn't have servants, so we can cook by ourself. So she tried to teach me about cooking. He doesn't help me.

Binh defends himself and tactfully praises his wife. Sometimes I bring the clothes to the washing machine, and we do the shopping together. Sometimes when I was young, because my family was poor — not too poor, but not too rich — and sometimes my family had a servant, but sometimes doesn't — sometimes when my mother was sick, I went to the market to buy some food, and I can cook, too. Yes! But now, she is a good cook, and I don't need to cook anymore.

NOVEMBER 1977

Their daughter was born at Kaiser Hospital in Oakland. The mothers' rooms there surround a central nursery area, and each baby is in a drawer that can be pushed through an opening in the wall beside the mother's bed. Dzung rang for the baby to be pushed into the room. She is a beautiful child, and Dzung says she will be trained to sleep through the night, according to the Vietnamese custom.

FALL 1979

Two years later, there was an opportunity for more people to leave Vietnam if they had institutional sponsorship. Dzung's sister and brother-in-law, a physician, and their three children were sponsored by a local church, in the hope of providing more medical care for the growing Vietnamese community in the East Bay. A committee of church members prepared an apartment, and when they took Dzung and her husband to the airport to meet the arriving family, they learned of a complication: as they were leaving Vietnam, the doctor had revealed that he

Binh and Dzung with their daughter, 1980.

had a second wife and other children who were to accompany them. Since the church sponsorship included only the first family, the second family was somehow routed at least temporarily to Hawaii. After some months spent in Oakland, the doctor and his wife moved to another state where he was licensed and works at a state hospital. The children stayed in California, went to school and university, and have prospered.

JUNE 1985

Dzung's parents have arrived from France, where they spent a few months after leaving Vietnam under the Orderly Departure program, and there is a luncheon for them and the various sponsors. Madame is elegant in a black embroidered tunic over black pants, carries a Dior leather bag, and uses a beautiful fan. She apparently speaks no English. Father is handsome, distinguished looking, speaks considerable English, fluent French, has very courteous manners. He and his wife were both born in North Vietnam. Before March of 1945, he was a district governor under the North Vietnamese independent government, which was allowed to function parallel with the Japanese occupation forces. After some intervals of removal and reinstatement, when the Viet Minh came to power, he was jailed for a period, and then retired to the country where he lived on family lands. At the time of the partition in 1954, they were fortunate to be able to fly to South Vietnam, but were deprived of their land, their principal source of revenue. In South Vietnam he continued his law profession in some capacity but held no post with the government. After 1975, they sold possessions in order to continue living in their house. Their son was in "re-education camp" for years, but has now been released. They refused to pay bribes to leave the country.

Madame has never done any domestic work and assumes Dzung will take care of her. When she arrived, she had heart problems, which have stabilized, and she has eye problems, so she can't do embroidery or read. This also excuses her from going to school to learn English. Dzung has written to her sister asking her to take *the parents. The brother-in-law has a good job now as a physician, and the sister enjoys socializing with her friends. He wrote back that it was impossible for them to take the parents.*

In a few months, Dzung's parents-in-law will arrive. Since her husband is the oldest son, he should properly take them into his home. The three-bedroom tract house now holds five people, three generations, and it will be difficult to add still another elderly and bewildered couple.

DECEMBER 1985

Dzung and her husband struggled with deep misunderstanding by parents still in Vietnam. Dzung was honest, and told her parents that she could not recommend their coming here, as she and Binh lived in small quarters and both worked all day. Other refugees sent back to Vietnam grandiose tales about their luxurious life in America. Dzung's parents, comparing her reports with those received by some of their friends, accused her both of filial disloyalty and of failing to do well here. There was no way to prove that this was untrue. When the parents arrived, just as they had been warned, they were unhappy at being alone all day in a crowded living space with no one to wait on them. Later the parents were settled with grandchildren an hour's drive away in San Jose where there is a vibrant Vietnamese community. Dzung visits on weekends, arranges for medical appointments, and shoulders the mundane responsibilities. Her sister comes to visit once or twice a year, takes the parents out to lunch, hears their complaints, buys them gifts, and convinces them of her devotion.

1990

By now, Dzung and her husband have succeeded by any measure: he as a pharmacist and she in a variety of jobs: teacher's aide, interpreter on call for the telephone company, interpreter in the human resources division of a major corporation with many Vietnamese employees, and court interpreter. She has also translated some of the writings of the Vietnamese spiritual leader Thich Nhat Hanh for publication in America. They have gone back twice as tourists to Vietnam and have traveled widely in other parts of the world as well. Their daughter graduated from the University of California and attended a cousin's wedding in Paris but has never been to Vietnam.

SEPTEMBER 20, 2004

Dzung has been doing difficult court translation for horrible murder cases, husbands brutally killing wives. She deals with these cases by meditation and simply deciding not to let herself become emotionally involved, but she regrets that it gives a bad impression of Asian husbands. Someone said, "What is the matter with these Vietnamese men?" She wanted to remind them of a recent much-publicized murder case involving a Caucasian couple.

Dzung's father has Parkinson's and dementia. He is confused and anxious about having to meet deadlines for his taxes. When he hears the loudspeaker calling someone, he thinks he is in an airport and must rush to catch a plane. Although he sees his son regularly, he frequently becomes alarmed that his son is still in "re-education," and he wants him to come here to be safe. Now he has been taken to the hospital again with pneumonia and is unconscious and on tube feeding. Her brother, who lives near and visits him regularly, is opposed to letting him go peace-fully, as she wants. Her brother-in-law also chides her for not wanting to prolong his life. She is under dreadful stress.

JANUARY 2005

Dzung and Binh want to be interviewed again, "to let people know what we have been through, and what we have achieved here." Twenty-eight years have passed between the first and second interviews; they have now spent more than half of their lives in America. Their daughter has a Ph.D. and is a successful pro-fessional. They have weathered painful times with family misunderstandings; rel-atives they sponsored had conflicting expectations and resentments. This time, they interviewed separately, and they tell in more detail of their family background and escape from Vietnam.

Binh was born in North Vietnam into a family descended from a distin-guished scholar. In 1954, when he was entering the fourth grade, Vietnam was partitioned; the Communist government took over in the north, and his family migrated to the south, adjusted to reduced circumstances, and learned a somewhat different language. This had been his first refugee experience. After coming to America, his second time as a refugee, for years he got up at 2 A.M. to drive to work and held two jobs while hoping to be licensed again as a pharmacist. As a result of the favorable impression he made during an interview, he secured a paid job at a hospital pharmacy near his home that provided the internship hours he needed. When he became a citizen, in 1985, he sponsored his parents to come under the family reunification program. His only brother, younger than he, escaped on a boat after 1985, came to the United States as a refugee, and now owns a furniture store. Binh credits his successes to luck, downplaying his own efforts. This is his recollection, recorded in 2005:

Everything is — we have to make decisions, right? But another one is luck, or whoever, you say that your angel protects you or that kind of thing. Luck is involved, too. Always, luck is part of something in our life. We do it, but the final result is always there is some luck involved.

My name is a 100 percent Vietnamese last name. My ancestor roughly in about 1700, he was the — now we call that a Ph.D. But in the old days, each year only about a few graduated, and they have a tradition, whoever got that degree, had the name carved in like a national cultural monument, and every year they carve the name and where that person came from. The Oriental cultures, the Chinese and Vietnamese cultures, promote education. My father was a post office worker under the control of the French government. He had the high education. He reads a lot; that's why he knows about the Communists. He gave for some of my relatives examples: Communism, it means you combine everything from everybody and divide it equally. If they're not that poor, it means they lose. If you combine the poor and divide equally, will be poorer. That's why he left the north. At the end of 1954, my family left Haiphong; it is a port in northern Vietnam about 50 miles east of Hanoi. The parents had to leave behind the house they got, the land they got, the heritage of my grandmother on my mother's side. They were merchants, and they were relatively rich. When we went to the south, of course they became the renters.

My father got the airline ticket for me and my brother and my mother [*in 1954*]. And we flew to the south before he came. He worked for the French-Vietnamese government then, and for the post office in Haiphong, and Haiphong is a large city. The French government would have to transfer to the Vietnamese Communist government. That's why he stayed there until the last minute, I think around summer or spring of 1955. We flew to the south, and we stayed in the refugee camp for a short time, one or two days. Because my mother had a cousin; he was a merchant; he was relatively rich, four- or

five-story building, near by the big central market in Saigon. And we stayed there with them a couple of months until my father came. And he rented a house in the suburb of Saigon. I was in fourth grade. The language in the south is the same, but the pronunciation, a little bit different. At the beginning, harder to understand, but you get used to it. Dzung can speak with the southern accent, but I can't. So when she speaks with her friends, the southerners, Vietnamese southerners, she can speak in the southern accent. But now, normally we talk to each other in the northern accent. In Vietnam, everybody had to learn two foreign languages. We call that the first

Binh pointing to his ancestor's name on a stele of scholars, Hanoi.

foreign language, French, and the second foreign language is English, like one hour a week, and only in the last three or four years of high school. I loved to do something like become engineer. But very hard to get into those schools, very selective. I couldn't pass the entrance exam. Some of my close friends went to pharmacy school, and I said, okay, just go there. You have to go to college, especially during the war; if you go to college, they postpone the draft. If you go to college three or four or five years, they postpone it, until you graduate from college.

The pharmacy course was five years, like here. I graduated in 1970 and joined the army and worked for the army [Republic of Vietnam Armed Forces, ARVN] as a pharmacist in Central Vietnam, like in a depot, to supply the medications for the armed force. They send the medication to the field hospitals, to the hospitals everywhere. It is only the minor things I learned through that time, because most of the medications in Vietnam is import from France. Except in the army, supplied by the American government. I left, because they need some high school teachers in some of the rural areas, and because I didn't want to stay in the army, I said, okay. They had some special programs, because they needed some science teachers for the — here we call it high school, but over there the second level is from ten to twelve years, and they were short on the science teachers.

I met Dzung before I went to the Vietnamese army, through a friend of mine, met her somewhere at one of the parties, and then the next few days, during before Tet [lunar New Year holiday], he asked me to go to see her at her house, and my friend took me along, and I met her. It was not arranged by our parents; no, no, totally not. No. Because she is from a wealthy, well-to-do family. Her father was one of the vice-chairmen of the Vietnamese congress.

When I came here, they required the license to practice here, and my English was not good enough, is one thing, and at the beginning we are not qualified to take that exam yet. In the United States, you have to have the transcripts or documents sent direct from the university or from another county. You cannot bring it because anybody can create it. And they have to evaluate if the program in Vietnam is equal to the program in the United States.

I got my first job just by accident, because I tried to get a volunteer job for the Highland Hospital, in the pharmacy, and the nice lady, the director of that pharmacy, Mabel Lu — she just passed away a few years ago — and they had a party with all of the drug company and the pharmacist association, and she asked me to join her, and she put me to sit at the same table with the branch director of drug companies in Oakland. We sat at the same table. And after a few conversations, he offered me a job like the sales people, but I said my English was not good enough to do that kind of job, and he said if I want I can be a delivery person for that drug company. That is a drug wholesaler.

I worked for them for 13 years until I got my pharmacy license. Roughly about 1980, a lot of Vietnamese pharmacists, a lot of Vietnamese professors in the Saigon pharmacy school, sent all the documents to the California State Board of Pharmacy here to prove that the curriculum is equal to the American curriculum, and after a couple of years, the board of pharmacies here approved it. But the Vietnamese pharmacists had to take the equivalency test and that means the national, similar like NAPLEX, but for the foreign students. And after you pass that one, you have to have 1,500 hours of internship in the American pharmacy. That's a lot of hours. I need some in the retail, and some in the hospital.

When I was working for the wholesaler, I knew a lot of pharmacists because I used to deliver the medications for them, and after I passed the equivalency test, the gentleman in Oakland agreed for me to do internship there to have enough hours. In the beginning he agreed to me to work there without pay. The salary I got with the wholesaler was enough for us to live with. And after I worked there for a few days, the pharmacist in charge told him, "You have to pay this guy." And he agreed to pay me at the internist salary. And back then, I used to come to work at five in the morning, and get up around two I think or one-thirty, because the warehouse was in San Leandro, and I drove to the pharmacy to work from two to six, normally three days a week: Monday, Wednesday, and Friday. I couldn't work every day at the pharmacy. From Vallejo, it was not that bad; about 45 minutes.

Roughly in 1989, I had about a thousand hours of internship with the retail pharmacy, and I could take the California State Board of Pharmacy test already, but I couldn't have a license yet, until I have enough, 1,500 hours, of internship. I took the test when I got more than a thousand hours. I didn't pass; almost made it, almost. And after the exam, they had a job fair, with all of the hospital or the pharmacy or drug chains to hire the applicants there. I took the interview with Kaiser. And a few weeks later they called me and offered me a job in Kaiser-Napa, and after the interview they accept me, but I refused it. I decided; let me do the study. And then I told Dzung I couldn't work that much and study at the same time. I said we could survive with the saving we have. Let me do the study. But a few days later, Kaiser in Walnut Creek called me, because they say I got the good reference from the one in Napa, and they offered me the job as intern for the hospital inpatient, and that is the internship hours I need. They accept me, and after that I left the wholesaler. Just luck involved again. When I did the internship with Kaiser, I got enough number of hours for the hospital internship hours, and after that I took the board exams, and I passed the second time, and I got the license.

My father at the beginning refused to leave Vietnam. He is the one who left the north, but he knows, because like I told you earlier, he read a lot; he knows the Western society is very hard on the old foreigners. That's why he didn't want to come, but finally, he suffered with the Communist government, economically. That's why, and he saw so many people, relatives, left Vietnam, and my mother convinced him to leave. My father was very good in English. He attended every night for six or seven years, roughly when he was 50, with the Vietnamese-American society; they opened a class every night. His English was much better than mine. He got the French high school diploma; it means his French was very good. He could speak both French and English.

My parents lived with us a short time, and they moved to San Jose and lived with my brother. In Vallejo, they don't have anything in the Vietnamese. But in San Jose, a big Vietnamese community; they can go to the Vietnamese market. They stayed with us a very short time. Because my brother was already in San Jose. He took care of them, and he was single. Much easier. Like with us, in-laws, that kind of thing is harder. That could be culture. Like the daughter-in-law, for example: of course she doesn't like it, but still, you have to accept it. Here, the Americans might say, "No, I don't want it;" they say directly. But the older culture, they say, "Oh, we have to accept it." But Dzung and I, especially Dzung, we are the new generation, the education from the French school; of course it's a little bit different. They both passed away: my father about 10 years ago; my mother about 5 years ago. My father was 77; my mother was 80-something. The ashes, now we leave in the Buddhist pagoda in Palo Alto.

Prejudice and discrimination is sometimes indirect. At work it is less, because the nursing staff is like 40, 60 percent Filipinos, some Chinese, Mexican — it's not in the hospital setting, because so many foreign-born workers there. But that is life. It's everywhere in the world. Not just here in the United States. But here in the United States we talk about it. Just like for example, in Vietnam, there is discrimination, too. They say, "Oh, the Chinese, the Highlanders;" that kind of thing is everywhere. Or the southern, the northern accent, the central accent. That kind of thing, I think that is the human nature.

In 1977, we were afraid to have the government in Vietnam know that we had left. But now we know, during that time the Communist government didn't care who left the country. They were afraid only the ones who go to the jungle would fight them. If they knew you were in the United States or in France, they didn't care. During that time, 1977, everybody was afraid of that, but now we know the story from the Communist people. They didn't care, the one who left the country.

It still is a division in the Vietnamese community here between the Communists and the non–Communists. Once in a while, you see the people oppose with the exhibition of Ho Chi Minh's pictures, or painting. I didn't go to the exhibition in the Oakland Museum because I heard that it was not that fair.

More from the northern side of view. Not from the side of the southern Vietnamese people. The same thing like the war in Iraq now — the things we see is the point of view of the American media and the American government. We don't see the point of view of the Iraqi people. They might interview some Iraqis who say, "I'm glad that Saddam Hussein was not there." Of course! But they didn't ask the second question: Do you think that is better off now than before? You learn the American people liberate your country; some things, they never raise the questions. Of course we say, we want to liberate the Iraqi women, too; do they want it? I don't know.

And that's why the Vietnamese say, I think they hear back then, it was by propaganda to support only one side, anti-war. Of course, nobody wants to go to war, because they didn't see the both side of the story. I have to use the example: the northern Communist government, they say they liberate Saigon. They tried to liberate like we tried to liberate Iraq. I think the same. I think we tried to find a cause. Saddam Hussein was just the cause, for us to have a just cause to get in, but I don't think that is the really cause. And nobody knows exactly why we wanted to have that war, or the Iraq war now. Nobody knows. Only the government says that, but I don't think that was really the reason. Why we cost fortunes to have a war? It might have some purpose, but nobody knows exactly.

Just like the old days, the missionaries in California tried to Christianize the American Indians. Did they want it? That kind of thing — why we have to put our religion on somebody else? Let's say that the people who didn't have a TV; why we fought there to watch TV? They might have their own god, another god. Do you want to put your god on somebody else? That is the point of view about religion, the same. Well, this society, we say that one wife and one woman; that is the Christian thinking. And it will become the law, and of course I live here; I have to obey the law, but is that better? Look at the Mormons: in some family with one man and five wives, and they live happily. They don't have divorce. Is that better? I don't know; I don't have the answer for that, but they think that we need to Christianize everybody. The Lutheran is different; the Baptist different; the Mormon different; and the Catholics different. Because this country started with those early people, back then 95 percent is Christian. And we think everybody should be Christianized, have to have a Baptist, that kind of thing. I don't have it. Why do I need it to go to heaven?

Our daughter speaks with the northern accent, from us. She can speak fluently. I can say 98 percent. But when she writes, she writes Vietnamese without the accent signs. Because she went to the elementary school that was the Christian school, and they have a special method to pronounce first, and the way you pronounce, you just guess in writing. That's for English, but she used the same method, and because the Vietnamese now, writing Vietnamese, is based on the pronunciation. She took only one or two Vietnamese classes in UC–Berkeley.

Being a parent is harder, because the kid goes to the American school, so they absorb their culture, of course. It is hard from one generation to another, and then we have two difficulties: the cultures and generation gap. Double. Like we all know: the first generation of immigrants have to work harder; the second generation is really the American, and life is too easy here, relatively speaking; everything is ready, handy, from paper towels to everything, Coke machine. It is very hard, because for example, she says, "Oh, that car was so cheap, only 25,000, only 30,000." I say, "Wait a minute!" I think she recognizes it a bit more because now she really has to work. Analyze it, and I say if you are making like five thousand a month, for example, after tax, how much you would

Dzung and Binh's daughter in Ho Chi Minh City (Saigon) on her first trip to Vietnam, 2007.

bring home, how much for the rent, how much for the gas, how much for this; finally she figures, nothing left. The main thing is the happy, because she can support herself. That's all we need. Because we all know that as parents if the children don't make enough money for living and they come back and they ask for it, it might become the problem. Sometimes money becomes a problem.

Sort of it was my decision [*for her*] to go to the University of California. Because she has been accepted when she was in eleventh grade. That's why I said, "You are accepted, and why have to think about it?" And it could be the first generation of the immigrant: I say, "We paid our tax for the state, now time to use it." And that's not a bad school; that's one of the well-known school in the world. Everybody and my relatives in France, they praise UC–Berkeley. I said, "Why bother to send applications, 60 dollars each, for 4 or 5 schools, and for what?"

She lived at home, one or two first years. I think I am more liberal, and more conservative. I don't know; sometimes I am more liberal. I said, "Fine;" she will have her own life. Only the first year I decide not to send her to be far away because I feel like she was immature. She is one year younger than her class, because she got into school one year earlier. And I feel the first year is usually like temptation, when you leave from high school to the big university like UC–Berkeley and you need to control a little bit, but after that I said, "Okay, it is fine;" she can handle it, the pressures. Boyfriends, I say, "Fine," whatever she choose. This is the American society. The chance is 95 percent she marry to the American, you can call that Caucasian, or Black; the chance is very high, 95 percent, okay? And physically, the Caucasian man has more appeal than the Asian man. Because you see all of the examples, always the Caucasian man is taller about 10 percent more or 20 percent more. The Oriental, about 5 percent more. That is biology, talking about that. And she is taller; of course she will choose a tall guy. Because our marriage is the same. Because free to choose; she from wealthy family; I was not.

I don't think I want to go back to Vietnam to live there, at this age. But when I am super old, very old, and here you have to stay in the nursing home, for example, it's very hard. Because I am sure that when we are older, the native language will come back, and in your dream or something, I am sure that I still speak Vietnamese. You see? That's why when you ask if I want to go back and live there, we might; in the final stage of our life, we might.

Five years after we came to the United States, we had the right of applying for citizenship. We became citizens in 1985. Because we were the ones without a country. Our case might be a little bit different, because we didn't come here because really it was our wish, because if Vietnam was there like before, we never — not like some people; they love to come over here to apply for it, and very hard to get in, and of course they celebrate it. I say we are the ones like no country. America is not really my country. It could be because I wasn't born here; I didn't absorb all of the American culture; I didn't enjoy baseball games like American people. I went there a couple of times, people that like baseball. Football, they go to drink beer; that kind of thing. I think one time I try baseball with the people at work. I say, "Okay, just want to go and see." And some of the culture is very hard to absorb. Especially I came here when I was 28. That is harder. Because the culture is language, the way we do things, food, music.

He has traveled widely: to Europe, to Canada, in the United States, to North Africa, and three tours to Vietnam. He still feels he belongs to no country. He is a citizen of the world who combines the best of several cultures.

When this interview took place, Dzung's mother had died not long before, and her father was in fragile condition in a nursing home. At times she wept at painful recollections. She began by recalling the earlier interview.

We were married in December 1974, so just four months, newly wed. We left from Newport, in Bien Hoa, near Saigon; we went to Subic Bay; from Subic Bay we flew to Wake Island, and from Wake Island to California, Camp Pendleton. My husband's aunt worked for the Americans at that time, so she had the paperwork to go out. Looking back at that, it was a cargo ship so we didn't have any place to stay. They planned to pick up more people in Vung Tau, but when we left and they heard that the Communists had come to Saigon, so they decided not to stop in Vung Tau. Just on the top deck, no cover, nothing, and when it rained, we used the boxes of Coca-Cola as a shelter to cover us, and some plywood to put on top. But looking back now, we were lucky, because compared with a lot of boat people who came to the United States in 1978 and 1979, they had lots of horrible stories on the sea with pirates; oh, terrible things.

We left because of all the bad experience from our parents who escaped the north of Vietnam in 1954. So we knew my husband was in the army, and now he might get killed; he might get in prison or anything. And actually all his friends and even like my brother, who were not as lucky as us to escape Vietnam at that time, they had to go to the re-education camp for several years. We just want to have freedom; that's why we left.

My parents had planned to leave Vietnam, too, but unfortunately they couldn't leave at the last minute because of all the events at that time in Saigon. Like the boat that our family had purchased, at the last moment, other people took it. They stayed back, and we sponsored them over here in 1985, so after 10 years we were able to reunify with my parents first, and then his parents. My sister and her family escaped by boat in 1978. My husband's brother escaped by boat in 1979, so slowly all my family and his family were over here. When we left, I missed my family. But after 10 years they came over here, and we had a lot of differences.

My father was an attorney. Under the first Republic of Vietnam, he was an assemblyman. That was why I was afraid for his safety when we arrived here and couldn't get contact with the family, but somehow, I don't know, maybe God or Buddha protected our family, but the last few years he was only an attorney, so that was what he reported to the government, so he didn't have any involvement in the government, no political things, so that's why he was safe. But my brother was a doctor in the military, so he had to go to the re-education camp for seven years.

He had a wife and two children, and when they tried to escape Vietnam at the end of 1975, beginning of 1976, they were tricked by the government, so his family were put in jail. After a few months, he had to give his car to the government so that they would release the two children, but his wife was still in jail until one or two years later that she was released. He was in the re-education camp. He was a doctor, and they felt that they needed doctors at that time, so he didn't have to do hard labor. Recently, on our last trip back to Vietnam in October 2004, he just told us that one day the wife of the supervisor of the camp was sick and he was able to save her, so after that they let him handle a small clinic in the camp. During the day he would work in the clinic; at night he was back in jail. Even they wanted to keep him there to work for the government down there because they didn't have any doctors.

In Saigon they needed doctors also, so my parents were able to ask someone to make a request to get him back to Saigon to work for the government in Saigon, or Ho Chi Minh City they called it at that time, instead of working down in Bac Lieu, a small city down in the Mekong Delta area. So that was why he was able to get back to Ho Chi Minh City.

They never told me how they were treated in jail. I only learned that the children were the first ones to be released, and then his wife. They came over here later, in 1990 or 1991, and he got the Master's degree in public health and became the San Jose branch director of the Vietnamese Community Health Promotion Project, a division of UC–San Francisco. His two children are now pharmacists, Pharm. D.

My father is 88 years old now, so at that time, he was 60-something, so maybe with his age and because he didn't involve in politics anymore so they just let him stay in the same home. They lived from their savings. My mom sold most of her jewelry. We also sent money back home to support them, through my relatives in France.

My grandfather went to France, but my grandmother stayed back because of all the events during 1975. Actually, I mentioned previously about the boat that my family purchased. So I think on April 26 or 27 before that the Communists came into Saigon, my family went on the boat and all the relatives also, but somehow with the curfew and all the firing, my brother-in-law decided to return back to Saigon to wait until the next morning to go. It would be safer during the day; that's what he thought, rather than traveling at night during curfew time. But the next morning, with all the chaos in Saigon, when my grandfather and three of my uncles went to check on the boat, they saw other people climb into the boat and took it. So they panicked and they jumped on the boat, too, so they left the family back home. That's why my grandfather went to France because I have one aunt and one uncle in France.

My brother-in-law went back home. So that's why my whole family went back home, on the night of the 29th or 28th; I don't remember the date now. That was what my family told me later on. My brother-in-law was also in the re-education camp for a few months. He's also a doctor. After that he was released also, and he escaped in 1979 with his family. My grandfather died before I was able to go to France, but I visited my grandmother. She was in France. After a few years, my aunt was able to sponsor her.

I remember that we only stayed in Subic Bay a few days and then in Wake Island about one week, and by the first of May, or like the first week of May, we were in Camp Pendleton. Even though it was May, Camp Pendleton was chilly for us because we got used to the hot weather in Vietnam. The

Red Cross gave us thick jackets to wear. They put up a lot of tents. We stayed in the tent with other families, 20 to 30 people for each tent. But we are lucky that my husband saw some friends, so they just decided to get all together to stay in one tent instead of staying with strangers. And my husband's cousin, who was married to a Caucasian, came to Camp Pendleton and sponsored us out. When we left Vietnam, we had the addresses of our relatives in the United States and in France, and that was why we were able to get in touch with them. The things, the film of our marriage and also our birth certificate and the photocopy of our degree, that we packed in our backpack, we just believe that even if we had to go anywhere even in Vietnam, we believed that those would be the important things for us to bring with us.

We stayed with his cousin, and then we got a studio apartment. We started school, learning English. We already knew some English, and French. And then I got pregnant in 1977. By the end, when I almost reached the due date, the manager told us that we couldn't stay there after we had the baby, so we had to look for another apartment. We applied to housing in Alameda, but it was for like a middle-income family; you had to reach certain criteria; you had to work, but your income cannot be over a certain amount. I don't remember all the details now. So we applied for that apartment, but it was not ready yet, and the manager had already rented our apartment to another couple by the end of the month, so even though that we asked them to let us stay for a few more weeks, but they couldn't. So my cousin let us stay with them in their apartment in Alameda while we were waiting for our apartment.

Our daughter was born at Kaiser Hospital, and recently my husband took a picture of a poster showing the kind of drawer that she was put in, so the nurses could push it back and forth between the mother's room and the nursery. Following my cousin's advice, I was able to train our daughter to sleep through the night very soon. My cousin said, "Let her cry; don't pick her up, and she will get used to it, and she will sleep through the night. If not, then you won't be able to do it later on, so just try it right away." So I followed it, and it worked. My cousins, seeing that I didn't have my mother over here, considered me as their baby sister. All my cousins escaped Vietnam in 1975.

I graduated from Merritt College. I was studying the paralegal class, and for the last semester some of the finals were research, so I was able to turn in the essay before the due date, and I remember that two classes the instructor allowed me to turn in late my test because I had the baby. I was a probationary attorney in Vietnam, working with my father. But I had to learn some new courses because the legal system over here in the United States follows the common law while the Vietnamese law is similar to the French law, Napoleon law. A little bit different.

Our daughter was born the end of 1977. I stayed home for two and a half years, and March 1980, I started to work as teacher assistant for the ESL program of Mount Diablo Unified School District. We bought our first house in Vallejo in 1978, and then in 1980 I started to work for Mt. Diablo School District.

My husband worked for a pharmaceutical wholesaler. Then in 1983 or 1984, they allowed the pharmacists from Vietnam to take the equivalent exam similar like the doctors, so he studied, and he had to do the internship, so after work he also did his internship at a pharmacy in Oakland. It was kind of hectic for him to commute from Vallejo to Oakland and San Leandro, so we decided to move to Walnut Creek, because of the school system. In Vallejo, our daughter went to a Christian school. They didn't have high school; they only had for elementary school, so we were looking for middle school and high school at a better school. So we think that Walnut Creek would be better, and it is convenient for me to work for Mt. Diablo School District, and my husband will have an easier commute to go to work and his internship. So we moved to Walnut Creek in 1986. Our daughter was in fourth grade. We moved to Walnut Creek during half the school year because her fourth grade, the first part, it was in Vallejo, but I remember the second part, she was going to Bancroft School in Walnut Creek. She struggled at the beginning when she went to the public school in Walnut Creek. Bigger and more difficult, but she did get used to it, and after that she was able to catch up. After that, my husband found a job at Kaiser. I remember it was Tet, our Vietnamese New Year that year, and he just said he wished that the internship position would be in Walnut Creek; it would be wonderful for him to take that position. And then a few days later, he got a call from Kaiser–Walnut Creek because the supervisor at Kaiser in Vallejo called Walnut Creek to let them know, because I think he did well during his interview with that lady, so she recommended him to Kaiser in Walnut Creek. So he got his internship.

My parents came after ten years, when we were still in Vallejo. We were like high-middle class in Vietnam, so my parents got used to have maids at home, who cooked for them, and — they couldn't understand the way that we eat over here. Even though we still have three meals a day, it's only dinner that we eat at home, but for breakfast and lunch, like for breakfast to be a glass of milk and some cereal or something like that, and for lunch it's just a sandwich. And they used to buy fresh food each day and cook for lunch, for dinner, so it was hard for me, because even though at dinner time, I could cook extra for them to eat for lunch the next day, they wouldn't eat that. When they first came, they lived with us in Vallejo, but they were not very happy because of the conflict of the culture.

And with his parents, because my family and his family were from different classes in the society, so his father always considered that raising the children but after that they graduated from school, they would have to work and support the parents, like paying back for all the years that they raised us. So many people over here would write things that were not true; they thought that we were rich because we didn't tell them how we lived over here, so they thought that we would have a lot of money, and especially my in-laws thought that my parents were able to smuggle, to exchange a lot of money over here so I would inherit all that money from my parents. So they kept asking us to send a lot of money, which we couldn't do it.

So when they were still in Vietnam, we had problems with our in-laws, and when my parents came over here, it was problems with my parents. Maybe they just consider that because I am the baby in the family and they still consider me as a baby all the time, and seeing that we didn't have enough, so my mom wanted to support us, but my husband didn't like that. My mom had been the boss in the family, and I can now understand why. She is a strong woman; somehow she can predict the future. Maybe her sixth sense or something, and so she always does the things that she likes, and I think that is what I am doing now, the same like my mom.

My parents lived with us for eight months, and with all the conflict between my parents and my husband, minor tension, nothing serious, but my husband's job was not stable; he had a lot of stress from his job. My mother would do things her way, and he didn't like that, but he couldn't say anything, so we asked my sister to invite our parents to come to live with them in Louisiana. But my brother-in-law refused; I think they are smart, because maybe they knew all the problems that could happen if my parents live with them, so they said no. And we had to really hurt the feelings of my parents when we confronted my sister, and after that my sister had to let my parents come to stay with her children, the grandchildren, and since then my parents stayed with their grandchildren in San Jose. For my sister, she considers that's the same. She's not here in California, so her children represent her to take care of my parents. But I know that my mother always said that living with the children and living with the grandchildren are different; they are not the same. Thinking back now, I believe all the conflict was due to a lack of communication in the family. In the Asian culture, you cannot disobey your parents; you have to listen to them no matter what. Even when there is a family feud, you have to pretend that everybody gets along very well to save face.

When my mother died, because my mother was a religious person, her wish was to have a lot of monks to come to pray for her at the funeral. And she kept saying a lot of things about preparing for her funeral. But she only told me, and I said to her that my father was still alive, and I am the youngest one in the family; whatever she wanted for her funeral, she had to write it down to let everybody in the family know. Because if not, I cannot do that, because I would become again an unfilial daughter. And so somehow one day my cousins came to our house, and my mother was also there to visit us, so I recorded her wishes, having my cousins as witnesses. Maybe something from the lawyer's skills made me do that. So when my mother died, I just turned on the tape, and my father refused at first; he was panicked. He thought I would cause a lot of problems. I said, "No, this is what Mom wished, and I just want the family to listen to it." And it was just about the arrangement for the funeral.

So I was able to fulfill my mother's wishes, and I think maybe because she had prayed a lot, maybe she had become a bodhisattva, that was why her funeral was that. At that time, it happened that there was like a convention or something of all the Buddhist monks from all over the United States, in San Jose. So even monks in Canada and everywhere, they came to that convention. And somehow that was why I was able to invite them to come to my mom's funeral. We had three ceremonies for her, three memorial services for her, before the cremation, so there were like 10, 12 monks who came from all over the places. One monk, who is very famous among the Buddhist community, came from Canada. Actually my mom's friends are still talking about that and how lucky she was to be able to have that monk come. The Venerable Thich Tam Chau is almost like the pope and still lives in Canada now. And other monks came from Texas, from Louisiana, and in San Jose I was able to ask one monk, an old monk — the Venerable Thich Thanh Cat — and other monks from the Giac Minh pagoda in East Palo Alto, the place where I have my parents-in-law's and my mom's pictures up in the pagoda there, and also the Venerable Thich Tu Luc from Hayward and monks from San Jose, so different monks.

It was amazing that I was able to arrange the services, one after another, and there was no conflict between the hours of those monks. Even though you are religious, you still have competition; no one wants to be the second one. So somehow we had that, and my husband was laughing because we had to kneel down for hours after hours; he said that my mom knows that we are not religious at all, so she made all of us suffer for her on this one day. He was joking like that. Like for one service after another service. That made up somehow, so I just believe that mom just planned it, and I just followed her; she guided me. I am not that smart to be able to do all these things.

Somehow still I have faith in Buddha, and whenever I have any problem, I would pray to the Kwan Yin bodhisattva, the compassion goddess, and somehow things would just go smoothly for me. Because like when we left Vietnam, as a newlywed couple, we didn't have any money to pay the way to leave Vietnam, because each ticket to leave, it would cost you like a thousand dollars for an airplane ticket, with the American people, or a lot of gold bars (each bar weighs more than one ounce) to get a place on the boat. But I remember it was my husband's grandmother's memorial anniversary that day. I just prayed to her to help us find a way to go out. And then it turned out that we went to his aunt's home, just to ask if she still had dollars to buy for my parents. And she mentioned to us about her way to leave Vietnam; she had the paperwork, and now her son didn't want to leave because his girlfriend was not allowed to go with him, so he decided to stay back with her, and we told her that if she was able to take us, we would share half of the price that she had to pay the chief of the Newport harbor, the Vietnamese chief, for her paperwork — so she told my husband that he would take her son's place, and I would take her place, because she had the ID card to go into the Newport area, the Newport harbor, without any problem.

So she agreed about that, and somehow we were home, and my husband's mother came, saying they were ready to leave, so somehow that evening his mother went to see his aunt, and she saw that the American van came to pick them up, but because his parents didn't want to leave Vietnam at that time, his father said what would he do over here, and he didn't want to be a busboy or anything in the United States. He said, if the Communists came, he would take cyanide to suicide. Well, he didn't; saying is easier than doing it. And he said that. We didn't know that they would have programs for the refugees over here and other things.

That's why, because his aunt offered to take them with her, as my father-in-law was the oldest son in the family, but he didn't want to go, so his mother came and told us. We just rushed to her house, and at that moment, the girl-friend decided to leave with the family, so his aunt said just follow her; if we were able to go through the gate, then we would go; if not, we would stay back. And we followed her as on her affidavit, the list of the people's names was longer than the people who were at the gate at that time, and because of her talent for bribing the guards at the gate. They would check your ID card with the name on the affidavit, but she said all the ID cards were in her purse, and her son took it with him when her two youngest sons followed her super-visor to the ship. So she didn't have any ID card right now; none of us had any ID cards. And she kept crying that if you didn't let us go through the gate and if I lost my sons — she made a big deal about that while she was giving out her hands with all the different currencies: dollars, gold bar, or Vietnamese money; meaning whatever you want to choose, you can take it — so they just called the names. So the first two names, she pushed us through the gate. My mom always told us, whenever you have any problems, just pray to your husband's grandmother.

Like I told you previously, I worked as a teacher's assistant, and then my supervisor told me to get the teaching credential to become a teacher. So in 1991, I took some classes at St. Mary's College, and I got the multiple cre-dential. I worked as a fourth-grade teacher for two years. First it was in Oakland, and then in Pittsburg, California. I was teaching in Oakland, but my car was broken into one time when I parked on the street next to the school, so after one year in Oakland, and Mt. Diablo Unified School District offered me a job in Pittsburg, so I took it. Then the principal said because I have an accent in English, she doesn't believe that I can control my students. After two years of probation she refused to let me become a permanent teacher. She said that she wished that the probation year could be longer, that she would be happy to keep me as a probationary teacher, because as a probationary teacher, then I had to do all my effort to improve my accent, but once you become a permanent teacher, you don't care anymore, because you know that nobody will be able to lay off you, so she refused to let me become a permanent teacher. That was why I went into the translation field. So now I'm thankful. I would like to thank her now, because being a teacher in Pittsburg with all the at-risk students who are there, I might quit after a few years with all the stress for teaching over there.

I worked for Levi's, just for one or two years when they closed all their plants in Texas, and there were a lot of Vietnamese workers there, so they needed a translator to explain to them all the benefits that they would get once they were laid off by Levi's. At that time, my mom just passed away, so my husband let me go. But he didn't want me to stay away from home. The first two times, only two weeks. But the following year I was away for a month.

I still work for the telephone company whenever I have free time. Because I can work as a contractor so I can log in and log out whenever I have time. I don't have a fixed schedule. I work for different courts, for Contra Costa, Solano, Alameda, Sacramento, and also for different law firms, for civil cases. For the law firms, civil, but for the courts, criminal. Right now I work full time for Alameda County. I joined the Northern California Translator Association, so my name is on their website. With the internet nowadays, so whoever needs a Vietnamese translator, they just check it, and then they contact me. Mostly I do translation for the medical field: The Alameda Alliance Health, Cal Optima.

The Thich Nhat Hanh book is just like my hobby.[1] Because my husband's cousin is a dharma teacher of Thich Nhat Hanh teaching, and six years ago when Thich Nhat Hanh came over here and had one day of mindfulness at Lake Merritt, he encouraged the attendants to form different sanghas so we can get together and practice the meditation together. So she organized one at her house in Walnut Creek, and every Sunday we'll have a session at her house, and she got involved in the La Boi Association, which is for reprinting the Vietnamese books for Thich Nhat Hanh. We have to re-type the old books. So I help her with that, and then Vietnamese books that Thich Nhat Hanh likes to be translated into English, our sangha helps to do that. He has two organizations: the La Boi, to print these Vietnamese books, and Parallax Press in Berkeley is the company that prints all his English books.

Our education mostly followed the French system. I went to a French high school. And I think most of us, like the people who live in Saigon, in the big city, we are all Westernized. We follow the Western medicine, and some would use the herbal medicine from the Chinese. Because of the Chinese influence, they would think about a certain kind of food. Because of the yin and the yang, so for women, you should eat or drink some different food, and for men, you should use different things, but mostly Westernized. Of course we wished to keep our culture, and try to teach our daughter our culture, and hope that she will keep that in her family, but I think that for us, actually right now, I don't think that our generation would belong anywhere, in Vietnam or in the United States, completely, truly belong, because there are still things in the United States that we don't understand, we don't know, so we cannot get into it, even though we try, and now after a few times going back to Vietnam as a tourist, we can feel that we don't belong there anymore. We have been back three times. The first time was only in North Vietnam, the second time from North to South, so we traveled the whole country by bus, and the last time only in the South. The first time was in 1998, the second time in 2002, and this year, 2004.

I like to travel, and I think that traveling will open your mind, open your eyes. Knowing about different cultures. We went to Italy, Spain, France, England, Morocco, Portugal, Switzerland, Holland; I think that's it; and then to China, Mexico, to Chichen Itza. And the first few years, we traveled in the United States. I just try to do whatever I can, because I am thankful for what we have now, looking back. At least I didn't have to have the experience to go to the re-education camp to visit my husband, like my sister-in-law, or like most of his friends' wives. Because we had an education, that was why we tried to push our daughter to have a good education. Education is something that nobody can take away from you. Even though going to a different country, at the beginning you struggle with the new life, but after a while, having an education, you can step up in the society. Gradually we have what we had before in Vietnam, the same lifestyle.

Our social life is both American and Vietnamese, because we live in Walnut Creek now. So that's why like over here, going to San Jose, we don't belong to the Vietnamese community there either, as they are different from our group in Walnut Creek. There are the communities of people who are non–Communists, anti–Communists, so they refuse to go back to Vietnam, and they still dream that one day they will be back and get back the control of Vietnam, but I don't think that will be a good idea. The Communists in Vietnam now maybe they have changed the concept so they are not so strict or so oppressing the people, the citizens anymore; like my friends who went to law school with me, they were able to become a lawyer now, and in Saigon, going there you don't think that you are in a Communist country. But of course you can still see the big difference: the poor people are still poor, and the rich people are still rich.

We all talk about maybe we would like to retire in Vietnam, but then we think about it; it's easier said than done, because now looking back, I have been in the United States longer than I was in Vietnam, and my daughter was born here, and she will have her family here, and if we retire in Vietnam, I don't think she will have time to visit us all the time, and so it is like, when you are still healthy enough to go back and forth, that will be okay. There is one old man that we knew. He was single, and he worked over here, and when he retired, at first he planned to go back and live in Vietnam. So he went back, bought a house, and he let his relatives stay there. He just had like one room in that house. But after a few years, he returned here! He was not happy to live over there. But six months ago, he returned to Vietnam, and then he got asthma, and he died in Vietnam. We just went to his memorial service two weeks ago. He actually went back, when he knew, he feels that his time is coming. Dying in Vietnam is quicker, easier than in the United States due to the lack of the new medical technology.

Some of our friends planned to do business, but none of them has been successful so far. We don't think that will be easy, because with the Communists, even though now they are open, but who knows? They can change the rules every day and confiscate everything if they want. They are welcoming the expatriates like us to do business. They say, "Oh, you can invest here, there; you can buy land here; it is still very cheap." However, when your business becomes successful, you might get into trouble. Actually, I never think about going back. Because when I left, I think that's it; I lost my country. That's why coming over here, I have to accept this as my second country.

SPRING 2005, AN E-MAIL MESSAGE FROM DZUNG

I believe with faith, hard work and support from your family, you can always start all over again. I feel so blessed for what we have now.

NOVEMBER 2005

Went to mortuary for viewing of Dzung's father. Brothers there from France. Hundreds of flower wreaths from all over the world. Family all in white gauze robes, with headbands and/or hoods. Dzung looked like a wimpled and coifed nun. Big altar with fruit, large picture of Buddha and seven stages of Nirvana. Dzung very concerned at making me comfortable with the ritual procedure: lit incense for me; I bowed three times to Buddha, then moved to another altar at the side, more incense, bowed four times to photo of her father, then viewed his body, behind the altars. Handsome gentleman. In the foyer a beautiful little girl, very courteous, brought me a glass of water on a tray, and we viewed a continuous loop video showing scenes of his life: in black judicial robe with velvet bands on sleeves and white jabot; strolling in Saigon with his elegant wife; presiding over legislature; in a gondola on a canal in Venice; in a square in Belgrade; many photos with VIPs at world conferences. I recognized Gamal Nasser, Haile Selassie; others were heads of state of Korea, Taiwan, Japan, etc. Last one in Dzung's home, Tet holiday. Very moving to think that he began life in North Vietnam when it was French Indochina, and Saigon was "the Paris of the Orient," and died in a California nursing home where the attendants may have had no idea of his former eminence.

I did not attend the cremation ceremony, but later saw photos of it and admired that Buddhist tradition of saying a formal farewell as the body takes its final leave. In my own family, precious and beloved bodies were taken away without ceremony, neither for my solace, nor to pay honor to them.

JANUARY 2006

Periods of about forty days recur in various traditions: Jesus retreated to the wilderness, Mexican mourners wear unrelieved black for six weeks, and Christians observe Lent. For 49 days now we have prayed for Dzung's father, and today he entered Paradise. The ceremony lasted about an hour and reminded me of a Roman Catholic high mass, with chants, incense, and occasional bell ringing. After the ceremony, one of the relatives said to me, "His spirit is now in the pure world."

The pagoda is open to the weather, and the garden has beautiful potted jade plants and evergreen trees, as well as ceramic elephants and lions. Steep steps, painted red, lead to the main sanctuary. I left my shoes in a cubby by the door and took my place at the rear of the room, sitting tailor fashion on the floor. Most of the people knelt before wooden bookstands. The people around me at the rear sat as I did, and after a while I noticed they, too, were squirming and shifting uncomfortably. There are altars on three sides. The central altar is dominated by a very large gilded Buddha with a brilliant halo of continuously radiating red and gold neon lights, an up-to-date electronic effect. On the altar are flowers, and mounds of oranges and apples. Round fruits are important in Buddhism, to symbolize the continuum of creation. A large photo of Dzung's father was centered on a side altar. On the side walls are panels with small photos of people who have been consecrated there, and his will later be added to the display.

Someone handed out green booklets with the words of the chants, 48 vows commanded by the Buddha. Since Vietnamese is written phonetically, I could follow the text. Some of the words were written in large letters and were followed by a brief pause. The priest or monk, hidden behind a screen at the front, occasionally rang a bell or beat a drum. From time to time, Dzung stood up, lit an incense stick from a candle, and put it in the container of sand at one of the side altars or at the central altar. A young man, perhaps 15 years old, did the same at the other side altar. Dzung wore a white robe of coarse gauze and a white headband. A seam down the back of the robe indicated that she is a first-degree relative. Her brother wore a crown-like headpiece of white cloth wrapping what appeared to be a bamboo frame. Sons, daughters, and sons-in-law had gowns with the seam, but daughters-in-law did not. The edges are frayed, to signify their haste to mourn. Little great-grandchildren wore sunny yellow headbands. The chanting, interrupted with occasional tinkling of a bell, was soothing, and although unable to understand the meaning, I prayed in my own way for this dignified man, his spirit drifting now in another sphere, at peace and freed of his troubled body.

Dzung and her husband believe that if one lives a good life, there will be reincarnation at higher and higher levels, and finally an end in paradise, with release from all struggle. Dzung's father might well have achieved this level of health, wealth, and prestige on earth to guarantee him an end to suffering. This is a profoundly appealing idea: if good fortune results from a previous incarnation, those who are lucky have no right to feel proud, and they can be admired rather than envied.

I saw no outpouring of grief, and afterwards, when we went downstairs for a vegetarian lunch, all seemed cheerful. There were about two hundred guests, seated at round tables for ten. Dzung, now wearing a stylish black-and-white tunic sweater over a black-and-white ao dai [traditional Vietnamese gown], shouldered the responsibility of seeing that everyone was properly greeted and seated. There were two speeches: a brief one by Dzung and a very long one by the older sister's husband, recounting in detail the life of the deceased. We ate a delicious vegetarian meal: soup, rice, fried spring rolls, stuffed pieces of bitter melon, mock chicken wings, mock roast pork, all made of tofu or gluten, and several salads. Most of the dishes were on the lazy Susan in the middle of the table, large soup bowl in the center, and other plates ranged around it. One guest served the soup to everyone at the table. Drinks were a choice of sparkling water or sparkling cider; a bowl of ice was passed Western style. For dessert, first plates of cookies and French chocolate truffles were brought, and then at the very end, small cream puffs beautifully decorated with swirls of tinted whipped cream. Much of the conversation was in Vietnamese, but the other guests also spoke excellent English. There was some talk of another relative who lives in France in a very modern house, heated with oil flowing through floor ducts. None of us would ever have dreamed we would be together in a pagoda in California, eating tofu and cream puffs. Dzung, once

Binh and Dzung, New Year, 2010.

bedraggled and sallow in the olive-green uniform issued in the refugee camp, is now chic, healthy, and self-confident. Except for graying hair, Binh looks much the same as he did then, solemn and very thin. I remember that one of the first times we rode around the city in my car, he was surprised that there were so many pickup trucks in residential areas. Today he said that now everyone in the family moves up; he is now the patriarch. We talked of old people who exercise to stay fit. In former times, life was so hard that they didn't need to exercise. He recalled when his mother was ill and as a boy of eight he had to cook rice, building the charcoal fire, waiting for a long time for the water to boil, stirring it constantly; now people can buy food from vending machines, and it is avail-able with no exertion. We talked about world affairs, the oil situation and energy; he thinks that evolution will take care of future generations; those who are strong will survive. He is of course is a superb example.

Dzung and Binh in front of their house, 2010.

JANUARY 2007

Dzung has come to terms with another inter-cultural challenge. It has been a year since her father's death, and they had to waffle on the anniversary ceremony because if they calculated the year of mourning according to the lunar calendar, it would have conflicted with the wedding plans of one of his grandsons; the wedding date was set by the solar calendar. Somehow they compromised; Dzung's brother usually is a stickler for tradition, but in this case he yielded. They have all learned to be adaptable. She laughs about it.

The beloved Vietnamese epic poem, "The Song of Kieu," ends with this:

> Our karma we must carry as our lot—
> Let's stop decrying Heaven's whims and quirks.
> Inside ourselves there lies the root of good.[2]

Now, Anywhere Is My Country

I think of H. T. often, recalling the day he drove my Volkswagen to apply for his driver's license. He said he had a lot of experience driving in Vietnam, and was confident with a manual shift. When he came to a near stop at a green light, I was afraid we would be rear-ended. I suggested that this wasn't necessary, and he calmly explained that it was the safe thing to do, in case someone was coming the other way and ignoring the red light. While we were waiting at the DMV, I called his attention to the sunlight in the new spring leaves of the trees, and he said that in Vietnam, sunlight is not considered beautiful; it is very hot there, and people sweat a lot, so they don't like sunlight. Now, more than 25 years later, he is a career employee of the California Highway Department. His education as an engineer in Vietnam and the network of professional colleagues has helped him to succeed in America. His eventful life falls into three episodes: the good childhood years in North Vietnam, the exile to South Vietnam when the country was partitioned in 1954, and the second exile to the United States in 1975. The first interview was in January, 1977, and the notes say, "Single man, born in 1943; the influence of French is noticeable in interviewee's pronunciation, vocabulary, 'chemise' for shirt, etc."

In Vietnam, when Americans came, sometimes we went to some restaurant, we drank Lipton tea with sugar and lemon. Somebody told me Americans like sugar in food. I drink coffee. But coffee in Vietnam is different from American coffee. It is stronger and smells more good, and we put sugar and some milk in it. Vietnamese coffee, we took the seed which drops from the coffee tree and dry them, and make them for powder, but there is too much caffeine in Vietnamese coffee. In Vietnam I could not drink coffee in the evening because I could not sleep, but with American coffee, I can drink it. They grow coffee in the highlands in Vietnam and also tea. There are many coffee and tree forests in highland. I visited the highland. I traveled in South Vietnam, but not the center, because of war.

EPISODE 1: NORTH VIETNAM, 1943–1954

I was about ten or eleven when I left Hanoi. I remember most. I have good memories of childhood, teenager. In the childhood, my family was very rich, and I can have a good life. When we left Hanoi, we became poor. I remember the day, beginning I studied A-B-C, and I remember when the Chinese lunar New Year, the Tet, my grandmother gave me a gift of money, and I asked her, "More, more, more." She gave me more because I am the favorite grandson. I was the first grandson in my family. She was the mother of my father; we lived in the same house. She gave me money and clothes. The money was in a red paper.

In North Vietnam there were more than ten: my grandmother, grand-father, uncle, aunt, and their children. The family of my mother lived in the next village. We came to visit them every month, the father of my mother. The mother of my mother died a long time; I didn't know her. My father was a teacher. He taught me ABC's at home.[3] I have five brothers and one sister. Two brothers are here, and three in Vietnam. I miss my sister.

His younger brother is a talented violinist who played concertos with the Saigon symphony. He says he is the brother "my parents love." I suggest that surely they love all their children, but he insists that this brother is the one they love the most, because he is the most intelligent and obedient; he stayed behind, along with the only daughter.

EPISODE 2: 1954–1975

He tells of leaving Hanoi and going to the port of Haiphong after the Communist takeover. The grandparents had gone first and bought permits for the rest of the family to join them. Haiphong was only 100 kilometers, about 60 miles, away, but there were so many checkpoints that the trip by train took all day. They went in three groups: H. T. on one day, with his brother, eight, and the sister, six; followed later by the father alone, and the mother with one son. It was H. T.'s first train ride; this seems a heavy responsibility for a boy so young.

I cried in the night before going to Haiphong. I cried and I walked with two friends from my house to Hwan Kim Lake in the center of Hanoi. And I cried when I walked with them.

We went to Saigon by American ship. In that time there were two American ships, one the *Adder* and the other the *Shepherd*.[4] *Adder* was about 60,000 tons I remember, and the other, *Shepherd*, was about 70,000 tons. We went to Saigon by ship, and lived with my grandparents. I went to school. My father was a teacher again, but we lost our money. In North Vietnam, my family had a lot of farms and a lot of gardens, a lot of planting of grain, rice. In Saigon, the whole family lived on the money my father made from teaching. In Vietnam, the father is working for all the family. I think my family was very sad at this time. My mother cried, of course.

Most Vietnamese hoped that two years from that time, we could come back, come back. We lived in Saigon for 20 years. About 10 years ago, we didn't hope anymore. My grandparents are about 80 years old now.

They use different pronunciation in Saigon, but in four or five months we could understand. The weather was different, and the food is some different. I went to the university in 1963. I finished, and worked, and I went to the army about three months. The highway department needed me again, and the army sent me back to my work. We weren't glad to be in the army. Most Vietnamese didn't like the army.

EPISODE 3: ESCAPING FROM SAIGON AND GOING TO
THE UNITED STATES, APRIL 1975

I had this idea about one week before the Viet Cong took over Saigon. I had some connection with Americans, because each office in Saigon had an American advisor. The American advisor left Saigon about three or four weeks before. I had three plans to leave: one is, my office wrote my name in the list and maybe Americans would pick us up to the United States; the chief told me this. The second: my friend and I put together money for buying a small ship made of wood, a boat, can contain about 15 meters long, and three or four meters wide, and we could go to Singapore. But Viet Cong took over Saigon, very soon we could not do this. And the third plan, because I read newspapers, when Cambodia was taken over, the marine [navy] went out by ship, and I thought that when Saigon was taken over, the Vietnamese marine do the same way.

But I think when Saigon was taken over, the ships would go out, but the ships went out one day before. And when Thieu, the last Vietnamese president — I don't know how to explain — read something for changing the government,[5] then I listened from radio, and I went to the port, and nothing there! The ships were all gone. But there was one small ship; I saw somebody in the small ship, somebody climbed and I and my brother climbed in that ship, but we didn't know if this ship would go to the ocean or not. We didn't know, and we climbed, climbed.

My parents knew. My family sat around the table for listening the radio. Yes. My mother, me, my cousin, my father, my grandfather, my grandmother [*pauses after each name, recalling where they sat*], sitting around the table. When Mr. Thieu read — I told my mother — "Mother, I go." Yes. My mother spoke with my brother. I took one small suitcase, one pant, one chemise, and my diploma. That's all.

When I left my house, my mother didn't touch me, and I didn't say goodbye to my father. I said goodbye to my mother only, because some neighbor was standing next to my house, and we didn't want to talk about that, and I could not say goodbye to my family. I said goodbye to my mother. I said, "Mother, I go." To kiss, is not the Vietnamese custom, never. If a foreign person touches me, it's okay; I feel comfortable. In Vietnam, we shake hands only. But if a Vietnamese or other yellow person touches me, we don't feel all right. It is not the way.

The ship was a Vietnamese military ship, but it was broken before. I left Saigon at 11:30, and I came to Vung Tau about 6 P.M. and we went to Con Son Island. In that night, my ship was broken two times. But there was one mechanical engineer; he fixed it three times, but the fourth time he could not fix it, and the water came in, and the ship inclined, and we didn't have anything to announce the other ship. And there was one ship passed it, but we could not claim [*hail*] it because it was overloaded. But they called to the military ship about three hours distant from me, and it came to my ship, and we climbed to the other military ship, and we went to Subic Bay [Philippines]. From Con Son to Subic Bay took about five days. The first two days we didn't have enough food. We had enough sweet water, but we had to take the shower by salt water. I wasn't afraid; I don't know why. At Subic Bay, some American ship supplied food for us.

We changed ship. We took the business [*merchant*] ship. We had to — it was very terrible, taking that ship. I think about five or six thousand people, and we had to live like sardines. In the floor and — because in commercial ship there are many floors to put something there, like shelf. We had to sleep on the shelf, like sardines. We made toilet outside. Ship here, ocean here; we make toilet over there. And most people had eye trouble, most people. We had to spend six days from Subic to Guam. All Vietnamese people. It was American ship; it was very dirty. We can live because of some fruit, orange and apple. We don't have enough food. Terrible.

But in that ship we met one more brother and one cousin. We didn't know that they left; they left the same way, but a different ship. Their ship left at 2:30, but the Viet Cong took over at 12:00. We went around the ship and met them. We were happy. Surprised and happy. We didn't touch. It is not the way Vietnamese.

I stayed on Guam for one month. Very hot. In Guam we had three meals per day: breakfast, lunch, and dinner, but I could eat only two meals. At noon, it was too hot to eat lunch. I was on Guam for one month with no fresh food, meat, fruit, or vegetables. The skin around my fingernails all came off. But I still felt lucky. I was in Camp Pendleton for four months. The food there was all right. Every day I had to go to some VOLAG — voluntary agencies — like the UCC, Church World Service, or ARC — looking for a sponsor. I go to VOLAG and ask them for a sponsor. My sponsor was the Jewish Family Service Agency. I don't know why they sponsored me. I had to fill out many forms.

I haven't met my sponsor, the president of Jewish Family Service. He sent the money by mail, and when we arrived, an employee met us and took us to the apartment by car. He was a young student, about 22 or 23. He invited me sometimes to his home, but he is single and lives alone in Berkeley, and he picked us up to visit some place in San Francisco. I wrote one letter to the Jewish Family Service when I was unemployed, two or three months ago, and I wrote to JFS, and they answered that they are not an employment agency. I said that for one year I tried to study English and to study one skill, and now I graduated, and to please help me to find a job for improving my life. They answered that they cannot look for a job for me, because JFS is not an employment agency. They sponsored five families. The other family told me he called up the president of JFS, but the *telephoniste* answered, "He is busy, busy, busy, and cannot answer." So we know that he doesn't want to talk. Some other Vietnamese person went to his office, and they didn't let him come. Yes.

They gave us the rent for two months, and that was all. I think they sponsor for us, two years, and at November 1977 they stop. Because the VOLAG told me when I left Camp Pendleton, they told me that, but I think in November 1977 I will call the JFS, or I will write a letter. They don't want to talk to us; they don't want to answer us. When I came here, I asked the employee of JFS, I want to come to see the president to thank him, but the president didn't want to. Now the employee has gone to study at Columbia University. Sometimes I write to him.

I was on welfare for eight months. I know it is not legal to send money to Vietnam, but I have to do it. I sent money when I was on welfare, but I had to do it. Nobody in the United States is very poor. I saw them in Oakland, but if they don't drink alcoholic and whiskey, they can live and can have enough food and clothes for living. If they have no job, they can get welfare. I know that the welfare comes from tax from the people who get jobs and are working; I know that, but when someone gets the high salary, he has to pay the high tax, and the low salary, a little tax, and nobody is too rich or too poor. It is like Communist; it is the purpose Communist, we think. Most Vietnamese think the United States has social Communism. It is a good system: nobody too rich, nobody very poor, because if somebody very rich puts money in the bank, nothing. The rich man has enough food, enough clothes, enough house for living; no problem. I know many American people are angry that we got welfare money and send to Vietnam, but we think we send to Vietnam a little bit: a little bit, about 20 dollars, 50 dollars, a little bit. When you go to San Francisco for enjoy, you can spend one hundred dollars; it's nothing. I have to try to send money; they wrote that they got it. I have to send them money again. I sent to Japan or France, and my friend there sent it. I don't want to write to my parents that I give them money, so I write that my friend gives them. I am afraid the Communists get the bad idea. They read the letters. Most Vietnamese do that the same way.

I met some people who were unkind to me, just some people. Most people are friendly, but some are unkind. They don't want to speak to us, or I see in the eyes or the face or by some action. They know I am Vietnamese. I don't know how they know. I think American people who don't always contact with the yellow people, they can't distinguish different Orientals. I cannot speak about the Chinese people because we don't have contact with them. At school we study, and we go home. I try to make friends with everybody, but there is the trouble with the language.

In Vietnam we don't have birthday ceremony, and we remember only the year. When I get married and have a family I will have religious cere-monies, but now I am single so I don't try, but some of my friends have cer-emonies for New Year's and for anniversaries. I don't try, because in the Vietnamese custom, it is the parents' responsibility. I don't want to do it, because one day I am here, maybe next day I go out of town, because I can go anywhere at any time. Today I visit you; maybe this afternoon I visit the other. Sometimes I visit my friends in San Jose, or Monterey, or San Mateo. Sometimes at midnight I visit my friends. They have ceremonies, and I visit them. They invite me, because I live alone.

We celebrate Tet [*lunar new year*] and anniversaries of death, grandfather or father, and some birthdays, because we study American customs. Christmas and Thanksgiving, too. The anniversary is a solemn celebration because we look up to the old people. We pray, nobody speaking, and eat. Do we sing? No, never! There are flowers, fruit, and sometimes liquor, wine or beer. In Vietnam that is a very big ceremony. The rich families serve one ox and one pork, and all the village comes to eat.

I knew these friends in Saigon. Some of my friends were in Camp Pendle-ton with me, and some came here from Fort Chaffee. Some of them are mar-ried; some are single. They were married in Vietnam, and brought all the family. There are more men than women among the refugees, but most of the men were married in Vietnam, and they could not bring their wives and fam-ilies. In some cases, the men left the wives, and in some cases the wife came here and left the husband. I have one friend, his wife is in San Francisco, but he stayed in Vietnam. The child is here with his mother. Maybe in the future the wife will marry again. I think he will marry again in Vietnam, maybe four or five years from now.

I think I will get married. I want to, but now I don't have a choice. I want to find a Vietnamese girl. I meet them sometimes in the ceremonies, at the parties, but I don't like them. I have some friends, but they live very far from here: one in Canada, and one in Oklahoma City. The girl in Canada works in a factory, and the one in Oklahoma is studying biology, chemistry, Ph.D. degree. I write letters, and sometimes I call them. They left Saigon at the same time I did. If I met a Vietnamese girl I liked, I would follow the Vietnamese customs. I can go to visit her home. I can take her to the movies if she is my girlfriend.

About Americans, I think, I'm sorry, I think most Americans resist minority. My friends who study in college told me that they don't have any American friends, because maybe they resist. I don't think the Vietnamese resist. Because my friend told me, when they ask them, they answer, but it is a rare case the Americans ask the Vietnamese or Filipino or Chinese. The other classmates are very hard to make friends. I work with Chinese, Japanese, Hungarian, and some Americans, one black. I can talk at break time. They all speak very good English. I try to make friends with them. They have lived here a long time. They didn't resist, but we are different in age; I am the youngest worker. They don't have much education. They don't know that I have more education. I don't think they are polite, because they — I don't have vocabulary to explain. Because they speak dirty words and use too much slang. I asked them about the words, and they explained to me, and some actions are not polite, with feet, hands. Because in my company the workers, in the office, there are many kinds of people. Some are very good; some are very bad. I can't explain. They jump, and they talk too much, and I don't have vocabulary to explain. They talk about me, and about other people. Sometimes they laugh at me because I am the new worker. And I feel bad; I don't like it. They laugh at my English and my customs. Because when I feel cold, I put on my jacket, they laugh at me. I think they want to make me feel bad, because maybe they are jealous. They don't want the company hiring the new worker. I work very hard, and I am very careful. I think the workers are all honest, because everybody wants to keep his job. They don't steal.

A man hit me in the street, but I think he drank too much. He hit me. Maybe he drank too much, and maybe he took some medicine or drugs. I think American people are as honest as Vietnamese, the same. Sometimes I believe Americans; sometimes I don't. In Vietnam and the United States, there are some good people, some bad people, and I have to decide. I decide by experience, and it depends on the case. For example, when I apply to some company, they promise, "Yes, you go home, and I will call you," but I don't believe. If they want to hire me, they answer right now, immediately.

A counselor at the Skills Center introduced me for this job. I don't know why he hired me because I don't know anything about repairing. I don't want to keep this job; maybe I will look for another to replace it. I hope to get another job, but not now. I have to save some money. I am putting some money in a savings account. I live with a roommate. He is studying at the Skills Center. They pay for him. He wants a bookkeeping job. My friend introduced him to me.

My brother went to Oregon. Our other apartment was too expensive. I had to pay $165; here I pay $100. One other friend lives in the same apartment, and he introduced me. It is an old building, not comfortable. There are three Vietnamese: one old man, and me and my roommate. Sometimes we read the newspaper or listen to the radio, and we talk about Vietnamese news. I cannot listen to the Vietnamese program, because VOA and BBC talk very early, so I can't hear it, but some friends announce it to us. In the United States there are many Vietnamese newspapers. One only is Communist, but there are more than ten non–Communist. I think some of the refugees are Communists. Most Vietnamese Communists have lived here a long time; they are students in Berkeley and Long Beach.

My brother in Vietnam is in "re-education" camp. I received a letter from my parents; they said sometimes they get a letter from my brother. I have received two letters from my parents in two years, but I think they don't want to write. I still write to them every month. I write to Japan or Australia or Canada or France. I received a letter last month. They are alive, but they don't have enough money for living. They asked me about money, if I have money, to send to them, because my family has seven members, but two people working. Two grandparents, two parents, and three brother and sister, and my father working, brother working, but the others stay home. No work, no job. My sister studied banking, but now she had to stop. No bank is open in Saigon now. In Saigon there are many, many people unemployment.

My friend introduced me to the school. He and I had the same sponsor. He came here one week before me. I think he went around and looked for a school. He is a good friend. Sometimes he invites me to his apartment; sometimes I invite him. If I go to visit him, I have to telephone first. In Vietnam, most Vietnamese don't have telephones. The offices have telephones, and we can call from the office. I like it here, to have telephones. In Vietnam we said "Allo," like the French, but now we say, "Hello."

When I go to visit, we talk, and sometimes we watch the baby playing on the floor. My friend's wife is busy, but sometimes she sits and talks with us. My friend's father doesn't have any friends. He is very happy when a visitor comes. Sometimes they give me special food, but not always. We drink orange juice, tea, or coffee. Sometimes we eat fruit, but not candy; we don't like candy. Cookies here are too sweet. I like apples and oranges but not American bananas, because in Vietnam there are very many, many bananas, but I think some Americans don't like bananas.

I am very comfortable materially, but not in the spirit, because we feel alone in the United States. It is better when we group the Vietnamese. We feel happy when some Vietnamese are talking, but we feel alone. Most Vietnamese don't want to become American citizens; we want to come back to Vietnam, and we want to become immigrant; it is enough condition for working, but we don't want to become American citizen. It is the American law, if we live here for five years, or two years, we can become immigrants, but now, we have enough condition for working.

The food in America is enough, but it is not delicious, because here we don't have fresh food: beef, pork, chicken, is not fresh. You put it in the freezer first, and then sell. In Vietnam, the beef and pork are killed at night, and the dealer sells it in the morning, very fresh and delicious, more delicious than here. Different kinds of fish, too, very fresh; I miss fresh fish, because the fresh meat and fresh fish is sweeter than here.

I didn't have Chinese friends in Saigon, because the Chinese people had Chinatown, very separate. They had schools, business, and we don't mix at school. Oh — I had one Chinese friend. He speaks Vietnamese very well, and he received the M.A. degree in Saigon. We went to Cholon [*Chinatown*] for buying.

My brothers and cousin are in Oregon. I would like to meet them, but I like the weather here. The most difficult thing is language. If I speak English better, I think it would be better. I study at home. I listen to the radio and read a bilingual newspaper, but I don't have enough time to study, because I come home at 6 P.M. and cook and eat until about 7:30. I read the newspaper and speak with some people, and about 9 or 10 P.M. I go to bed. Maybe I will register in Laney [*Community College*] this semester. They have ESL classes in the evening from 7 P.M. to 10. And when I drive my car, I turn on the radio to try to understand.

Maybe five or ten years from now I will go back to Saigon, because maybe Saigon and the United States will contact. Maybe the United States will help Hanoi to drill the petrol, the gasoline in the ocean. When Hanoi becomes rich, we are not afraid. Now they are very poor, and they have many differences from the United States, but I think the social in East Europe — Hungary, Poland — is better than China, because they have more freedom, because they have become rich. If Hanoi becomes rich, there will be more freedom.

If I went back today, they would put me in jail. I went away from Vietnam for two reasons. First reason: I want to go out; I want to see outside of Vietnam. I am not afraid of Communists, but I don't like this way. In the childhood, as I said to you, I wanted to take trips, I wanted to see outside, but now I want to go to the East, like Syria, Lebanon, this area. I dream to get there. But now, anywhere is my country. I think, I hope I get the degree here and I move to the Middle East for a few years, and I move to Africa, Europe, or South America. I want to live anywhere a few years. I think this is possible. And in my job, I don't want to sit in the same place; I want to go out. In Vietnam, I like; every week in Vietnam, I went out of Saigon at least two times for controlling. I want to go far, very far, and come back.

Sometimes I don't like to live here; I want to move, but I must get training for a job skill. I have studied drafting. They found jobs for me, but I have trouble about English. They told me to interview about 10 places, but most of them told me I have trouble about English, so I have this job just for now. I am single; I don't need anything. Sometimes — sometimes I feel crazy. I think about my family, my country, my future. I am not afraid, because I am single; I don't need anything. I am unhappy. And most Vietnamese dream while sleeping, dream to be in Vietnam every night, every night, meeting family, friends. Some Vietnamese told me at day he live in United States; at night he live in Vietnam. One Vietnamese refugee cut his finger off. Some of them have tried to kill themselves. I go to visit my friends, and then I feel better.

In the apartment, we think we are in Vietnam. In Vietnam, a few people went out; I went out always, but most Vietnamese stay home, because in Vietnam we had trouble about war. When I went out of Saigon, maybe the Viet Cong would keep us; we cannot. But I think here to go to the park, we have to have a group of people; it's better, but I go alone, I feel sad, sadder. In Monterey sometimes we go to Carmel Beach or Pebble Beach or Pacific Grove. We go to the beach about one or two hours, take picture, come back, because it's very cold. On Sunday I always go to Monterey when I have time. When I bought a car, I go to Monterey from the evening at Friday, and I come back at night Sunday. Sometimes I have to stay here in Oakland for working something, for visiting friends or cousins, or cleaning the apartment. I have cousins in San Francisco, in Oregon, San Mateo, San Jose, Los Angeles: not the same grandparents, the same ancestor. This car belongs to me. Remember I got my driver's license in June. The younger Vietnamese do exercise. I make exercise at home. I bought an exercise string. I don't go around the lake; it is too cold. I don't have enough friends for playing games, ball games. I don't play card games. In Vietnam I played volleyball. We don't go to the park or the zoo. We stay in the house on the day off, because here, about spirit, nothing good here. It is not delicious when we eat; it is not beautiful to see the scene; nothing, nothing for spirit. Yes.

H. T. was married in July 1979 in a Japanese Buddhist temple in San Francisco. There were many guests, all smiling and very well dressed, and several movie and flash cameras recorded the event.

In 2004, he responds to my request with an e-mail message:

I am very glad to hear from you after 25 years. Although without contact with you, I am always thinking of you and remember the time you taught me English, driving the car without automatic transmission, and asked me some questions about Vietnamese culture as well as civilization. That time was very wonderful to me.

He lives in a suburb of Sacramento and works for the California Highway department as an engineer designing bridges. He and his wife come to my house, and although he is happy to interview, he does not want his real name used. Now 60 years old, he is round-faced, balding, and with a grey mustache, and wears glasses. She is lovely, gracious and composed; they both seem comfortable and relaxed. They have traveled together in much of the United States, as well as Europe and Asia. Not surprisingly, he has had health problems caused by stress.

In this interview, he was more explicit about his education in Vietnam, and the support network created in America. The graduates from Phu Tho University, the only engineering school in Vietnam, created an alumni newsletter to help each other when American sponsorship failed. He was enrolled in a job training program at first, and although he had a degree as a civil engineer, he was put into electronic drafting because there were immediate job openings.

This is what he recorded in October, 2004:

When we got here, we tried to connect with relatives and friends. Before we leave Camp Pendleton, and leave for Fort Chaffee or somewhere else, we leave the relative and friend the address of sponsor, and after that we send letter to each other, to the sponsor address. In our school we still have one magazine, since Vietnam, and we get the news to make that magazine, until now. I have one friend, graduate before me about five or six years, and he working at that time in Louisiana, and he start to prepare that one. First time, just a few page, and make copy and send it to the friend, what friend he have the address, and after that, you know more people, and we contribute some funds.

I studied about six months, at the East Bay Skills Center, for electronic drafting. I graduated in Phu Tho University next to Saigon. I got the B.S. engineering degree in civil engineering in that university. I want to study civil engineering drafting skills, but they don't accept, because at that time, civil engineering is difficult to get job, and they ask me to study electronic. And after that, I get job in Dictran Company, in south San Francisco. I do some drafting, and they trained me to test the machine. At that time they produced the answering machine. They modified the cassette tape deck to be the answering machine for the telephone. And after that I worked for Remco Company and they trained me to — because at that time I had the EIT license, Engineer in Training — and they hired me and trained me to technician to test the machine to duplicate microfilm. In 1980 my friend in Richland, Washington State, called me over there and said they opened some positions for civil engineer working for the Hanford Two nuclear power plant. And they interviewed and accepted me to work. At that time I worked for the WBG Company, joint venture.

My friend was already working over there. I worked at Hanford. At that time, I just had EIT, and they accept that license. After that, I get license PE, Professional Civil Engineer, in Washington. I worked for WBG for nine months, and then Bechtel Company took over that job, and Bechtel hired me. And after that job complete, they sent me to Diablo Canyon. I worked over there about two years. The same job. I designed in civil construction the steel frame, pipe support. In nuclear power plant, they need a lot of pipe, and we have to design the support for that pipe. I designed pipe support and support the construction. This means when we have a plan, have to prepare the document and give them to the track men, and they will build.

I enjoyed. Because you know in the construction we have limited time for after the job the contract complete; they just ask me, "Now I want to send you to somewhere." You say yes or no. That's it. But yes, they send me there to the new job; but no, they lay me off. They off me. That's a problem. And that reason why I have to say yes, to follow them to go somewhere else, like

Hope Creek. [My wife] followed me and had a good job, and everywhere she had to start again.

Asked about finding housing, the wife speaks:

They let us stay in the hotel the first month, and paid per diem. We rent furniture and submit the receipt, and they pay. Some place I can find a job, and some I cannot. Because when I live in San Francisco, I work for Bank of America, data processing, so when we go in a big city I can find some. Usually the job site is far from the city, but some job site, I can find a job in this job site. So sometimes I have a good job; sometimes enjoy stay home.

H. T. continues:

Actually in Bechtel, there are a lot of Asians, and we treat each other nicely. Over there everybody is a professional, and they treat each other very nice. The people is nice, too, very nice. I don't get any discrimination anywhere. I hear some, but I never get that problem

Because we follow the job, and the job is always in the small city. And some cities, like Hope Creek, and in New Jersey I live in Pennsville. Have only one Safeway and one K-mart. And I enjoy living in small town. I work over there two years, and they send me to Bay City, Texas. I work for the South Texas Project. And after that they send me to Chattanooga. Over there about four months. I lived in hotel four months, working for Sequoia nuclear power plant. But after there is the worst time for me because I have to get in the old plant; they call a dirty plant — it means that they already contaminate — but fortunately, I just get radiation very small amount. I have to wear the special suit. And before get in, get out, have to use a frisky to detect contamination. For four months. But fortunately, the amount to get radiation very small. From there, I get back to Bay City again. Until 1988, they send me to Gaithersburg, Maryland. At that time I worked for Brown's Ferry and Watts Bar. Belonged to TVA. Over there, there are about five or six nuclear power plants. Sequoia, Brown's Ferry, Watts Bar, I forget. After that they ask me to go to Turkey Point, in Florida. But I deny. Because they ask me over there for two months, but they didn't pay per diem, jut regular salary. And I say, for two months I go over there, and I don't know where I go. And I accept to be laid off.

But in Texas, when I was working in Texas, I know that I have to leave Bechtel, and I begin to prepare for myself, and I apply for the PE license in California, and I get the PE license in California. I flew back here to take the test. I went back to Sacramento in May 1990. And I apply for Caltrans, and I start to work on January 1, 1991. I ask my boss, "Why? Because January 1 is a holiday, why you hire me on that day?" He says, "Easy for the accounting."

He and his two brothers were the first to come to America, in 1975; they were joined by the rest of the family, who also escaped by boat in two groups, in 1979 and 1980. As they left Vietnam, following one expensive failed attempt, the

parents were held up by boatmen taking them to the ship, and they lost their last
possessions. Eventually they were all reunited in California.

Two brothers went to Portland, Oregon. They studied over there and
get job over there and in 1987 came back here to San Jose, and they applied
job in Sacramento. And now work for Franchise Tax Board, computer science,
program analysis. The youngest came here in 1979. All of them are boat people. My parents came in 1980. They have to pay for one organization they
prepare boat and brought them to Indonesia. First they paid 12 taels of gold
each.[6] They had to go to Long Huyen Province, and they waiting over there
for one year, and they went over there for one year, waiting to get in the boat,
but at that time they don't know why they cannot get the boat. And that
organization had to refund them almost. They went back to Saigon, but not
living in the same house, living in the rural area, and my brothers looked for
another chance, and they success. And they paid only two taels of gold. The
people ride the boat from the land to the big boat in the sea. The big ship
hired these people to bring my parents to that ship, but they said, "Give us
your money and jewelry because in the foreign country your life is better; you
don't need these anymore." And my parents have to give them everything. If
not, water taxi driver wouldn't bring them to the ship. That's a problem. My
parents gave them all reluctantly. Fortunately, they got on the ship in time.

Total family now is 32 people. Not real big, because I have two brothers
have no family, and the two of us have no children. The sister is not married.
Six of us living in Sacramento, and one in Los Angeles. We get together each
time for birthday or children. Or sometimes like Tet [*lunar new year*]. My
mother doesn't know about English because she came here, old already. She
came here, she is 64 years old. But my father is very good English. He can
read novel, and now he is 80 years old, but he is still reading and studying
mathematics and physics also. And he bought this book and study himself.
He know English and French. He was a teacher in Vietnam. But now I am
happy my father is very healthy. He is still jogging and lift five-pound weight
every day, two hours, and cycling also. Two hours a day.

I exercise every day. Swimming and jogging. I swim in the fitness club.
We have inside swimming pool. I do about 50 laps per day, for 50 minutes.
Sometimes 60 laps if I have time. At five o'clock I go over there. But I just
swim about four or five times a week, but I do jogging on the treadmill, at
the fitness center. Actually, before about six years I did not have good health.
From 1994 to 1996 or 1997, I suffered three major surgeries. One stomach,
one colon, and one gall bladder. But after that, I feel very good now. And
fortunately, is not cancer. My stomach ulcer is because of stress. Because my
character always nervous. That's a problem.

I still have the 401-K from Bechtel. With Caltrans, I have a 401-K and
retirement, too. I can retire now, but if I retire now, I have a problem: I cannot

4. Looking Back, Years Later

get full benefits about health. At least I have to work for 20 years. Six more years.

H. T. explains how he has acclimated to life in America, and he now laughs at differences in food and religious practices:

I think I changed, but not easy to figure out how I changed. Coffee: now the same as Vietnam. But before, the coffee in 1975 is instant coffee, not fresh coffee. American chicken now is okay. Not me, but my friends, when they said they come back to Vietnam, they don't feel good when they eat beef and pork in Vietnam because the taste is different. They don't feel good. Religion, we still follow Buddhism, and we read and listen to tapes about Buddhism. But we believe — as you know, Buddhism has no god; we just consider the Buddha is a teacher that teaches how to live and how to escape, self-rescue, and about life's problems. It helped me a lot. I don't go to temple. If I have a chance, I go, but not every month. But I read the Buddhism books. And some evangelist monks explain the Buddhist Bible. In Sacramento, there are five temples. So if we need it, we go there. Because Buddha doesn't say we have to go to the church. You can stay home and can study everywhere. At home, we have an altar, and we light incense sometimes. Not every day, just special occasions. We already have a Vietnamese cemetery in Sacramento. When my parents die, they want to be buried here.

H. T. and his wife have traveled extensively in recent years, including two trips to Vietnam. He no longer thinks of returning there to live.

Vietnam has changed a lot. I don't have family over there, and when I left Vietnam, total population, north and south, about 40 million. And now is 80 million, and very, very crowded. And while the Communists still control Vietnam, I don't want to live there. You know, I went to France in 1990, because at that time I left Bechtel, and Caltrans didn't call me yet, and at that time I say I will travel, because after that maybe I will have no chance to travel. And we just travel in tennis shoes, t-shirt, and just small luggage, and we went to Paris. Over there I bought the Eurail pass and took the train for 35 days. At that time, we didn't go with a travel agent, just with ourselves. I like that way. Now in Sacramento, we have a small group, about 10 people, and when we travel, we go together. Last year we go to Alaska. Before 9/11, I planned to go to Spain and Portugal and Morocco in the same trip. But after 9/11, they cut Morocco.

I went to Mt. Rushmore, very interesting and very beautiful. I admired the architect, and that idea. I took the picture of Crazy Horse. It's not complete yet. I went to Yellowstone, and to Canada, to Vancouver, Edmonton, Toronto, Niagara Falls, Montreal [*pronounces it in French*]. I went to Europe also, Spain, Portugal, and France, Holland, Munich, Venice, and to China also. Next year I plan to go to Japan and Cambodia and Thailand. When I retire, I will plan to travel to Australia by cruise ship.

He travels with a group of Vietnamese companions, but also has friends who are not Vietnamese.

We have friends and go out to eat together and some entertainment. I went to Reno several times, but I never lost more than 20 dollars. Because I just spend 20 dollars for fun. I know I cannot win. You never win. But after that, I can say that I win, because they cannot get more money. That is winning. Actually, my family normally does not like gambling. No gambling, no alcohol, no tobacco. Actually, we do not have time to watch television. Just time for the news and some classic movies and things like that. Even now because maybe I am behind everybody, I don't know who is the famous actor and actress and what movie is a good one. I watch CNN and ABC. And the art channel, A&E. I like that one. And classic movies, because we still like Joan Crawford and Clark Gable. We like that. Did you read *A Thousand Tears Falling [by Yung Krall]*? It's a novel, but looks like the memory of a Vietnamese lady, and her father is a high official in North Vietnam, but she and her family stay in South Vietnam, and how she handle the situation in South Vietnam, and after Vietnam collapsed. She left her father in Japan and asked him to leave Vietnam and the Communist party, but he denied that. I think if you want to understand the society of South Vietnam before 1975, I recommend you to read that book. She married an American, and now changed to an American name. I like to read that kind of book because I was born when the war began, and really half of my life was in the war, but I didn't understand about the war. But now I have time, and I have a chance to study and understand about this war. I read a lot of memory of South Vietnam and North Vietnam officials, in Vietnamese, and also the book written by McNamara.[7] Because each party wrote in their part, in their opinion, not the whole thing. You know, reporters like Dan Rather, they just come to Vietnam and stayed in the center of Saigon, very safe place, and after that they wrote the news and send back to here, and sometimes they don't listen well about the situation.

An e-mail message from him in the summer of 2006:

Last month we went to Montreal, Canada, for high school classmate reunion. We came from USA, Vietnam, Australia, French and Germany. I met someones not seen since 1963 and some teachers too. Everybody changed so much, I could not recognize someones until they tell the name !!!! We lived in same hotel for one week. We visited Quebec, and some interesting places together, and teased each other by "nickname" to remember the years in high school.

Twenty-five years earlier, he had said, "Nothing for the spirit here." He seems now to feel that there is after all something for the spirit in America.

I Don't Want to See Sad Again

Vanny, 43 years old in the fall of 1980, had been a teacher in Vietnam, and already spoke Chinese, Vietnamese, and French, as well as some English. She was sponsored and came by plane in 1978 under the family reunification plan. She was unfailingly cheerful and self-confident and quickly became a fluent, although erratic, speaker. She assumed a role as my interpreter and colleague. When she transferred out to a job training program, we kept in touch as she regularly called to tell of her progress.

The Chinese zodiac has a 12-year cycle of years, and the belief is that one's birthday to some extent influences personality and fate. Each day is also divided into a similar cycle. Vanny explains that because she was born in the year of the ox, she was destined to work hard all her life, but because she was born at noon, in the hour of the rat, she has not had to work at the worst kind of drudgery. Her life, nevertheless, has not been easy. Her family, well educated and prosperous Chinese in North Vietnam, fled first to South Vietnam in 1954, and to America in stages after 1975. By 1985, her family was all together again. She was first interviewed in 2001 at her home in Oakland. Her husband had died a month earlier, less than a year after retiring from his job as janitor at San Francisco airport. There is a wrought-iron security door at the front door and a "Far East Realty" for-sale sign in the front yard. She walked away from one house in Hanoi, and a second in Saigon, but this one she will sell, and she will move to San Jose to live with her son.

The house is spotlessly clean and quite bare. We sit on a Scandinavian-style sofa with orange cushions; there is also a large leather puffy armchair. In the dining room is a glass-topped table with brass supports and brass chairs, which she bought at Salvation Army for $100, one of the few furniture purchases she ever made. Everything else was handed down by relatives. On the mantel there are a large ceramic swan flower holder, a clock, and a couple of Chinese vases. In the dining room on a shelf is a small Buddhist altar with an orange, some flowers, and a picture of "Lady Buddha." Prominent in the living room is a large folding game table, with mah jong tiles laid out, and a tray of poker chips. In the entryway is a stack of boxes and a chair; these and the living room furniture are to be picked up by Salvation Army.

Vanny, looking younger than her 63 years, is dressed in a blue-and-white striped shirt, black pants, and flip-flops that she soon removes; as she talks, she massages her bare feet. Her sister-in-law stays in the background after serving a steaming cup of tea; she is 74, never married, and speaks only Chinese. When she walks me to the car, Vanny says that she doesn't want anyone to see her cry; she gets up early in the morning and cries at the breakfast table alone. This is her story as she tells it in 2001:

My parents were born in North Vietnam, in Hanoi. They were both Chinese, Cantonese. My grandfather was a Chinese doctor in North Vietnam; Grandfather had Chinese education. My older grandma, she came back to China because we had a lot of property in China. Once in a while she come to visit us, but my second grandma stayed with my grandpa. My father and my uncle go to the French school in Hanoi. You know at that time the French controlled Vietnam, and if you don't know the French language, it's not easy to find a high job. My grandfather gave both of them to go to school and study French language. My grandparents passed away a long time ago, before I was born. I only know about them because my father talked to me.

You know, the Chinese culture before, girl education was only elementary school; that's all. You know, they think only for the boys everything good. They don't care the girls too much. That's the Chinese culture. Usually the man goes to earn money, and the wife stays home to take care of the family; that's all. Until me, no! After marry, I still continue to work. I am a teacher.

My father, I don't know how to say it; in French language they say "comprador." It's a business; they have a catalog from France or somewhere, and the comprador take to the businessman, and they order, and if you sell more, you get more commission. Perfume, because in France, the perfume is perfect. And wine, and material. If they order more, my father gets more commission. And he had his own business. But you know when the Communists came and they cut Vietnam in half, then he went to the South in 1954.

I was born in 1937, in Hanoi. My mom had five girls, two boys. I am in the middle. You know, my father, because he studied French language and he had the new idea, he is very fair for boy and girl. He's not like my friends, the boy is more important than the girl. But my father, everybody have education. I went to school when I was three years old, to pre-school. Chinese school. Step by step, I just go up until high school. I graduated from the Chinese high school. You know, the last two years before the Communists took North Vietnam, we went to the seminary to study French language, because at that time we are teenager, and I took that class two years. In the Chinese school, only teaching Chinese language, but when I study at the Catholic school, they teach both languages. Vietnamese language and French language.

My mom hired the maids in Vietnamese. And we worked with Vietnamese. When we were little, learn is easy. We speak Vietnamese language well. We don't know reading or writing Vietnamese language, but my father make school, teaching seven kids sit there, teaching all. And he bought the newspaper, he circle and write the number 1-2-3-4-5-6-7. And then my older brother reading newspaper first, and make a turn to the last one. We reading newspaper for daddy, mommy, and they sit there and listen, and we reading. The first time, you know, the first week, slowly, and later we reading quickly.

My father had his own business, a big business. When we left North

Vietnam, the three younger kids, they were very little. And the three older, didn't have any skill, just school boy, school girl. We went to Saigon in 1954, before Christmas. By boat from the north to South Vietnam. You know, that's an American boat. They helped the people move, the refugees. Only with the suitcase; that's all. Because the boat had only one space, so we cannot carry everything.

My older sister stayed in North Vietnam. My father took six kids, eight persons, go to his sister's house in Saigon, but the house not enough space for us. We have a tent, and we live outside the door because the house too small. But my aunt's neighbors are very good, and you know in South Vietnam it is hot, and they are sleeping there, too. At that time, no Communists yet. And later, have Communists, almost 10 years later. At that time, we just immigrate there, it is a new place, everything new, no business. So the kids, me and older, no go to school, and try to get a job. You know at the bakery someone come to buy, and we sell, and we have lunch and dinner there, in the morning until evening. We work a long, long day and get money, and my mom stay home and take care and my father teaching Vietnamese and French language at the high school. And the three younger kids could study at school, and they don't need to pay the tuition because he was a teacher.

Five years, everything is okay. At night, at seven o'clock, I go to school, seven to nine, two hours, study. I studied about the Vietnamese language, and I went to teaching adult school at night. In Vietnam you don't need a certificate or something; if you want to work, okay. And that time, I started teaching, and I stopped work at the bakery. Then I was teaching at night time, and daytime, I go to school. Then when I had more time, I go to tutor at home. Because some people they saw I teaching well, and they are so happy; they ask me, "Do you want to tutor the kids at daytime?" and I say, "Yes." And they introduce, and the kids study at school, and after school come back to the house and teaching at home. Make money and help family.

I met my husband because my third sister is a secretary at a Japanese company. Then she passed the test and went to work at the Saigon American Embassy, and she passed her secretary job to me. She practiced me two weeks; at that time my typewriting is not too quickly. And after work time, I go to the school and practice my typing. Working and studying. She caught me from the school to do her secretary job at the Japanese company. They sell Japanese material. They have a catalog, and someone orders. I liked that job, and since that time, I know my husband. You know, the office, at the front is one company, and in the back is the other company. That company they sell everything about the electric, and we are in the same office but in front and in back. He is a seller and got a commission, and he was a good friend of my sister. I know him since 1960. He is old than me, two years. I worked at that company not too long, only two or three years, and then they closed the business and I went back to teacher job at the elementary school. Morning kindergarten, afternoon fifth grade, French school. At night time, I'm teaching adult school.

We had dates for 10 years. On weekends, after eating with noodles, sometimes go to the park, take a walk. Sometimes we take a trip go to the beach. We go with some friends together. After three or four years, then he took me come back to see his family, and they know me, too. He came to my house, too. He had a Vespa, a motorbike, and he came to pick me up. For 10 years, we cannot marry. You know why? Because in Vietnam they catch the Chinese at the young age, under 32 years, to go to the soldier, and he need to hide. That's why we cannot marry. He hide in the office. All day, all night. They have a bathroom there, and they order the food, and they bring to the office. On the weekend I go to his house and bring some clothes and take there for him and bring his dirty clothes home and wash. Sometimes at night I iron clothes there for him. That's all. It's very hard time. He hide two years, and then need to pay someone and talking with the government and say he is the only son and he cannot go to the soldier army; then he have to stay home and take care the older father and mother.

She explains that she cared for her dying father, and because they had waited so long, before he died, he gave her permission to marry without observing the traditional years of mourning after his death.

Then after Chinese New Year, February, 1972, got married. And in December, got my son. My son was my Christmas gift. Before the Communists come, I had my son and my daughter. My daughter was born in 1974, February 10. I only stay in the hospital one or two days, and I come home. At day time I took the kids, and my sister-in-law they take care. The two sister-in-law stay home; they cooking; they take care. And I go to work. At night time, I took the kids home. My husband still work, and he do his own business.

After Communists come, took all my husband's factory, make the tubes for electric. I usually talk to my children, say, "You're rich. Daddy have a big business, have a factory," and the Communists come, and with two hands I give to them. You know why, the Communists, they hate someone rich. They said, "You pay someone money, you took something from the poor people because you are rich." My husband say, "Okay; the Communists want; give to them. If you don't give, they will give you a lot of problems. You have to go to the jail, and they will take you go to the forest or go to the farmer."

I teaching at school only 50 dollars Vietnamese money. That time have father-in-law sick, mother-in-law sick. And my sister with two kids and my husband and me, 10 persons! And my salary, hide it, and I bought the gold, and hide somewhere. And we sell and hide and bought the gold, sell, hide. Hide, hide, hide. Finally my diamond ring and everything, sell, sell, sell. For buy the food. And waiting five years before I left Vietnam. We only close the door, hide inside the house; that's all. All families like that. They fighting on the street or somewhere; we don't care; we close the door and stay inside, and we don't stand up — we sit lower. Sometimes they fight and got hurt. Everything stopped. Everybody hide at home.

In 1975, the Communists came at May fifth, and my second sister worked at the embassy, and before the Communists come, they have a list; they count, and my name there, and my mom, my sister and brother, whole family can go because if you work with government, your family can go. But too late. They came to airport too quickly; we cannot left Vietnam at 1975. Then I wait and wait and wait until 1978; I got a passport. But the final, I have to wait one and a half more years, and then they let me out of Vietnam. Finally the last year, when I got the passport, I sell all. Everything I can sell, I sell. The first thing, I sell the baby clothes of my children. I sell, someone buy it! I sell, sell, sell. And the last minute, I sell my furniture. All furniture I sell out. Everything you don't use it you can sell out. Sell everything for the life.

I come by plane. With USCC. That's a group with the Catholic. At New Year they help refugees out, and they lent them money for the airplane ticket. At this time, my son eight years old, and my daughter six years. The kids under 12 years are half price. They pay three tickets; that's all. Because at that time airplane ticket cheap. Sit in the back of the airplane; that time very cheap; $320 one ticket, and three tickets over a thousand dollars. I owe only half; that's all. And in 1993 I got the assembly job; I pay more and more. Only one year, paid off.

In USA life, husband and wife have to go to work. I study and work. What kind of study, I study about the child care program. I got 24 units now. I studied at Laney College about the ESL. I studied in your class, and then I went to OCC about the assembly job. The first job was the assembly job, full time. They make the Walkman. I take bus 40 or 40L go to downtown Oakland, go to 14th corner, take 72, and we change the bus two times, then go home. And I still go to Laney to study every night and Saturday morning about the ESL and grammar. I got citizenship in 1982, and my son and my husband, too. And we vote all the time. I paid tax since 1984, make the W-2 form and put together.

I bought this house in 1989, December. I paid 20 percent deposit. You know why? I go to work child care and babysit, cash. Because my husband and we still work something, sewing. And my husband and we have some time, do it. Take to my house, and when we have time, do it. Got cash.[8]

When we come here, he take two classes, adult school, and I take two class. Morning, I take your class, evening because I not enough one year got green card, I study at the EOCC adult school at night time. And my husband take two class. Morning, he take adult school at Berkeley. And afternoon he take refugee class because he the household; he need to take the refugee program at Laney. And he graduation there two years. But he could not find job. And finally you know on weekend he go to study, this job about the janitor. We study every, anything! He studied about the janitor, and I studied too at San Francisco every Saturday. And we got 105 hours training, and we got the certificate from the City of San Francisco. He studied first because I need to take care of the child, and when he graduated I go to study. He got that job at the airport in 1984 almost June or July. He worked over 10 years there. He work 11. Nine-thirty leaving home. He eat dinner, then he go to work. I make a box for him for eating. At daytime he's home; at night time I'm home, take care two kids.

Then my husband night time could not sleeping, at daytime could not sleeping, and he work there almost two or three years. At night shift. And he very skinny, skinny. And he talk to the supervisor and the reason, and the doctor sign it, and he could not sleeping and after they saw like that and let him work swing shift. And he work three to eleven. One-thirty he have to leaving home. He got more weight, a few more pounds. When we move here, he drive to work. We bought a car, but we bought the second-hand car. In Vietnam he had a driver license, drive the highway. But in Vietnam they have not easy this one automatic.

This year I work only one week, and then I stay home. I saw my husband the legs so weak, not strong man; I told my boss, "I cannot go to work anymore," and I told him, "This Friday is my last day." I stop to work, stay home, take care my husband. This year I have only one week pay, no income now. Social security, not yet because I'm not enough 65. They want to give me, but they cut some; if I got now, all my life, only like that. I'm almost 65; I wait until I'm 65. I want to get full.

My husband, this year after his birthday, he tell the airport, he retire, but he sick. The last birthday, February sixth, they make a birthday party for him; he so happy that day. And February seventh, he passed away at midnight, the day after his birthday. He got the last birthday, so happy. My son bought the big cake for him. He so happy. You know we got the ambulance January second, go to hospital. Then he was there at Chinese New Year, the first day of New Year; then he stay there a few days, and they send my husband home, and 10 days he passed away. The social worker came, and then the nurse came only three times. And I saw him passed away, and when he passed away, whole family, and my children and me around him.

And my son talk to me and say, "Mom, I want to give Daddy his funeral at Fremont. And bury him there. And when you come to visit him and give him some flowers, it is close, easy." Because he is the older son, he decide, and I say, "Okay, you are older; you decide." And he decide everything for Daddy. My son graduated from Oakland Tech High School and studied at

San Jose State until he graduation, and he got a job with Cisco, computer company. He got that job a few years, and he got good pay; he buy a house in 1999. Before last summer he got the house, three bedrooms.

My daughter went to Columbia, at New York. She applied lots of universities. My son and daughter, they decide by themselves. I told her, "Why and Berkeley accept you, and you go too far?" She said, "Berkeley is not too good. They protest too much and I don't want. I need to study something." She said, "That school is good." I said, "Wow! That school so expensive!" She said, "You don't need to worry, Mom." She got a lot of scholarships. She apply about $25,000. She want to work 15 hours for work study, I say, "No! Ten! Because it's important for your life. You try to get a good grade, and easy to find a job. If you want to work, okay, but only 10 hours, no more than 10 hours. Take the time for homework." Then I paid dorm fee. And she got work study, 10 dollar an hour. They pay every week, 10 hours, 100. She can help herself a lot.

I don't need help. I don't want to talk money to my child. Because that's my duty to take care of them; they get good education, and now, they make money. I say, "Don't spend too much, you need to save money for your future, and you buy house." You know, I tell them, "When I get old, if you give me, I say thank you. If you don't give me, okay; I have enough for my life." We don't know what day we're gone. They told me go to the lawyer and make the will. I said, "I don't need a will." Because anything from the bank, I put my child's name on there. Because my husband's retirement now I rolled over to my IRA. If I pass away, they got 50 and 50. I don't want they argue. They still good brother, sister.

I do everything because of my children. You know what they said? They said, "You don't need to worry, we will take care of you like that." I feel better. And she said, "If you feel boring, come to live in my house, stay a few months, and if you want to go somewhere, call the tour company and take a tour. Take a trip!" My children said, "Don't do like Daddy, work, work, work, and later got nothing, nothing enjoy the life. After sell out the house, where you want to go, go." I say, "Okay, thank you."

They say Las Vegas is so beautiful. They go there and see the show. Lot of show, so beautiful. My son say, "Mom, in May I have vacation; I will go with you. Because last time you didn't go, you stayed home with Daddy." I say, "Okay, I will." They let me see the picture, and so beautiful. They said, "You want to eat Chinese food, they have Chinese food. They have anything there." My daughter say, "Maybe I will take a trip to Taiwan with you." I say, "Okay." Maybe if I can contact with a tour, I would go to Vietnam. I don't want to go to the North, because it's too dirty. Maybe I go to the middle, to Hue. I didn't go there because we immigrate from North to South. I lived in Vietnam but we seldom go to the tour because the life in the war city, we need to run here, run there; every time we lost something. North Vietnam, cannot sell the house; we need to run. South Vietnam, have to run, throw away, and we run. And come here, and my child says, "Mom, no need to run. You sell your house." They joking, they say, "This time you don't need to lose your house; you sell it."

I tell my daughter, "If you really in love and marry, you need to decide; you need to prepare your heart." You know, this time, and that time when I was young, is different. Everything change, change, change. Parents, we cannot tell them, "Do this or that." They have their ideas. Each century is different. My parents very different; let me choice by myself. You know, I'm lucky, because in love I choice a good one. Some days I only pray to the Lady Buddha; that's all. I don't want to stay home alone. Alone, and sometime thinking, make the head heavy. I had bad luck because I was born in lots of war. Run around, around. I was born in the year of the ox. The ox works hard. But I'm lucky because I'm in the rat time, noon to one. That time is break time. It's hard, but it's not too hard. I want to have a good life; I work hard. I don't want to see sad again.

I want the kids to have a good education. The good idea we need to accept and put in the brain, we need to prepare and listen to do it. If something we think a bad idea, we need to throw away. Because all my life, I'm thinking of education. I talk to my children, said, "You see your Daddy; he have big business, have property, finally got nothing. Something out of your body they can take easy. You need to study. Good education, that's your property; nobody can take from you. If they take away from you, your life is gone." Someone look you low, I don't need that person. But if you look me low, okay, I try to work hard, and let you look at me. I don't mind you look down me; I want you to look up at me. I push myself. I say, "Yes, if you don't kick me, I don't mad. If you kick me, I am mad, but I don't kick you back."

JANUARY 11, 2002, PHONE CALL FROM VANNY IN SAN JOSE

Vanny, loquacious as always, is enjoying herself. Her children want her to "go anywhere" now, and then she will go back to school to improve her English. Her mother is happy in a "nursery" in San Jose that houses more than 200 people, many of them Chinese Vietnamese, so she plays mah jong frequently and has a daily visit from one of her children. If it is a nice day, they take her out for dinner. She speaks only Vietnamese and Cantonese, no English, and the family has made a bilingual word list for her so that, for example, when she has a headache, she can point to the word on the list. She only went to Chinese school for a few years, and in that culture, a girl's body was not discussed, so she doesn't know any body parts in Chinese, only in Vietnamese. Her son is not worried about the current "dot.com" layoffs; his boss told him he is so valuable that he will be the last one laid off. Vanny went to Taiwan in October; to Yosemite, Grand Canyon, and Las

Vegas in November; and this month plans a trip with a tour group to Beijing. She loved Las Vegas, especially the shows. Next she will go to New Jersey and tour the East Coast with her daughter.

MARCH 6, 2006

I drove to San Jose to visit Vanny at her son's house in a typical tract with bucolic street names, broad concrete driveways, and two-car garage doors dominating the front of each house. I take off my shoes as I enter, although she tells me I don't have to. A large aquarium separates the front entry from the living room. A leather sofa faces an enormous flat-panel television, and another even larger aquarium bubbles quietly. Next to the television is a stack of auxiliary equipment. On the mantel are some artificial flowers and porcelain figurines: a Kwan Yin, and a Buddha holding a cheerful child. Everything in the house is immaculate. In the small garden area, at one side a raised bed made of artificial stones contains an assortment of succulents and showy plants. At the other side is a mass of potted orchids and cactus plants.

We sit in the living room and look at her photo albums. Her daughter's house in New York has several bedrooms and a swimming pool. There is one photo of their civil wedding at the San Jose city hall. The wedding couple, Vanny, and the best man are the only ones there. The bride wears rather ordinary clothes and carries a bouquet. There are hundreds of photos of the wedding, which took place two days later at the house. The intervening day was taken up with preparations. She had decorated the stair rail with garlands, and above the mantel are red paper cutouts of the Chinese symbol for "double happiness." The garage was cleared out to accommodate a table for refreshments. The bride wore a beautiful white gown, heavily embroidered and with a full skirt. A hairdresser came to the house to do her hair and that of her brother's girlfriend, formally dressed in blue. Vanny wears a Chinese-style brocade dress, black with dark red design. The ceremony begins with the groom knocking at the bride's bedroom door for her to come out, and they come down the stairs together for a tea ceremony. The bride and groom offer tea to everyone in order of status in the family. A pretty female relative, dressed in white, holds the tray with tea cups. First they serve tea to Vanny, who as the mother of the bride has the first rank. She explains that if her husband were still alive, they would sit on the sofa together. She then "says something," giving her daughter to him and wishing them to have a good life. They serve her the tea, and she gives them a gift, money in a "red bag." I think she means envelope. She gave them a check for 10,000 dollars. I ask whether they opened it then, and she says no, but they already knew what it was, and the bride said she didn't want to show off by opening it then. The next in rank is her brother, as eldest son of his father, who is served tea and gives them his gift. All the gifts are money in a red bag. The next person is Vanny's sister-in-law, who as the bride's father's family has the highest status in this pecking order. All of the relatives then follow in indis-

putable order of age and status. There are some photos of the groom's family: his father is a retired dentist originally from Peru; his mother, of Italian extraction, was a nurse. The groom, a medical doctor, is their only child.

Then everyone goes to the Japanese park in San Jose for still more photos, posed in romantic settings. Then there is a time for resting, and during this time, Vanny prepares champagne and balloons and other decorations to take to the restaurant where guests are entertained at a banquet. They hired a photographer to take a lot of pictures, and she designed a thank-you card that has a photograph of each guest to be sent later as a souvenir. The only photo of this event shows a large red cloth, which each guest is invited to sign as a memento.

The next album is of photos of the granddaughter, taken a couple of years later, beginning at the hospital when she is just a few hours old, and continuing up to the present, when she is nearly two. She is a beautiful healthy little girl who can already speak English, Spanish, and Cantonese, as well as international sign language, which her mother has taught her as a further stimulus to brain development.

Vanny frequently uses the phrase "Chinese custom." Before her husband died, he told his daughter that she could forget all about Chinese custom, which would dictate that she could not marry for three years after his death. Now that they are in America, that shouldn't matter. She doesn't speak of her mother's death, and I am reluctant to mention it. She says she doesn't want her children to be jealous of each other. She helps each one as she can, but they can't expect that she can do exactly the same for one as the other. Now she helps her daughter with the grandchild, but she can't promise to do the same for her son and his wife when they have children.

FEBRUARY 26, 2009

Vanny is at her son's house in San Jose for two months, having her eyes tested and her teeth checked, and cooking for her son and his wife, both of whom work long hours. She proudly shows the latest photos of her other home in New Jersey. Her daughter works in New York City and now has three beautiful little girls. The parents-in-law live near them, and the grandmothers take turns with child care. The children speak Chinese, Spanish, and English. They call her often on the telephone and say they miss her very much. Vanny is especially pleased that now they are so prosperous that she regularly donates castoffs to the Salvation Army; she refuses to take a receipt for the donation because they were good to her many years ago, and she is happy to pay her taxes. She will not, however, allow her photo to be published, because she does not want to "show off."

5

THE SECOND WAVE, THE "BOAT PEOPLE"

You Can Go Anywhere, You Can Speak Any Word

Minh's family has been on the move for three generations, learning new languages and starting new businesses. He was born in 1958 in Cholon, the Chinese city that is part of Saigon, now Ho Chi Minh City. His grandparents had left Southeast China in 1940. His maternal grandfather was a farmer; the paternal grandfather, a rice merchant. The protracted war with Japan had left them starving and dependent on the help of friends. In Vietnam they prospered until the Communists came, and their life was shattered again. Minh was one of thousands of Vietnamese, many of them ethnic Chinese, who fled in boats in the late 1970s. In America, Minh found freedom exceeding his expectations. In 1981, he told his story:

Because in main China, always war, and they afraid the Japanese. And another reason, no food in China, so they hear some people say in Vietnam, easy to keep living, so they move to Vietnam. My mother just a baby. By boat, big boat, 15 days on the ocean. They say this ship moved slowly. And they learned a little bit of Cantonese, not very well. You know, Chinese, they can pronounce many words, in Chiu Chow, Cantonese, or Mandarin, and the writing is all the same, but the pronunciation is different. My grandfather knows how to write and how to read Chiu Chow; my grandmother, no, she can't. In China, most of the people seldom go to school, except rich people. Farmers never go to school.

The first time in Cholon, they worked as employees, and they saving money, and many years later, they make their own business. Making the dress, making the clothes. I think medium degree, they are rich. I lived in my father's family. My father's father — that's my grandfather — they were from China, too, but they were not living in Chiu Chow; they lived in Santow City. In China, my grandparents deal with a rice store, grocery store, then 10 years in the war, just eating in the house. My grandparents had a warehouse, stocked a lot of rice; 10 years just no business, just eat, eat, eat. At last, one day,

123

finished, anything gone! So my grandfather alone went to Cholon, and he knew the friend, and he knew another friend, and his friend told him in Vietnam easy to make money, so you have to go back to China and bring your wife and your children, come to Vietnam. So my grandfather, he lent the money from his friend and come back to China and pay the fee for my grandmother and my dad, and they went to Vietnam. Before that, my grandfather is a rich man. Stock big, a lot of rice. But 10 years in the war, no business, just live in the house, eat, eat, eat.

When he went to Vietnam, he make a business with his friends, because my grandfather, he know how to make the t-shirt, so my grandfather's friends gave some money, and my grandfather went to Santow and ordered some machines to Vietnam because in that time, in Vietnam is no machine. Anything is by hand. So my grandfather, he know the weaving machine. Then my grandfather make a business. First time, the factory is so small, just three or four machines; then my grandfather make a good business, more than 20 machines.

In China, even you don't know [*to read and write*] the Chinese, you just know how to speak, and you study from the people — we call in America apprenticeship — a short time, you know how to work, so I remember, after I was born, my grandfather, he hear some people say make the candy is good, easy to make money, so my grandfather, he think it over: yes, make candy is easy. So he close the factory, and he put the money to make candy. But because he didn't know how to make candy, and my grandfather hire the people make candy, but sometimes my grandfather was arguing with the people make candy, so the employees make the candy all no good. So oh, my mother said, just three months, the store closed, so everything gone again.

So then no money. So he borrow his friend some money and make the t-shirts again. So I think after 1963, my grandfather's business good again, so he applied the license to import the cotton and nylon and sewing machine, something like that; he import a lot of machine. At that time, oh, he make a very very good business. In my family, they hire more than 30 people work in the factory. Then he import a lot of product and make a lot of money.

My father just helped. You know, my grandfather didn't know the Vietnamese. You know, in Vietnam, every business, you have to know the Vietnamese. Every document, you have to sign by Vietnamese. So my father, he know the Vietnamese, so he can help my grandfather to decide something.

I am the first son. There are eight; four sons and four daughters. I lived with my grandparents and my parents. You know, at Chinese, children always live with parents. Even the first generation, and second and third, they like to live together. Usually, in Chinese, the girls get married with the husband; they have to live with the husband's side. Our religion, I think Buddhist. In Vietnam, they had a picture of the ancestor, but in America, I didn't bring.

In California, I hear some people say the government is prohibit to fire the incense because easy to cause a fire, you know, so I didn't pray by incense. In Vietnam, the house by brick, very hard, so didn't catch fire. In California, most house by wood; so we don't pray my ancestor in California, in America. In Chinese, most the pray by woman, the man seldom, so I didn't pay attention to pray.

Before 1975, I am a student, so went to high school. This school is the Catholic conference, Taiwan Catholic conference; they build a school in Vietnam, very, very big school. All the students Chinese. More than 1,500 students, this school. In class we always speak Mandarin and Vietnamese. Outside the class we can talk any way; we can talk Chiu Chownese and Fukienese and Cantonese.

I remember 1968, the year we call by Vietnamese Tet Mao Tun. Oh, in Chinese new year, every family is very happy! At the first day of the year, you know, every family play the firecracker; very, very loud the firecracker, so a lot of people to watch the firecracker and watch the lion dance, so they were very happy. But later, I hear my friends say, "No! That's the war; that's the gun, not the firecracker." So every family was afraid — "Oh! Viet Cong coming to Saigon city!" So my family refuse me to go to anywhere, just stay at home; we can't go anywhere; And my parents, they bought a lot of food, keeping in the house, and we live in the house three days. The war was happened. A lot of gun, ooh! — pum, pum, pum, every night, so we were scared! Oh! So the police and the army, Vietnamese army, come to every house, to check the number of the people in the house, how many children, how many young men, and see who is a Viet Cong. You know at that time, every young man 18 years old have to join the army. And the police come to check how many young men in your home. So in 1968, my father had joined the army many years, so the government gave my father I think a license, so he didn't need to join the army again, so I'm lucky. My father is lucky. But the police still bring my father to the police station and check the paper, is the real or the phony. At last my father was in the police department three days; then my father came back. My father became hungry, very hungry, because in three days no food, no water.

In Tet Mao Thun [*January 1968*] because the war is prolonged I think seven months. And we live in the third floor, and at Tet Mao Thun we saw the helicopter; they put the shot to the country, poom — oh! We were scared. The helicopter was fired near by my house — ak-ak-ak, the sound is very clear. Oh! We were scared, and my mother talked, "Everybody go downstairs! Don't stay upstairs!" So we run downstairs. I stopped school for one year, because for war. And at that time, my father sent me to a private teacher, a private English teacher. I study English at that time. At that time, I was 10 years of old. So I just study English, about three months, and then I can attending class again.

At that time, my grandfather's warehouse was fired [*burned*]. A lot of products were fired; anything gone, so business closed. So then my grandfather had to change his business, and he ran the business as dying fabrics. Make paint, and order some machines to dye the fabric. It was more quiet in Saigon City, but another city, we had all this years, a war, the Viet Cong come in this city, and the Vietnamese army attacked them. We hear from radio every night. Most people listen to England, London, and channel Australia, because these two channel, they report the real news. In Saigon City, you can read by the newspaper; you don't need to listen by channel. Every day the newspaper report which province had the war, something like that.

In Saigon City, I saw a lot of American army; they like to come to the bar, many, many bar, and we go across these streets, we saw the army; they go with a girl, but I heard the people say the American army, they are very rich man; they sit on the three-wheel bicycle, man-powered bicycle, and they pay a lot of money, so the drivers very happy, yes. But at that time a lot of American product, too, in Saigon City and we can eat American foods. But I hear the people say the American army is very nice people, very friendly, talk with the people. They are very nice, but I don't know why they like to go to the bar, but I think because they have the money. I think in 1972, 1973, I know from the Chinese newspaper report that Kissinger go to China, mainland China, and ask Mao Zedong, and talk with China, then President Nixon had a visit in China. That's interesting. I heard about that; I'm very happy America and Chinese be friends.

I was supposed to graduate the high school in 1975, but the principal was gone before 1975; they heard maybe Saigon will turn to the Communist, and they went back to China, Taiwan, and some teacher went to America, to Los Angeles. In 1975 the government was changed, so every school had to learn, not learn the knowledge, just learn about the Communist. I hate that study. I don't spend the time like that. I stay at home, help my father to run the business. A lot of problem is to apply the license again. Everything have to apply again, so I had to fill up a lot of forms. Before 1975, they have a lot of money; they can hire the accountant, the computer to do anything. But after 1975, you can't hire the accountant; everything you have to do by yourself. So I help my father to apply the license again and to contact the government to sign the agreement to dye the fabrics for the government. So my family was lucky. Yes.

At 1977, the Vietnam, the Communist government, they announced every young man had to join the army again. Before, after 1975, every people was happy, oh! New government coming; we don't need to join the army again; we don't have the war again. So every people was happy. The first time, every people was happy; then after that, the Communists, they changed the dollar bill, and no business, no salary, so every people, the living, was very hard to keep living. Very bad, bad, worse than before 1975, so everybody hate government. So in 1977, I think 1976 or 1977, the Communist government announced to the people. They say every young man 18 years old have to join the army again, and if you over 16 years old, you have to join the — we call the free labor — it means you go to the country and you work just three months, for free; you have to prepare your food yourself; the government don't pay anything to you. You have to go outside the city, and dig the stream, something like that. So the people get angry to the government. We don't pay anything, so we have to prepare the food and money to live in the outside the country. You know, outside the country a lot of mosquito, sting the people, so they get the disease in the country. So some people was dead in outside the country, so every people was afraid. So that's why I escape from Vietnam; that's my father's idea because he scared that I young man maybe they call to join the army. Join the army, no money, just a little bit money for month, no foods, just eat the potato and something like that, no rice. So every soldier's family, if you join the army, they will give you one week go home to visit your family. Everybody come back, they become skinny, oh! So every person was scared their children would join the army again.

My grandparents, my mother's parents, and my first uncle, they left with me, same boat, but they paid by their own. My father paid for me and my two brothers and young sister, total, 32 pieces of gold. One piece is more than one ounce. Half is for the government, half is for the boat. My second uncle, he escaped from Vietnam earlier than us. That day I left, the tears running. I can't speak, I can't talk to my father and mother that day. Before that, we talk, talk, talk, talk, talk, talk. At that day, we very sad. We want to talk something, but the words in the throat, yes. We can't say. Just the tears.

We got on the bus, and the boat owner had told me the bus stop, and the boat owner had a car to bring me to the boat. I took some clothes, a little bit food. No money. Any money, had paid to the boat. Seven o'clock at night. The Vietnamese, the Communist police called every one, your name, okay. My name is put on a list, and the police called your name, and if he called your name, you can come to the boat. We was afraid. Because we hear someone say, even the government let you go, when the boat is running in the ocean, somewhere, from Saigon City, we go about one day — maybe the government they will check your boat, and they will arrest you again, so we were afraid.

After three days, the boat cross to Malaysia. Then we going to come in to Malaysian island, but the Malaysian navy, they don't agree, and they pull my boat out to the public ocean again, so we had to run to the public ocean again, and then about three days, we come to Indonesia. And we land on the Indonesia island. The first time, we land on the Indonesia island, not refugee camp. The government in Indonesia, this small town, they settle the place for a few thousand refugees just settle, live here, but not real refugee camp, no immigration, no come to interview anybody. This place just live here, just keep going to provide the food, water, but not the real refugee camp. After three months, we had to move to another refugee camp called Binang refugee camp.[1] Then we met immigration of Australia, America, Canada, and Austria, a lot of other country. And after we live one month in Binang refugee camp, we have to remove to Galang refugee camp — that's the new island. The first we came to the Galang refugee camp, no house, but a lot of people build the house for the refugees. Just the walls, we call the barracks. Every barrack for 100 people, so my boat is the first boat come to Galang refugee camp. Oh! At that time, everybody was afraid, because everything was new in this island, the barracks just built, no rest room, anything no. Just the walls. We were afraid. After three days, then we call the IRC [*International Rescue Committee*]. So they bring the foods to the refugee. Oh! We are happy, yes, because we watch the foods. Then the Galang refugee camp, they built. Right now, the Galang has more than 300 barracks, very big. And right now, the refugee camp has water, has electricity, very nice. And has TV! But when we were there, didn't have anything. I was there in Galang Refugee Camp about five months.

I tried to read the English newspaper. They did have classes, but you had to pay money. So I don't need to attend the class because I think maybe several months I will come to America, so I can go to school in America. I decided to come to America because more freedom. Since I was in Vietnam, I study, I study; I hear the teacher say in American, everything was free, was freedom. You can speak free, and you can go anywhere by your — if you decide to go anywhere, you can go, so no one can refuse you, so I think is more freedom. I was in Vietnam, I expect everything in American was free. But in right now, I was in America, was exceed from my expect, you know. I was in Vietnam, I think America is like that, but right now, is bigger! Yes, more free. I think right now, I see the homosexual can apply and the state government to allow they can go to work like that, so — oh! I can't believe that. I didn't believe in United States we go to school for free. I didn't know that, so I just believe that America everything was freedom, not free. You can go anywhere; you can speak any word.

I came by airplane to San Francisco. My aunt was already here, before me, seven months. I lived with her a month, until I find the house, and then I moved with my two brothers and sister, and in this house, many people broke into the house and steal something, so they're afraid; they moved to another where. Right now six live together, with my grandparents. They came in the same boat, but they came to Minneapolis, Minnesota. They lived with my uncle. So because the weather in Minneapolis is very cold, so my grandparents, they sat at home a year, very sad, because they can't go anywhere. They won't go anywhere. Because my uncle was still young, he can go anywhere, but my grandparents, they are old, so when go out, oh! Have many, many jackets and wear many hats. Very inconvenient to go out.

I came, my aunt sponsored us, but my aunt sponsor from the United States Catholic Conference. So after my aunt sponsor us, USCC, they have paid a little money for refugee, for living for month. So everybody can receive $250 for month. So four people, we receive $1,000, so we have money to pay the rent. After that, we apply welfare. And we bought the clothes, because the weather sometimes cold, sometimes hot, so we had to buy the jacket, clothes and shoes, and bought the pans, something for cooking. A thousand dollars spend on the rent and for anything.

Minh studied in the ESL class for four months before enrolling in a CETA (Comprehensive Employment Training Act) program; after completing the program, he was hired at a large bakery.

The first time, they told me it's not a permanent job, just on call that time. At most American factory, the first time, you got a low seniority so you have to on call. So I say, "That's okay; right now I need a job, so I don't care, any job." So I work a couple of months, still on call, sometimes two nights a week, sometimes three, sometimes one. The first time I always work in the graveyard shift. Oh! Too bad! Sometimes I slept midnight about two o'clock and my telephone is ringing — "Are you available to work right now?" Okay, okay, I have to wake up! Very bad. So right now, my supervisor, he schedule me for day shift, so I'm very happy. I still good pay. I am on probation now, so I have to work a short time; then I will got the regular rate. First time I work, oh! Very hard. You have to work fast! I can't believe the people work with the machine as fast as the machine. Oh, sometimes I was slow; the bread would drop down, no use, dump in the garbage, so I was scared the supervisor, maybe, maybe they will tell me, this employee is no good, too slow; they will fire me. I was scared, so I have to try to work fast. Right now, I think fast is okay. Easier now. Right now, some new employee come in, so I have to teach another. Sometimes I have to work overtime. The overtime, I have to work 18 hours a day. Oh! From 9 o'clock to midnight, or three. Oh! After I work, oh, I get tired, very tired.

Maybe in the future I saving a little money, I will running a business. I would like to be in business; I would like to be a businessman. You know, if you work your money is every month like that. If you run a business, if you have a good business, maybe your money is more than the salary. I just send a parcel to Vietnam. My family receive the parcel, but the tax is very high, so right now my parents wrote a letter to me, "Don't send a parcel to us; we are going to plan to escape, so you don't have to spend money on that. So you keep the money; when we escape from Vietnam, when we are in refugee camp, maybe that time, we need the money, so you have to send us." I received a letter recently, and my father and mother say they will escape from Vietnam maybe after 1981.

I would like to learn English, because I think the English is very important in my life. But in this several months, I won't improve my English, because I get tired. After work, oh! I get tired. After work, I eat lunch or dinner; I have to sleep again. To keep my strength. But in the factory, after the break time, the lunch hour, so I read the American newspaper, and when I find out which word I don't understand, so I make my memory to spell this word, and repeat, repeat many times after I go home. So I take the dinner, and I look up the dictionary and look up this word. So, I like this country. I plan in the future I can learn English good, improve my English, so I plan to attend the college to learn some knowledge.

2008 — Minh didn't attend college, but he set up a successful small business, recycling plastic. He bought a house, married, and had two children.

In Our Life, We Learn
Something from the Trouble

Linh and her husband entered class at the beginning of the term in September, 1979. They both tested very high in the placement test. He only stayed for three hours; his English is good, and he qualified for the Skills Center training program at Laney College. Their classes, restricted to Indochinese refugees, are funded by federal funds under the IRAP, Indochinese Refugee Assistance Program; the ESL students have specific pre-employment vocabulary instruction, must pass a test to go from one level to the next, and then are put into the training program for machine operators and clerical workers. Linh, whose name means "gentle spirit," is a pretty woman, terribly thin. She has a wide face, with a slight overbite, and a sweet smile. She speaks Mandarin and another dialect of Chinese, but no Cantonese, so she doesn't socialize much with the other students. She can read and write English very well but is shy about speaking. She chose the seat in front in the farthest row from the door, over by the window. This seat generally is taken by someone eager enough to want to sit in front, near the teacher, but still timid enough to sit as far as possible to the side. She often stopped by my desk on the way out to converse on some pretext, to practice her English. She told me she had known English in earlier years but she had trouble remembering it; her memory wasn't very good anymore, which bothered her. Then on her last day before she also transferred to the Skills Center, she told more about her life, to explain her lapses of memory. I was amazed that she retained any shred of sanity when I heard what she had been through.

She was born in 1937, in Fukien, a coastal province in southeast China. When her paternal grandfather died, her father was working in Vietnam. According to their mourning custom, it would not be permissible then for him to marry for three years. There is an escape clause, however, if you are already engaged and marry within a hundred days, so her father, when he learned of his father's death, raced back to China to marry his fiancée, a medical student at the university in Shanghai. He stayed there while she finished her studies, and Linh, their first child, was born. By that time the Japanese army came into Shanghai, and they went back to Vietnam, now virtually as refugees. From infancy, Linh and her younger brothers were taught English by her mother, who thought this would always give them an advantage. Later on, Linh worked for 20 years as an accountant in a Chinese bank in Saigon and had little chance to practice her English. Her husband, on the other hand, practiced English because he was a school teacher and principal and also worked with Americans in Saigon.

Linh soon after her arrival in America, spring, 1981.

Almost as an afterthought, she told me another thing to explain her trouble in concentrating, that when she was in class she remembered the English, but when she got home, she couldn't.

She said very simply, "Unfortunately, my mother died in a boat." Then she told how she and her husband, who are childless, had escaped from Vietnam a year ago, and a month later, her mother, her brother, her sister-in-law, and nieces and nephews escaped in a small boat and were all lost at sea. Her family had been almost entirely wiped out at that point. I was stunned. What do you say to someone who tells you such a story?

JANUARY–FEBRUARY 1980

Telephone calls from Linh: Linh has been having great problems with her feet. They pain her terribly and swell so that she's unable to walk. She can't sleep because of the pain. A Chinese doctor gave her some salve to rub on, but it hasn't helped. Part of the problem may be that it's been very cold and she probably doesn't have heavy socks or heavy shoes. But there is something more going wrong; she is not silly.

Another day, Linh was alone and despondent. Her husband had gone to San Francisco to pick up a letter from Vietnam. His brother doesn't forward mail to them; they have to go over and get it. The letter was from Linh's only surviving *brother. Since he's still writing to them in care of the brother-in-law in San Francisco, she knows he hasn't received any of her letters giving him their address. The last letter that they had received from him said his child was very ill with a high fever, and they had tried to get him into a hospital, but there were no medicines. She said there is medicine, but it's only available for the people who pay extra or who have special privileges. She wanted to send medicine to the child but didn't know what kind to send or whether it would get through to him.*

In January she was promoted one level in her English but is not yet in the employment training program. Her husband is now in the top English class in the afternoon and studies accounting in the morning in the regular Laney College program. They're still on welfare, and he has been told that he must enter the job training program, an all-day program, which means that he will have to give up his accounting class. The training program, which they insist he go into, because he is now ready for it, is to be a machine operator in a factory; typical jobs are bagging potato chips or putting mayonnaise into jars. He would rather continue to take accounting in college and try to become an accountant. I talked to him then on the telephone. He was feeling pressured because by the end of the week, he had to make up his mind what to do. He is apologetic for being on welfare, and said, "If I take accounting, it does mean staying on welfare longer, but I think after a while then I can get a better job." He would pay more taxes and be a more productive citizen in the long run.

On the evening of February 4, 1980, I called them and found their spirits were much improved. He had talked to someone at Laney College who promised him a work-study grant so that he could continue to take his accounting classes and would not be forced into the Skills Center training program.

Linh's health had improved. A friend gave her some Chinese medicine, which she massaged on her feet, and by the next day, they felt better. The news from her brother in Vietnam is not good. He works in a factory that makes raincoats. It's very hard work, and he makes just enough money to support himself, just to pay for one person, but not for his family, a wife and two small children. The child who had the fever is now better, but they're constantly worried about the possibility of getting sick. They don't have enough food or medicine. The brother begs her to help him to come to the United States, and she said, "If he can get to a refugee camp, then I can ask my sponsor, and my sponsor will help him to come to join me." The problem is getting together the thousands of dollars of gold to get a family of four to the refugee camp. She thinks that in a few years she will be an American citizen, and if they can manage to stay alive that long, then she can get them here.

This is the interview recorded in September 1982:

I came to America to be free from a horrible country. I left Vietnam in 1978, and I arrived here in 1979. I came by boat and left from Bien Hoa province. The boat was 15 meters long, and there were 162 people on it. We had to pay gold to the owner of the boat, but the owner had to pay the government. It cost us 11 ounces, little bars of gold, for each person. Two pieces and a half. The first time we were on the boat for four days and four nights, and we still couldn't leave the Vietnam sea. We rode all the days around the Vietnam area, and the boat broke down, and everything in the boat, all the machines and everything electric on the boat is broke down, too, so our boat is very danger in the sea, and we had to come back to an island that belongs to Vietnam, Con Son Island, Con Lon in Chinese, to ask for help. And when our boat was near the island and troops of the Viet Cong, they asked our boat to stop, and they just fired guns at the boat, but our boat was out of control on the sea, and the Viet Cong had a navy ship that just hit our boat — a big noise — and we are so scared, and a lot of soldiers came up to our boat, and they are so mean, and ask all the men to jump down to the sea, and the men had to obey them, and after that they asked the women and children to jump down to the sea, too.

And at that time all the people are very weak because they had four days and four nights on the sea and nothing to eat and drink, and we are so weak, and I am the weakest one in the boat. My knees hurt, and I always fall down; I am too weak; I cannot move, so I ask the soldier to let my husband and the owner of the boat help me move down to the sea, and fortunately they let them help me. No food to eat. We just sit like that [*huddled with knees up*] because the boat is so crowded, impossible to move. We just sit like that, and when we want to move, too weak and fall down all the time. We had to jump out of the boat and walk to the shore. The water was cold, too. And meanwhile two Viet Cong put a lot of rocks behind our boat; they just are afraid our boat will move away, but our boat is out of control; we cannot move.

And after we land to the island, the owner of the boat showed the document to them, to show them that we bought permits from the government, because they have received our gold, and after that they have to call back to Saigon and to the government, and Saigon said that is true. Then they just treat us better, and they cook rice for us. At that time they cooked congee [*rice porridge*] for us. And at that time it tastes very good to us, like a big banquet. The island used to be a prison, and we just lived in the prison. We stayed 15 days on the island. The owner of the boat had to give them more gold, and some watches and some other things, and that's why they treated us nicely. We can go out of the room and they didn't lock the door, but we cannot leave the island.

Next morning our boat was gone, piece by piece, because there was a grade 9 and 10 storm, so our boat broke apart. The Communists sent another boat out. The boat didn't take too much people, and then they could fit us in. They came to Con Son to pick us up. So after the boat arrived in Con Son, and 162 more people got on, they already had more than 100, so it was very crowded, and very dirty. Too many people, and they throw up, and very dirty.

We were on the second boat four days and three nights. The first boat, the waves are very strong, and the deck and the sea is the same level, any time they can sink down, but the next boat is lucky, no waves, very still, but after four days and three nights the boat have a little trouble, and we kept on going, and we saw a big fire, and we don't know what that is, and we just keep going to reach that fire. And it is a big ship to take the oil from the sea. So the owner of the boat just go up to ask them for help; our boat has trouble, but they didn't help us; they just called the navy of Malaysia. Because then our boat is inside the area of Malaysia. So they send a navy ship of Malaysia, came and asked a lot of questions. And at first they didn't want to help us; first they wanted to tow our boat out of their sea territory, but they keep on, and we asked them to help us and told them our problem how we had to leave Vietnam. Then after all they let all the people in the boat transfer to their ship.

So we are so scared. If we have to go back to Vietnam, we have nothing, no house, nothing. Our money, our gold, is gone, you know. Nothing, no place to live. So then they took us to the horrible island. The first time we arrived at that horrible island, we don't have a house; then we live in the beach for 12 days; we sleep on the beach, and in the morning when we woke up, all our body is wet.

The living condition is much better at Kuala Lumpur, and the food is better. We stayed in Palau Bidong for seven months and a half. After that we left that island to Kuala Lumpur and waited for one and a half months, and then we took an airplane to this U.S.A.

Her husband interrupts: Our boat was the 83rd boat to arrive at Palau Bidong, and at that time there were about 10,000 refugees in the island. After we left, there were more than 50,000 refugees. The United Nations lent us the money for the airplane, $320 per person, and we have to pay it back. No interest. After two years they will send the bill to us, and then if we have the ability, we will pay, and if we don't we'll just tell them we will just pay part and then just pay installments. My father is a high officer of the Republic of China and a patriot of China, so we should go to Taiwan, but unfortunately my father has died before the Communists took over Vietnam. My brother and sister went to Taiwan after the Communists took over Vietnam. My nephew and my niece are students in Taiwan, and that's why the Taiwan government allow the parents of all the students to go to Taiwan.

My father lived in Singapore, but he worked for the Taiwan government. As you know, Taiwan and Singapore don't have diplomatic relations, so my father worked as a consul, to sign all the papers for the people to go from Singapore to Taiwan, but even when my father was alive, and the Communists didn't take over Vietnam, they didn't allow too much people to go to Singapore, unless we invest in Singapore, so I couldn't go there. When we came to the refugee camp, we are willing to go any place that they accept us, but because one of my sisters is in the U.S.A. for more than 10 years, she is an American citizen, so she sponsored us. My brother moved from Taiwan to U.S.A., sponsored by my sister, too, so that's why we were accepted by the U.S. government, and after we are accepted by the U.S. government, another government will not accept us.

When I was in Vietnam, after working hours I was interested in reading, so I read magazines and books and those books, included everything about every country in the world. I used to read many things about U.S.A. I read the "*Reader's Digest*," and "*The World Today*," both in Chinese. Sometimes I saw pictures of America. I am interested in reading, so I read every day. It's hard to compare, you know; some things in Vietnam are comfortable, and some things here are better.

Linh resumes: I wanted to go to Taiwan because I am Chinese, and I worked in the commercial bank for over 20 years, and our head office in Taiwan, so I hoped I could go to Taiwan to keep my job. When I was in Vietnam I thought I can get a job in U.S.A. It's not that hard to get a job. But after I arrived to the country this three years I realize that it's very hard for me to get a permanent job. Because I have been to interview, but the interviewer just don't consider my past experience and what I can do; they just consider my English and answering phone calls. They just pay attention to that and ignore my strong points and just saw my weakness. As I work in the cashier office at Laney College as an account clerk, it seems not different, the accounting field in Vietnam and here, and I worked in the accounting field for more than 20 years. I think there's no big difference. The machines I used before in Vietnam, except the computer. I have completed all the accounting courses except the income tax I will take this semester, and I also take the computer courses, because I know most job now requires computer. But you know when I was in Vietnam, I got the job in the bank when I was a teenager, I know nothing; I don't know how to type; I don't know about accounting; I knew nothing about accounting, but I still can get a job, and I work hard, and I am willing to learn, and I got promotions very fast, and my manager and my supervisor, they like me very much. They prefer and very happy for the performance in my job.

At first, we lived in my brother-in-law's house. We were in El Cerrito. We have the International Institute to take care of us, so the worker asked us to stay here in Oakland, because it is easier to take care of us. Because we are living here and we know nothing about this country, so for example we go to checkup, anything, we don't know where to go, and we don't have a car, so she just asked us to live in Oakland. They still help us if we have any problem. We just go over there to ask them, but if something is too hard for us to solve, then we go there. If not, we just solve by ourselves. We were surprised by this. We can't imagine that there are agencies like that to help refugees come from the other countries. In Vietnam they don't have agencies, but sometimes the people in Vietnam will help when people ask them for help. For friends or relatives, they just help the people; that's all. Volunteer, no agencies. But everything is for personal. They always volunteer to help people out of office hours. No pay, nothing.

Husband: When we first came here, we tried to look for a job. That's why we stayed in San Francisco with my sister. But when we cannot find, my sister took me to EDD [*Employment Development Department*], and then we filled out a form and then introduced me to the Embarcadero building, to a company there, and they also asked me to fill out a form, but just fill out the form and wait for the answer, and until now, we get no answer! So it seems very hard to look for a job in the United States. My sister is busy working, so she cannot take care of us, and we know nothing, how to go. That's why the International Institute told me if you need help it's better to come to Oakland. It's easy for them to help us, such as apply for Medi-Cal. That's why we came to live here.

[*As he talks, his voice becomes lower and more shaky, and his hands are trembling; this obviously has been very painful for him.*]

Linh: I like just the climate, and it's easy to go to school. The first winter is hard, but here is better than other places in the United States. Last week I just went to Los Angeles to visit my previous manager. He called me on the phone, and I was surprised. I have been apart from him for more than 10 years, and I didn't know he is here, you know, but he called me about three weeks ago, in the evening. I was so surprised! He said, "Can you recognize me?" I can recognize his voice, you know, even that it's more than 10 years. He said he heard somebody say that I am here. He's so happy, and he had to call San Francisco to ask a friend to give my phone number, and then he just called me right away and asked me to visit him. You know, I have lived in this country, but I never leave Oakland any time, you know. I don't know how to go to the other place. Then after one week I received a long letter. He said he feel just truly close, and he said, because he knows what happened to my family, "I will see you as my relative." Yes, so sweet. And he invited my husband and me to visit him. He told us how to get to the airport or take the car, how to arrive at his home. After that we had to decide to take the airplane to visit him and his wife. When we arrived in Los Angeles, he and his wife were very nice. He just took us like his relative. It just seemed like to come back to my family. They have been here since 1975.

I studied a little English in high school, and after I got a job I went to school to study English in the evening, but after a few years then I was too busy. We always worked overtime, and no time to go to school, so I just stopped learning English. I was assistant chief in the accounting department.

My neighbors are all Chinese and Vietnamese and some American. We just say hello to each other, and we can get along with them. When I go to school at night, I am so scared, but sometimes the class is not open in the daytime. And I go alone, but this summer I asked him [*her husband*] to go to class the same time with me. I have a friend, when she goes to work in the early morning, somebody want to —

Husband: Somebody wants to rape her, not just rob her, but want to rape her, and she refused, and then he hit her and broke her teeth. She had to go to the dentist, and when she went to the dentist, she [*Linh*] met her, so she realized what happened to her.

Linh: When I was 20 I went to evening school alone, I don't have scared, but here, even I am old now, but I am scared. In Vietnam, if people are older, they are not scared in the street, but here, older or young, they are scared. So I am so scared to go out alone, so we just all the day, except go to work and to shopping, we just stay at home. The food is no problem. We just eat some kind of food we like, but we just buy something depending on our income. We don't buy some food too expensive. Sometimes we cook Vietnamese food, Chinese food. We are easy to adjust ourselves. Just the English language, because I don't have more opportunity to contact with Americans. The first time I arrived here I cannot speak to anybody; I just stand aside and listen. The first year, at the beginning, I cannot sleep at night. Now is better; maybe I keep busy and no time for thinking. Sometimes I have nightmares.

I worked in the cashier office for seven months, but after that I was no longer eligible for the work-study program, so I stopped working. I think that's no problem with American customs. I don't like to make other people uncomfortable. I can adjust myself to get along with people.

Husband: In Vietnam we are Chinese, and we learned Vietnamese just like a foreign language, just like we learn English. We learn how to read and write, and then how to speak, because we had no contact with Vietnamese people, to practice. When I was a child, I seldom had contact with Vietnamese. After I was working, as a dean of the school, then there were a lot of Vietnamese teachers, so we have to contact with them. Before I became the dean of the school, I learned Vietnamese in the evening. So first I learned the word, and then how to speak.

Linh: At home we had some Vietnamese workers, and the neighbors were a few Vietnamese girls, too, and they preferred to come to my home to have fun with me, so I have more chance to practice Vietnamese before I learned how to write and how to spell. The Chinese who live in Vietnam, we speak the dialect at home, and we go to school we talk Mandarin.

Husband: Now we are no nationality. We don't like to be the people of the Republic of China, and also the Republic of Taiwan doesn't like us. They refused us to go to Taiwan, so we have no nation! So the only chance is to become an American citizen, right? They destroyed everything in Vietnam; they have to take time to build it again. Before the Communists took over Vietnam, you can say it's a good country, because they have built some new factories and they can provide the clothes themselves, and they have canned food; they have flour mills and sugar mills; they can provide everything for themselves, just a few imports from foreign countries, and the weather is nice, and the living is not that high. We don't have to worry if we are laid off or fired or something like that, no, so you see I keep my job. If the government is not changed I can keep my job until I retire. We don't have to live under pressure. But now they destroyed everything because the government is a different way. Maybe you can read in the newspaper how they did. And they always didn't do what they say. The way they say is very beautiful, but the way they do is horrible.

Linh: Women in Vietnam have equal life with men, but not 100 percent. In some offices, the men are first, then the women. But some offices are new-fashioned; they are equal. South Vietnam is different from North Vietnam. The North Vietnam Communists are more old-fashioned. In South Vietnam because we had lived in the new fashion for a few decades, so we cannot change our life just for a moment. We still lived in the new fashion, but sometimes they force us, we have to restrict ourselves. Vietnam is better than China, more equal. We can promote to the same job; we can get the same pay, for example. Some women were higher than me. They have a woman in the congress.

Husband: She [*Linh*] was almost the chief of the department.

Linh: In my family, it is equal. Just depends; some is new-fashioned and they are equal, because in Vietnam, before, they were under France, so they are influenced by Western. After that the Americans came, so they are different.

In Vietnam, most of charity organization come from the people, not from the government. The hospital is built by the people, by the community, not by the government, and the funds in the hospital or the school are donated by the people; they volunteer. For example, you have a business, and I work in that school or hospital, and I go to you — you just go by yourself— say, this year I will donate so much, and you write a check. Nobody to force you to donate, but just volunteer. In Vietnam we don't have Medi-Cal. We have hospital, but part is free, part have charge, and the people who are rich they just go to the same hospital, go to the rooms have charge, and who are poor, just go to the hospital the part is free. But if the rich people go to the hospital, they charge themselves, and you know why? Because they can pay, and they don't want the people to say, "Oh, he's a rich man; how come he goes to the free hospital?" This just keeps from the poor people, you know, so they don't have to do anything to make the other one criticize them.

The medical part is the same, but the room is a little bit different. Just the room have charge, have TV and telephone, but the free is not; no TV and no telephone. But that's not important, right? Just the medical is the important. And in the school, for example, you say, you are rich, you have to donate 150 or 200 students, free tuition. Then he will donate 30, depends on your ability. Then the school just collect how much they donate, the total amount, how much students. They print the form for the poor students; they go to take a form and fill out the committee to decide which students are eligible to take this scholarship. And they just sign for them, and they just go to school free, but some rich people, they have to pay tuition.

In America, just the first time, maybe because of the language problem, people get tired to talk with me. They are hard to understand, and they don't want to talk to me. Sometimes I met on the campus or outside of school, but just a few, but after that, when they understand me, there's no problem, and they like me. They were just impatient to listen. But some are very nice; they encourage me and make me comfortable.

Because we live in this country, we have to Americanize, right? And we have to keep our own culture, too, because each culture have their strong points. The Chinese respect our elders, and take care of the other person when they suffer, family or outside. We just put something for our parents' anniversary [*of death*]. We don't celebrate birthdays because the Chinese culture is when people are young, don't celebrate their party but the new-fashioned, even as a child they have a cake to celebrate, but the old-fashioned say don't do that when you are young. The children grow up here is out of control by the parents; they are free. In Vietnam, for example, they are married, they want to keep their marriage forever, but here they can divorce. In Vietnam they don't want to divorce. Just the old-fashioned people had more than one wife, but the new ones don't. What kind of people, I don't care, just they are nice and more education, just a nice person, good man or good woman. I don't care about what kind of color. Religion is just no problem. I think that all religion tell people to do something good.

In the future, I want to get a job, and then I will find a better place to live and bring my brother from Vietnam. If he comes here, then I have to ask him to look for a job, any kind of job he can do, and then he has to support himself. This is the Chinese tradition: you have to help the member of your family. Even if we have enough to eat and our living is good, we cannot see our relative in a bad situation. The first problem is to get a job so I can sponsor my brother.

MAY 10, 1985
Linh called with the news that her brother, his wife, and their two children have left Saigon under the Orderly Departure Program. They had to wait more

than a year, from April, 1984, to April, 1985, from the time when they were advised that they might leave, until they were actually processed. Then they flew to the Philippines, where they will be detained for six months, for orientation and training. They were given an English placement test, and the brother ranked in the highest group; the sister-in-law placed in the next highest. The brother is now assisting an instructor in the English classes. Linh is very pleased with this. She is elated of course to know that they are going to be safe at last. Until now, they haven't been able to communicate freely. They wrote to her, complaining about the delay and the conditions in the refugee camp. She then wrote to them, a very long letter, telling them of all the troubles she has gone through, leaving Vietnam in a small boat, three times stopped and thinking they might be killed, suffering lack of food and water, and horrible conditions. She said, "I told him all this, what I went through, how hard it was for us, and they should be thankful that they came on a plane, and when they come here, everything will be not so hard for them."

July 1985

Linh's brother thinks he may be arriving here as early as September. They are in the Philippines, studying English for several hours a day. He wrote her at first in Chinese, but she told him to write in English, so now he does, and she corrects his mistakes and sends them back. She is trying hard to prepare them, so that they will have an easier time than she did.

December 6, 1985

Yesterday I had lunch with Linh, after she called me and said, "I have some bad news to tell you." It was that she had quit her job at the law office, because she just couldn't stand the exploitation any longer. I assured her that this wasn't bad news, but on the contrary, I consider it rather good news. She invited me to her apartment for a delicious lunch—fish ball soup; stir-fried broccoli, mushrooms, baby corn, carrots; spring rolls; and fried rice noodles with shrimp, barbecued pork, and vegetables.

She is upset and apologetic about quitting her job. She was working far more than 40 hours a week, and never paid overtime. She had been losing sleep to the extent that it was really damaging her health, and her husband agreed that she had to quit. When she resigned, the lawyer at first refused to accept it, then asked her to work a few weeks longer, and was astonished when she really quit. He first said, "But you can't just quit like this," and then she reminded him that she had given notice, which he had evidently just not believed. She stayed on a while to train a replacement and then had a terrible time getting her final check from him. She calculated all the termination pay she was owed and submitted it. Then she didn't get it for nearly a month and had to phone several times. Then when it came, she was sent two checks, one of which was for something that was also *included in the other. So she sent it back, with a note explaining that it was an error (and a considerable one—more than $240), and that she should not have it included in her W-2 form.*

She gave an example of her work. Recently, an employee gave her a paper and told her she was to pay $25,000, but Linh read the document, and said that the amount owed was only $1,500. The other figure was in the letter, but it wasn't the final amount. She went back to the employee and explained it, with the result that the employee was disgruntled. The lawyer, who had been saved a thousand dollars, would never know about it and just blamed Linh for being slow. She said this same kind of thing happened numerous times; she admits she is slow, but it is because she is so painstaking, and she is sure that she has saved him great amounts of money. She handled a total of seven accounts, including his personal business. He and his wife use the same checking account, and she was keeping this reconciled, which was difficult, because they both wrote checks without keeping track of them themselves. He also has some partnerships as well as the corporation, with constant transfers of funds from one to the other, and she was able to keep it all straight. She feels that no one else will be as conscientious as she has been and that her successor will probably cost him a lot more money, which he will never be aware of.

Her co-workers gave her a good stereo system, with turntable, radio, tape deck, and speakers. She also has a microwave, which her husband bought for her. She looks animated and pretty, and she speaks of her mother now without breaking down. She said yesterday, "If my mother were here, she would do very well, because she knew English and would study and improve herself."

January 1986

Linh has taken a good accounting job with Alameda County; her supervisors and co-workers like her, and she is happy. She and her husband are hunting for a house to buy. I drove them around to look at some of the possibilities in different parts of the city. They want to be on a bus line and don't care about being near Chinatown.

March 1986

Linh and her husband bought a charming small post–World War II house in a good neighborhood. They paid almost half in cash. They still do not own a car.

March 2000

Linh's husband is helping me straighten out my checkbook, which has become hopelessly out of synch with the bank statement. When there is a discrepancy of a few dollars, my tendency is to assume the bank is right and I am wrong, and make an adjustment, but there came the point at which it was clear that I had to do

more, and I remembered that he had once said he would be glad to help me with
my bookkeeping if I needed it. He went back through more than two years of bank
statements and check registers, uncovering all the errors I had made, every one of
them foolish—subtracting instead of adding a deposit, mistaking a nine for a
four, dropping a zero here and there, writing a check I had carried loose in my
wallet and neglecting to list it in the checkbook. He has infinite patience and care
for details. I should learn from him; being more careful saves time in the long
run.

JUNE 2004

Linh calls to tell me that her niece, who was born here, graduated from high
school and has a scholarship to go to Yale. The father is distressed that she is
leaving home to go far away. Linh says, "I support her in her decision." She has
told her nephews, "Study hard, and be good boys. Your skills you cannot lose.
Everything else can be taken away from you, but your skills, no one can take
away." They have both graduated from college and have good jobs.

AUGUST 25, 2004

More than 20 years have passed when we record a second interview. They
are both retired, and every morning they go to a park near Chinatown to join
dozens of others doing traditional exercises. Linh enjoys tending their garden, and
she has planted several fruit trees. She has gained a few pounds. They have traveled
widely: since their first trip to Yellowstone Park in 1989, they have gone to China
more than once, to Vietnam, to Canada, to Australia and to Europe; and most
recently, they took a South American cruise. Their well-furnished house is immac-
ulately clean. I remove my shoes at the door. She rinses every dish before using it.
We sit at the kitchen island to drink dragon well [lung ching] tea from a small,
squat olive-green pot they bought on a recent trip to China. The tea is very expen-
sive, made from the tender tips of the leaves which first grow in the spring of the
year. She saves the leaves after making tea and uses them again as seasoning in
her cooking. They used to drink red tea, what we call black, but now they know
that green is healthier, so that is what they drink. Then they tell their stories:

Linh: This pot we bought in WuXi, China. This pot is made from special
clay, makes yourself healthy. Don't need to drink a lot, a little bit. It's a little
sweet, but not sweet like soda. The pot is called purple clay, but actually it
is not purple.

Husband: The purple color is under the earth, but the green color is the
clay. It is good for our health. We visited the northeast of China. We arrived
in Beijing first; then we went to Harbin, Xi Lin, then Chan Chung, then Da
Lien, Shantung. Xi Lan City is the birthplace of Confucius. We visited the
temple. And then went back to Shanghai and to WuXi and visited Tai Hu.

At first we came here, we just studied, enrolled at Laney College, studied and work and work. For 10 years. I went to Laney first, majored in accounting. The next semester, she also enrolled in Laney, too. Not special refugee course, regular class. Take about two years. We both graduated from Laney College, take an A.A. degree.

Linh: We got the highest honors in the class. He finished first. Because one class they don't have in the day time, so I took it at evening. And then the other course in this year they didn't have, so I had to wait.

In that apartment, the table too low, and not stable. And the chair high, so when we sit, when we read something, it was not right, but we have no choice. We saved money, no car. Usually people come here, they get car first. We didn't have. We walked, and no car. We stayed in that apartment until we bought the house. Didn't want to waste time to move here and move there, just stayed.

First got work-study job at Laney. Paid $3.99 an hour in the cashier's office. Minimum wage, account clerk. Money not enough, but I need a job. Before I came here, I worked at a high position, but when I came to this country, I heard that when I came here I didn't have local experience, so it didn't matter how much I was paid; I got local experience. Very, very simple for me. My boss didn't know that I worked in a high position before in a bank, so he thought how come I picked up so fast!

Husband: Very funny how we learned about Laney College. Actually, when we just came, we lived on Madison Street, close to Laney College, but we don't know where is Laney College, so at first we tried to go to adult school, at the Chinese Community Center. A lot of people also want to go to adult school, so the line is too long, and when it reached to us, there is no more space for us, but Linh is still on the waiting list. But I heard somebody tell me that in East Oakland there is also an adult school and not so many students there, so I walked over there, and I enrolled in that school, on East 14th Street close to Lake Merritt. And there I studied about one week.

The teacher said, "You really don't need to stay here; you need to go to Laney College." But I said, "Where is Laney College?" Then the teacher told me how to go to Laney College, so after class I walked to Laney College to enroll. Then they asked me to fill out a form and pay about two dollars and no fee. And then they sent me to the admissions office to look at my paperwork, and they said, "Oh, you are a new resident, so you have to pay tuition." I said, "I am a refugee; I have no money." Then they said, "Okay, you go to financial aid office and apply for financial aid." So they gave me a lot of papers to fill out, and it is almost closed in an hour. So I ask if I can take it home to fill out. And they say, "Yes, you need to take it home and fill it but not bring it back. After you fill it, you send back to the federal government. There is an address there. You send direct to them." So I fill out the form and send directly to the federal government. And the next week, the school is already starting, but I still do not get the information from the federal government, so I still cannot go into the class. So after two weeks, then I receive a letter from the federal government, and they ask me some more questions. So when I bring this letter to the financial aid office, so then the chief of the office looked at that paper, so they see that means that I did apply for financial aid and they are sure that I am qualified for financial aid, so they say, "Okay, now you can go to the office and get the permission." And it is already more than two weeks, so when I go to the class, maybe I cannot catch up. Professor let me stay in the class for one class, and then said I could try to catch up. So finally I enrolled in this class. It was easy for me. But for accounting, actually, I had never done accounting. My wife helped me.

Actually, that was very funny how I got a job. I didn't know there was work-study or any opening. One day a Vietnamese lady — I don't know her, but she knew me — she told me that in the financial office there was an opening, looking for a person who can speak bilingual, Chinese and Vietnamese, and asked me to go there. The second time I went to the financial office, I said, "I heard you have an opening here." So after the interview then they said, "You can stay here. When you have no class, then you can come to work. When you have class, then go to class." And they pay by hour, not pay by day. So that was a work-study job; that was my first job in here, too. Also the first time I can get in touch with computer. They ask me to input all the student financial aid information into the computer.

Before I graduate from Laney, after the first semester, in the summer time there is no class, so all the work-study students stop working. But the boss ask me, do I want to continue to do the job. I say, "Yes, why not?" Then they only let me continue. The other students, they all stop, so no more money. But after two days, also stop, because run out of money. So I walked over to Madison Street, to the county headquarters, and look at the list for openings, and there are some openings for bilingual account clerk, so I apply. And when I am scheduled to take the test, a hundred people are there to take the test! But they use a computer to get the score, so they get the score right away. So after they get the score, they say I passed the test.

They say, "Now you need to take a typing test. Do you want to take it right now or not?" I say, "No." Actually I did have some typing, but not enough, because here I never did typing. So I said, "Wait to schedule for another day." Then they schedule for another week. Next week. After that, I went to an office store to buy a typewriter. I come home and practice myself for about one week; then I went over there to take the typing test. Then they tell me, now there is no opening for bilingual Chinese-Vietnamese, only for Spanish, so I have to wait. So now I am in Laney College, so I don't mind to wait. I would like to continue my study. I thought maybe they do not want to hire me.

And next week the financial aid office call me to come back to work. So I come back to work in the office for a while, and then the next week, the first week, the county office notify me for an interview, send me to the social service agency on Broadway for an interview. So I went over there to see the chief of the personnel officer. And after he interviewed me, he called another branch in north Oakland, social service agency. I heard him call the supervisor there. He said, "You need a clerk, and now I have an applicant I want to send to you." Seems he doesn't like him to send anybody; it seems he has somebody in mind, but the chief says, "I think you need to see him, to interview him." So then he finally told me to go the next day to see the supervisor there. Then after I went to see the supervisor there, after the interview, he said, "Okay, I hire you." After they decide to hire me, I have to pass the physical exam. So after I pass the physical exam, then I decide I have to go to work. But I also have to study, so at first I schedule to have class at daytime, but now I have to work daytime, so I change all the schedule of class to evening.

Actually, the first day I went to social service agency to report to work, it is very hard because there are a lot of phone calls. My job is unit clerk, just like assistant supervisor. There are some workers that have their own job, but all the work comes to the unit clerk. All the phone calls come to the unit clerk. The first day I went over there, my supervisor is not there, too! She is sick! So I sit there, and the phone rings, and the most difficult for me is because what they are talking about not English. When they are talking, use all the code. Even the worker have their own code, their numbers; they are not talking, "This is Mr. Chan," or, "Mr. Hong," or whatnot; they talk "930" or "840." Even all the forms, all the agency forms, have not name, have a code, so use the code name, not the form name, so I don't understand what they are talking. So sometimes I cannot catch the phone. But fortunately there is a lady who sits across from me, a worker there; she is a black lady, but she is very nice. Sometimes she helps me. The first day, after 10 hours work, I come home and I say, "Maybe I cannot do this job. It is very, very stress, and I am very tired." But I tried next day, and finally I get through it.

Because that unit is to handle refugee cases, that's bilingual, Chinese and Vietnamese. I worked there for about one year, and during that time — because my major is accounting, so this is just a clerk position — so when the county has any other account clerk opening, I apply, too. Once you are a county employee, you can apply for other job and use county time; they don't deduct your salary anything. So when there is any account clerk opening, I apply, and I passed the test, and I got the interview from health care services. Then I went to work over there. And the chief financial officer is over there. And he is very nice. Before, he had been in Vietnam, so he had good feeling with me. So he talked to me a lot. He was in the army in Vietnam. So he talked to me a lot, and I think maybe he will hire me. And later he told me that this position of account clerk is already filled, so he told me, "You can apply for this position as billing technician." So actually I thought, *technician*? That means related to mechanic, and I am not good in mechanics. But I never heard about this position called "billing technician." But he asked me to apply. So then I just followed his advice, and I go to personnel office and apply for billing technician position.

And then again pass the test, so this time they send me to the health services agency to see the same boss, the chief. But this time under the chief the supervisor is a lady, and they both interview me. So after they interview me, they say, "Okay, you wait," and they will notify me later. Usually you only wait for about 1 week or 10 days. They should notify me if they hire me or another person. But I wait for 10 days and no phone call. But finally after two weeks, the supervisor called me and said they decide to hire me. So I went over there and got the job, so I quit the social service agency and then went over there. That was the job I kept; went from Billing Technician One, to Billing Technician Two, and then Billing Technician Three, and then I apply another job, Accounting Technician. That is a management position, Accounting Technician. It is in the same building, the same financial department. It was a management position, with all the management benefits. I worked there for 18 years.

Linh: If the family is poor, no income at all, can get work-study job. I cannot have [*any longer*] the work-study job, because he got the job with the county, and we are not poor anymore, so I can no more work there. Fortunately, the other department hired me, the disabled, disability, at Laney, they hired me, so I worked there for a while. Then later I went to work in the law office. At disability, I learned a lot there, too. The supervisor was very good. She let me understand accounting system. Everything should be accurate. A lot of problems in accounting, ask me to find what is the error. Cannot balance something, so I find a lot of them. After work, she talk to me, too, very nice. And then I took the accounting test, and she sent me to work for the law office.

I started to work there in 1982. At the beginning, I just worked part time only, because I was still in school. Full-time student, so I worked part time. They called me bookkeeper. There were four lawyers, a law firm. I was the only bookkeeper. And after that they gave me more work, and was a full charge bookkeeper. I had to do everything. I am doing the tax for the county and city. Before, the account clerk do it, but finally they ask me do it. So I did. And also my boss has his own business and ask me to take care, too. And also sometimes they have some people that are getting old and they cannot handle this, sometimes they have a lawyer to take care of it, and ask me to audit those accounts, too. Like a conservator. And I audit those.

Later he formed another law firm, and a house for rent, I had to deposit, and I had to handle those deposits and payroll, something like that. At the end of the year, a lot of things. Different business, I had to handle it. So too much work. Even the office supplies, this is not my job duty, but I need to do this. I check each one the price, to save money. I compare price, and order this way. And then at the bank — he trust me; I don't know why he trust me — I could transfer the money for him. I just call, say my code, and then I could transfer the money. At the beginning, I say I didn't promise to do this job; I don't like to do this, take the money and transfer it some way, he [*might*] think that I stole it, so I say no. He said, "No, you are quiet. Nobody can transfer and lose the money." He just let me transfer the money; so many accounts, it drive me crazy. But I still, I think I did well.

The day that the accounting firm told me that I passed the test, I was so happy about this, and then after a couple of days when one afternoon, heavy rain, that afternoon I have no class, stay at home, and hear a phone call, law office calling, ask me go interview. I said, "My God." Now heavy rain and go to interview, no coat, and I don't know how. I don't know how. I just take up the best coat I have, bring umbrella with me, and fortunately the office is not too far from my apartment; then I just walk to there and got interview. The boss ask me a lot of questions, ask me to tell about myself, and then he said, "I hire you," and he said he give me eight dollars an hour. Then I just — because my friends they work only about five dollars something but now I have eight dollars. And he said, "Too little?" I said, "No, that's okay. When I work and do a good job, you will increase my salary." Now it's okay, I think enough for me, eight dollars per hour at that time. The other employees there were very nice. At first I was scared.

I can use what I learn from the college. Later too much work, it doesn't matter, but some new employees and the situation changed a lot. Work is a pleasure for me. I work about 11 hours a day, seven days a week. My holiday, still work. And summertime I stay late, late, and I went home, but in wintertime, it is getting dark, so I brought all the documents and work at home. I wrote down my work hours that I work at the office, but the hours I work at home, no charge. Because nobody saw I worked, I don't want people to say I am cheating; I am honest. But I work at home, nobody knows. Sometimes I work until midnight. No charge.

After I graduate, I worked full time. Because I did the payroll myself, I wrote my time myself, so I didn't write down the actual hours I worked at home. Sometimes I was working, so tired, and I think everybody is sleeping; my boss and coworkers are sleeping; how come I am still working? But when I accept the job, I work; I just do my best to complete the work, and do my best and no error — this my personality. I am like that. It doesn't matter — pay me or not pay me; I told my boss, too — I said, "If I accept the job, I will do my best. If you know that I am good, increase my salary." I worked there three years. The situation not like before. I like to work, happy, and everybody getting along well, and only job pressure is okay, and you feel happy when you work in the office. Later, that changed. I moved to the other place of work.

After I quit this job, before I get the job in the county, I applied for unemployment. Because my health seemed not that good because too much work. I wrote down why I quit this job, so the employment department say I am qualified for the unemployment. And then of course they have to send the information to my former boss. So then my boss denied. But finally I won this one, so I got paid unemployment.

But he held my last paycheck. The last day I worked in the office, he didn't pay my paycheck. And after I finished, one month or two months, he still hadn't paid, and I wrote him a letter. And finally he paid me, but I already figured out how much he should pay me, but his manager paid me more than that. I think an error, so I sent it back. So I wrote a letter, and I said, "This is more than I should have gotten." So I asked him to void this check and don't put it on my W-2 form. And give me actually the right figure. But unfortunately, this check created a problem for me, because unemployment requires that after I collect the unemployment benefits, when I still got a pay-check from the law office, they asked me to pay back all that I got from the unemployment benefits, and include interest and penalty something. So I wrote another letter to the unemployment department, included the letter that I wrote to the law firm, my former boss, and send them so they know that this was the check I got when I was working, not this month. Then finally, nothing happened. But fortunately, I kept a copy of the letter. Otherwise, nothing can prove. But sometimes in our life, we learn something from the trouble. I learned from the law firm, everything, keep a copy. I never worked as a lawyer, but when you work there, you learn something more. I learned a lot from my work there because they let me do a lot. This one you cannot learn in school. Only really work and learn from there.

Actually, at the beginning I very like the law firm. At the end, the last three months, everything changed. I not only worked for the business group; his personal books I handled, too. At that time, I just think, "Okay, if I go to school, I have to study very hard; I have to take the quiz, the test; still very, very busy, too, but now I learn from work; it doesn't matter." I already comfort myself like that. Learn from job is better. So when he give me more work, I still say, "Okay." Sometimes too busy, and the deadline come, and sometimes I put a note on my door, "Please don't interrupt me." At night I feel very heavy. Fortunately, everything we got through. This is life.

AUGUST 27, 2003
Linh told me that she and her husband were going out for dinner that evening with friends, and I asked which restaurant they liked in Chinatown. They couldn't

answer the question, although I asked several times, in different format: Do you have a favorite restaurant? Which restaurant do you think is the best? Which restaurant do you recommend? No answer. Finally I asked where they were going that evening, and they told me. I asked, "Is that a good one?" Linh said, "We don't complain; we were refugees for years, hungry, so we don't complain anything." My questions had implied a derogation of some restaurants in favor of others, and they weren't willing to do that.

AUGUST 2004

I drove Linh and her husband for his post-op checkup after cataract surgery. When I took him last week, he was bothered that I parked in the garage and had to pay. Today we parked at a place he knew, a couple of blocks away, on the street with no meter. He is very careful not to jay walk and goes out of his way to a crosswalk.

APRIL 1, 2006

Linh and her husband came for lunch and brought the album of photos from their recent South American cruise on the Queen Mary II. They traveled with his brother and sister-in-law, and also a former co-worker and friend of Linh's. There were 100 photos in the album, showing one or both of them against the background of the luxurious ship or some feature of their day tours in Argentina, Peru, Ecuador, Panama, Costa Rica, Mexico, and Los Angeles. They didn't buy any souvenirs; Linh, ever sensible, said, better to take friends out for lunch. The photos included shots of them playing ping pong, relaxing in deck chairs, and dressed as I have never seen them, Linh elegant and pretty in black or bright colors, he in dark suit and tie. She told me she now weighs 90 pounds. She is photogenic now, with round cheeks and sparkly eyes.

MAY 24, 2006

Linh called this morning to tell me she is leaving next week for a long trip — 23 days — to Singapore, Malaysia, and Fukien. Fukien is where her family originated, and she is excited about trying to find their home. She will ask the tour guide for help and hopes to locate their home. We diverted into a long conversation about toilets in China. She says she tried to tell their tour guides on previous trips that if they would spend the money to have sanitary rest rooms, they would make a lot more money from tourists, not only Chinese but others. She says most of her Chinese friends say they will only travel by cruise ship now and will never go on a land tour to China because of the awful restrooms.

She talked about an experience on a previous trip to China — they were climbing steep steps to a mountain shrine, wearing jeans and walking shoes, and were amazed at the Chinese women who wore high heels and skirts, what she called "dressed to go to a restaurant." In the streets of the cities, likewise, the

Chinese were far more dressed up, not wearing walking shoes. Once she heard other Chinese tourists, the ones who were dressed up, and didn't know that she understands Mandarin, questioning where they were from because of their strange dress. They were saying, "Where are those people from?" She didn't want to tell them that they were from the United States.

JANUARY 31, 2007

Linh says she prays every day to Kwan Yin, and it always helps. The altar in the living room is on a chest covered with a lace cloth. There is one large statuette of Kwan Yin in the center, and several smaller ones arranged on each side. There are three bowls of round fruit—apples, oranges, grapefruit—and two vases of artificial flowers. There are two tiny medallions of Jesus, given by a Christian relative. On the wall is a beautiful calligraphy scroll. Several stuffed animal toys are on the sofa. Facing the dining area is a flat-panel television. The well-tended garden includes flowers, fruit trees, a vegetable patch, and a compost pile. Nothing is wasted.

SEPTEMBER 27, 2010

Linh wants to add this postscript to her interview:

After I worked in the county I kept taking tests. Finally I passed an accounting technician test, for a management position, with good benefits. I was retired in this position, with good retirement. I'm very glad we came to this country; the government takes good care of us. We met some good people, and there is a good government and good retirement. When we had trouble,

Linh and her husband, 2010.

we had help. My husband and I both had good jobs and worked until retire. After we retire, we are doing volunteer, helping people when they need help, such as take them to hospital, make appointments, do paperwork, etc. It doesn't matter what time — if they call us, we go right away, even five o'clock A.M. We hope we have good health; then we can help more people. We appreciate America, and we wish God bless America.

Luu Gets a Job

OCTOBER 5, 1985

Luu called this afternoon to tell me that she has a job and asked if she could come to visit. She was in my class last year; two of her sisters have also been my students. She is outgoing, has a square, flat face and beautiful teeth. She came by bus and arrived within an hour. She took off her sandals at the door, and then we had tea. She ate a large piece of mooncake and seemed delighted when I gave her the egg yolk from mine.[2]

Her mother and father both came from Hubei province in China, so she speaks Hubei dialect, as well as Mandarin, a little Cantonese, and Vietnamese. Her father and mother were already engaged when her father and grandfather fled from China to Vietnam to escape the Japanese, probably around 1939. For three years her father was alone in Vietnam, and in this time he married a Chinese woman there. Then Luu's maternal grandfather, the father of his fiancé, went to Vietnam and reminded him of his obligation, so his fiancé was sent for, and he married her, too. Both wives are about the same age and have the same status, although technically Luu's mother is the first. She sometimes refers to them as "tall" and "short" mother. In all, there are 11 children of one wife and 14 of the other. The father spends about half his time with each family. One family was sponsored by a brother who came here first; the father then sponsored the second family. They all came by plane, through the family reunification plan. In Vietnam, the family was evidently well-to-do. The father had a dental lab, and the daughters worked as dental technicians after completing school. He is quiet and serious, and doesn't want the girls to smile around him. All of her friends are afraid of him. He hates card playing. In Vietnam, he wouldn't allow any of his family to gamble, but here he can't control them.

One of Luu's brothers, the middle one, left Vietnam alone, and she refers to him as "lost," because they have never heard from him since, but she doesn't think he is dead, because a fortune teller told them that they would see him in America. This happened at the time of a ceremony held three months after her grandfather died. A Buddhist monk came to their house, when the grandfather's spirit was visiting between midnight and 2 A.M., and the monk told them they would see this son in America.

Luu attends the Jehovah's Witness Kingdom Hall regularly, the only one of her family to go there. If she doesn't go twice a week, they call her to find out why, so now when she goes to visit her "half-mother," her father's other wife, she calls them first to explain her absence.

The father attended our school for a while, and then "the welfare" made him change to a job-training class. He goes, but isn't progressing, and Luu thinks he will probably never get a job. The mother would like to go to China to visit her relatives there, so the children are hoping to amass enough money to send her. She is illiterate and gets angry if the children use any English words in her presence. She refuses to try to learn any English, yet she complains that she is living here "like jail." The grandmother, on the other hand, can write her name, studied English for a month in refugee camp in the Philippines, and enjoys trying to say "Good morning." The grandmother will go with the youngsters to the supermarket in Chinatown, but the mother won't. The mother is about 60 years old, and the grandmother is probably about 75.

The mother sometimes feeds as many as 48 people in their three-room apartment. On weekends they only eat breakfast and dinner, although anyone who wants to cook noodles in between is welcome to do so. The mother's obligation evidently doesn't include more than two meals. When other people come, the women help her. They have no yard, or place to overflow, so they all cram into the three rooms. Only two sons are married. The oldest daughter never wanted to marry, preferring to live with her parents. The others may want to marry, but probably haven't been able to make appropriate arrangements. In Vietnam, all of the father's earnings were handed over to his mother to disburse, and if the children wanted money, they got it from her. Now he keeps the money that he gets from welfare; this will expire after 18 months.

Luu studied soldering and computer assembly in a training program, and the instructors there helped her to locate her job. They looked in the newspaper, found an appropriate ad, and set up the interview for her. There were five applicants for two jobs, and she and her sister were both hired. She solders cables, is paid $4.00 per hour, and after three months, will receive some benefits. Her brother also works in Hayward, so he drives her to work and back home. Luu says that some of her classmates in the training program didn't want to get jobs until their welfare expired, and thought she was foolish to go to work now. She, however, is very happy to be working.

Grandma, We Listen to You

Phuong is satisfied: her three children are grown, all have good jobs, and all own their own homes and cars. She has seven grandchildren; the youngest will

*soon enter pre-school, ending her role as babysitter. Her name means "phoenix,"
one of the four sacred mythical creatures, and it suits her, for like that fabled bird,
she has shown great courage in re-inventing herself. In 2007, she says:*

I feel I'm lucky. When we go to get medicine, the pharmacist calls me
Auntie; he is the son of an old friend from Vietnam. I tell my grandchildren,
go to school, have a career, and make money; they can take care of me, and
they will make Grandma happy. When they win an award at school, I don't
give them candy; I give twenty dollars and tell them to save it for sometime
when they need it. They say, "Grandma, we listen to you."

*In 1981, Phuong was a newly arrived refugee, one of the ethnic Chinese "boat
people" who escaped from Vietnam. She stood out for her physical attractiveness,
her quick intelligence, and her self-assurance. She was tall and slender, wearing
a stylish ivory silk pants suit. Although she wore this suit to school every day, it
never looked soiled or wrinkled. She was interviewed first in August 1981, when
she still had limited English, and again in January 2004, when she was more
articulate. We were in frequent contact through these years. Sometimes we had
dim sum [tea lunch] at a restaurant she liked, outside of Chinatown. Once she
came to my house with ingredients for one of my favorite Vietnamese dishes, goi
cuon [shrimp roll], and taught me how to make it. What seemed simple to her
was insurmountably difficult for me. Nearly every year she brings me one or two
mooncakes, with a red Chinese character painted on the top. In America, she has
had to study two languages: not only English but also Cantonese, the language of
the Chinese community where she looked for work as a teacher.*

*Her father was a teacher who migrated with his wife and four children from
south China to Bac Lieu, in south Vietnam, sometime in the 1930s. Phuong was
the fifth and last child, born in Vietnam. When she was nine years old, her parents
died, and she was brought up by her brother. This is how she told her story in
1981:*

My brother opened the Chinese medicine business; always get busy,
thinking about make more money. I always lived with my brother. My brother
very loved me, and my sister-in-law very loved me. Now they are all died, in
Vietnam. When I little girl, I very lazy — I don't want to go to school. My
brother say, "I want you go to school;" he make me every day. Then, 15 years
old, I study very well. I am the head in the class. I read and write very well,
Vietnamese and Chinese.

*She became a teacher, and the son of an old family friend was introduced
and courted her for a year.*

We know each other a long time, maybe one year. In Vietnam, very different; the girls didn't go to the boy's house. My husband came to visit me,
every day, because he had a car. Every day he came to my house and came to
my school to visit me. When my husband came to my house to visit me, I
bring some food and tea and coffee. We eat all together in my family; don't

go to restaurant. Because if we go out to eat lunch, some people look like it's very terrible. Different in here. And my husband asked me, "When are you able to marry?" And I say, "Maybe, maybe. It's a long time, a year." And my brother-in-law talked to my brother. Then my brother asked me, and I say, "I don't want to get married." My brother say, "Why?" A long time, answer that. When I said yes, my husband very happy.

My husband helped my father-in-law every day, and he drove a car many, many places. We got married in my home. Different in here. My husband's old friends drove 10 cars to go to my husband's home. I wore a pink dress, a long dress, the same thing in here. And pink flowers.

In the traditional Chinese wedding, the groom and his friends escort the bride from her home to his, and then she becomes part of his family. Phuong wanted to continue her teaching career, and the school principal wanted her to continue, but her mother-in-law insisted that she needed help with her business, selling diamonds. They lived with several generations and 10 servants in a large five-story house in Soc Trang. Her husband's family was very rich, with a Chinese medicine business, and owned many houses in Soc Trang and also in Saigon, five hours away. Phuong's son was born two years later, followed by two daughters.

In Chinese, the first baby a son, the family very happy. If they have a girl, so-so. My husband's family very loved me. Before, is very easy living. The money usually do it. Before, my family kept the money. I help my mother-in-law, every day bring the money to the bank.

This happy and luxurious life ended in 1975 when the Communists came, closed the Chinese school, and targeted Chinese business. Her husband was taken to jail, her parents-in-law escaped by boat, and for six months she managed on her own, struggling with the effects of hyperinflation.

Very dangerous. Very difficult. Because I have the diamonds, every day I get more money, but it is very difficult to keep the money. Before I left Vietnam, the money changed twice high. Changed the new money, but I get the money at night; I bought many, many things. The money is all gone; I don't keep it. In the morning, maybe one time I change the money. Because all the family came to the office to change the money. Very difficult. I bought diamonds and gold, many things. The money is very small — don't keep it. I bought diamonds and gold; I bought many, many food. Because I was thinking, I make more money, I worry about my children's future. But every day I get too much money, I worry how to use the money, because change the money, I was afraid. Maybe two weeks we visit my husband, to bring the food, but we cannot talking. When we left Vietnam, we wrote some letters to my husband; we said we are going to school. We are afraid the Communists know we are getting out, so we said we are going to school, but my husband knew we were leaving.

She says that they could not take good food to him because he would have to stay longer in jail; presumably, this relates to the price of the bribe for his release.

My old friends bought the boat, a big boat — maybe five hundred people were on it. We paid 10 pieces of gold for one person. My husband's parents left Vietnam first. After half a year, we left, from Soc Trang. We were 15 days in the big ocean because the captain didn't know the way. After maybe five days we met an American big ship, and they gave us water. We need the water; if we don't have the water, we will die. They gave us water, and food, oranges and apples and milk. My younger daughter got a lot of milk, she very happy.

The ship was boarded by Thai pirates with faces painted white who terrified the passengers and stole from them. She and her children stayed below deck for three days.

I was sick. I was very afraid. They said, "Oh, the woman is very sick." All the diamonds is sewed up in my jacket.[3] Some people, all the jewelry is gone. Three days, and at night. The robbers stayed on the boat all the time. Sometime they got all the jewelry, diamonds. Sometimes the people are crying, and the Thai people hit the women. The women have a lot of diamonds, and the Thais took them, and they cried.

They landed in Indonesia, where they were treated kindly in "a small place." She studied English for three months and was happily reunited for a time with a brother who arrived by boat from Vietnam and then went to Australia. After a year they spent two weeks in the Galang refugee center "to check up the body," went to Singapore for three days, and flew to America. Here they were taken in and helped by relatives and friends. She enrolled immediately in school. She also welcomed an opportunity to break out of the Asian community and practice her English.

In my apartment are many friends from Vietnam and Indonesia. I have a Vietnamese old friend; she opened a sewing factory, and a Mexican friend works in there, so I have a Mexican friend, too. Because I enjoy speaking English. Sometimes I meet him because I can always speak English, but with my Vietnamese and Chinese friends, they always want to speak Chinese and Vietnamese. The Mexican, he is 21 years old, very nice, and he sews very well, and he speaks English very well. I don't sew; I just go to visit. The Mexico boy made my suit.

My older sister stayed in Vietnam. I write many, many letters, tell her United States very nice; I can bring books and go to school every day; she very enjoy, but now leave Vietnam very difficult. My sister family has a lot of money, but now very difficult leave Vietnam. She wait for maybe her husband buy a boat. My sister has three children, but the children all soldiers. Very difficult living in Vietnam.

In the future, I hope I can in here learn more English, and I hope in my future I can make more money, same thing in Vietnam, and buy a new house, and buy a new car. And last one, only I hope I can visit Vietnam again. I have my brother and sister stay in Vietnam, and my husband. I hope, and that's the last one — is too small — I may visit Vietnam again. My children will learn more English, and together will get a good job, too. They very enjoy the United States.

Two years later, the younger daughter, now in junior high school, answers the telephone and says in perfect English, "May I know who is calling?" The older daughter is an honor student in 11th grade, and the son is in a training class for auto mechanics. Phuong went to San Jose for her father-in-law's birthday celebration. Two years ago she said he was 81, but today she said he is 78. In any case, he is very old, but still goes to school every day to learn English. His wife, who knows very good French, has also learned some English. Their son, Phuong's husband, has been released from jail, and they are trying to get him to come here. She says she is very lazy about writing letters to him but still writes twice a month. She describes him as a "happy-go-lucky man" spoiled by his mother.

More than 20 years later, Phuong is interviewed again. Many of her wishes have been granted. Her family has prospered, and she has returned three times to visit Vietnam. She is at her older daughter's home, two doors away from her son's home, in a pleasant Oakland neighborhood. Phuong's son has a successful auto repair shop, is married, and has two children. Phuong's older daughter has two children and works as a secretary in one of the area's highest-ranking schools; her children can attend the school even though they reside in another district. Phuong's younger daughter has three children, lives in a fashionable suburb, and is building a new six-bedroom house in an even more stylish location. This daughter's husband and his brother have two successful furniture stores, one in a building they own and the other in a building they are buying. The children are musically talented and take piano lessons; one of the advantages of the new house will be a grand piano. This daughter does not work outside her home. Every weekend Phuong visits her and stays with the youngest child while the mother takes the older ones for their music and swimming lessons. Phuong has gone with them on vacation to Hawaii and to Puerta Vallarta, which she liked, because it reminded her of Vietnam, but there were too many flies. Next year they will go to Cancun, also in Mexico, where people say it is clean.

Phuong says when she came here, her life began again. Recounting her story in 2004, she adds more detail. After the Communists closed their Chinese medicine store in 1975, she sold in a market until that was closed. She had tax receipts, but they still said she could not sell. She took her three children and went after hours to the house of a high official. She curried favor with Communists of two opposing factions. To one she fed a lot of soup because he was very poor; to the other she gave large money gifts for his children; then they allowed her to continue her business. On September 18, 2004, she says:

I stood outside all night, until five o'clock in the morning, but cannot talk to him. Then went to his office, two guards stopped me, but I talked to them and went in. The high official saw me in the night and felt sorry for me. He said I can sell medicine but for outside only. I made him give me a permit on paper.

Her son, then 17, planned to escape on a boat with 12 other boys, but she refused to let him go without her. Then in one week she made all the arrangements to leave, paying the equivalent of $21,000 U.S. in gold wafers. When she went at night to pay, the man had a big box filled with gold and took them in a jeep as far as from Oakland to San Jose, about 30 miles. The boat held five hundred people and had no water. She took some rice, a cooking pot, a few clothes, and a small coffee tin with gold and diamonds hidden in it. She sewed gold in the hem of her pants and the belt. The girls had little gold earrings and necklaces. The Thai pirates robbed everything except what was sewed in the clothing but didn't harm them physically. In Indonesia, she bought a sewing machine for $1,500 from someone who asked for $5,000. She found a partner who could sew, made 10 pairs of pants a day, and made a lot of money. She gave the money to her brother, who arrived from Vietnam soon after she did; he went to Australia and died there.

In the intervening years, in addition to caring for her grandchildren, Phuong has worked as a teacher in the Chinese school in Oakland; for this she needed to learn Cantonese, so she took classes at the community college. For a long time, she has worked as a housekeeper for a wealthy American woman who has several vacation homes and pays well for Phuong to oversee the primary residence when they are not there. Phuong is grateful for the wages, and also for the trust placed in her. She misses her friends in Vietnam, but she says she has no desire to go back to live; the air is polluted, and the water is not safe to drink. She says everyone in Vietnam thinks all Americans are rich; they don't understand how hard people work here. She still sends the customary money gifts for New Year, although her friends and relatives no longer need them for survival. Her husband has left Vietnam and is in San Jose, but she does not depend on him, and her parents-in-law have died. She is now the matriarch, her children care for her, and her grandchildren respect her advice; she is content. She still, however, has lingering fears of the Communists and does not want her photo to appear.

We Have to Love Each Other

Her Vietnamese name, Be Thi, she easily Anglicized to Betty; other life adjustments have been harder. Since coming to America, she has gained weight, to nearly 90 pounds. She often says, "I think I'm very lucky," and maybe she is trying to convince herself. Early in her life in America, she said, "I dream of seeing my father and my brother every night. I don't know what happened; my mother

*died 16 years ago, but I still dream and see her. I think if I die it will be easy."
Once, she tried to kill herself with an overdose of medicine, an episode that cost
$1,000 in hospital bills, and made her husband, at least temporarily, stop going
to Reno to gamble. Her account glimpses the darker side of the sewing factory and
the thugs that preyed there. It seems that each step of her life has been from one
difficulty to another, and her problems — war, hunger, poverty, failure to bear a
son, loneliness, intercultural marriage — are beyond her ability to ameliorate. Still
she perseveres and finds comfort in her family and work as a housekeeper: "My
job is like my family. They all love me, and I love them, too. That means a lot,
you know."*

SEPTEMBER, 1980

*On registration day, September 8, at 8:30 the line of people waiting to
register for English classes at the adult school went from the front door around the
corner onto Webster Street and was as wide as the sidewalk. There are 211 seats
in the school, so those who were in line from 5:00 A.M. until about 6:45 were
able to get in classes, while the others, more than 400, were put on waiting lists.
I wonder how many of the earliest arrivals here are Vietnamese.*

There are 38 chairs in the room where I teach. Allowing for absences and

Be Thi (Betty) soon after enrolling in ESL
class, spring, 1981.

*students who leave at 10:30 to go to
work, I have registered 40 students,
all Asian. They include two Vietnamese women who don't speak
Chinese. All the others, whether
from Vietnam, Burma, Laos, Taiwan, or the People's Republic of
China, consider themselves Chinese. Some of them can't communicate directly with each other,
however, because of the variety of
dialects. The largest group speak the
dialect of Toi San, in the province
of Guangdong. The young ones
from the People's Republic of China
[PRC] and some of the Vietnamese,
speak Mandarin as well as a village
dialect. Among the Vietnamese,
several speak the dialect of the
southern Chinese district of Chiu
Chow. One of the two Vietnamese
women, Be Thi, does not speak
Chinese. She has medium-length*

hair, curled up at the ends, and wears pretty pastel pants suits. Her name means "Doll Poem" and it suits her. Her hips are so narrow it is hard to believe she has children; one was newborn when they left Vietnam by boat.

October, 1980

Be Thi told me that she has a lot of abdominal pain. The doctor's remedy didn't help her, so she was going to consult a Chinese herbalist. She explained that on the boat when she escaped, she was beaten very much and robbed. She wrote those two words on paper and said that because she had a nursing baby, she was not raped, one of the few strokes of luck she has had. In the refugee camp, they slept under the sky, with no medicine or cover, and ever since then, she hasn't been well. As she spoke of this, the tears streamed down her face, but she didn't change expression, just wiped them away.

She weighs 85 pounds and looks fragile, but she is sure of herself and what she needs. She is determined to learn good English, and she will. Her manner is modest and polite. She writes easily with exceptionally beautiful penmanship; clearly she has been well educated. Her husband is in another class, less advanced, at our school. He is nice-looking, rather tall, and terribly thin. I see them in the mornings when they come to school. She carries their books in a bag, and they stop at the door for her to give his books and papers to him. They smile at each other when they part.

November, 1980

The de facto class leader emerged soon—Mr. Yu, a handsome, silver-haired man who had been a general in the Chinese Nationalist army. He came early every day and sat in the seat nearest my table. One day in November, he was absent, and Mr. Ting, the other leader, announced quite formally that on the day before, Mr. Yu had died of a heart attack. We collected money for flowers, and Mr. Ting went to the nearby florist to order them. He made a down payment and retained the rest until after the funeral, to make sure that they arrived in good condition. Coming to school the next day, I was apprehensive about Mr. Yu's empty seat as a sad reminder of his death. I thought the students might be reluctant to sit there, but I had underestimated their pragmatism. The seat, in a choice location, was immediately taken by Be Thi.

February, 1981

I was alarmed by several dark vertical bruises on Be Thi's throat. She was wearing a mandarin-collared blouse, but since she sits in the front seat I could still see the marks. I asked her if she was all right, and she said the bruises came from vomiting too much, and she assured me that she is better now. A folk treatment that involves rubbing the body with the edge of a coin may leave bruises; this could be another explanation.

We have a lot of holidays in February: in addition to the American holidays, we also celebrate one day for Lunar New Year and another day for the anniversary of the Chinese Community Center, the building in which our classes meet. This anniversary date had escaped notice until recently, because it falls on February 22, and until the United States started moving holidays around, we thought the school was closed to honor George Washington. When we began to observe Washington's birthday on the nearest Monday, we found that the school still observed February 22 as its anniversary date.

On a Friday that was a holiday, Be Thi telephoned me at home. She was very happy because a friend had lent them money to buy a car and told them they could repay it whenever possible, without interest. This friend has been here for five years. She said, "Our friend loves my husband very much." She wanted to bring me some Vietnamese food, but I told her we were going out for dinner.

On Sunday morning, two days later, Be Thi called to tell me that in the night, they had been burglarized. The back door of their apartment can't be locked because it serves two apartments. Their black neighbors had a party Saturday night, with very loud music and marijuana smoking, and in the night someone broke the window to their bathroom, entered, and took her husband's jacket, which hung there. In the pocket was his wallet, containing 25 dollars, his papers, and the car key. They think the thief took the car for a joy ride and brought it back, because the door was open. On Monday, looking spectrally thin and very sad, she came to school just to tell me that they were going to the police. This was a trap, for they were robbed again while they were at the police station. Later, she tells of multiple exploitations — by their Chinese landlord as well as the black neighbors. At the same time, she recognizes a kind black neighbor and a good Chinese landlord.

SPRING, 1981

Be Thi got a letter from her father, who lives in Tay Ninh, 100 kilometers from Saigon. He had ridden a bicycle for three days to get to Saigon, after getting government permission to go, in order to mail the letter to her. She hadn't heard from him for about a year, although he had been sending letters, but they hadn't gotten through. She has four brothers, and as the only daughter, she is valued. The father is 52 years old, and she explains that in Vietnam it is very old because he has had to work so hard as a farmer. He has lost all his teeth. He begs her to send pain-relieving medicine for a brother who was injured when a buffalo cart fell on him and has been in pain for two years.

JULY, 1981

I picked up Be Thi at the home of her mother-in-law. She said that about 10 people, sometimes 12 or 14, live on the ground floor of the old house that has been chopped up into apartments. By the front door is a tin can filled with sand

*with some incense sticks stuck into it. Inside, next to the door is a shelf piled high
with all the family shoes. Floors are bare; the living room is furnished with a sofa,
a chaise where the mother-in-law was resting, and a large TV with VCR. The
dining room has a large table, and on a small table are a thermos and some cups.
The kitchen looks bare. Several little grandchildren are running around; the old
lady greets me politely, although she speaks absolutely no English. She has a lot of
gold teeth. Be Thi says that in addition to the family, there are many young single
men who came from Vietnam with them who live there sometimes.*

*She was wide-eyed at seeing my house. After seeing the downstairs, she asked
who lives upstairs. She was astounded that this house was for just one family. She
especially admired the washing machine; she washes all of their clothes by hand,
and it's very hard, but her husband told her when they have enough money, he
will buy a washing machine. Clearly, the TV-VCR had higher priority. She was
nervous at first about being interviewed; she had her dictionary with her and had
enlisted the help of a friend in Richmond who speaks very good English. He told
her that he would be at home, and if we got into trouble about language, she
could call him. After the interview, before leaving the house, she called him to
tell him that she didn't need his help.*

*In this tape-recorded interview of July 8, 1981, she tells of her childhood in
a war-torn country, how she was nearly sold into prostitution, tricked into joining
the army, and how finally she found love and the hope of surmounting cultural
and religious barriers.*

I am 28, but I lost two, so I am 26. My birth certificate says I am 26,
because my parents got it when I was two years old, in 1955. When I came
here, I like United States very much. When I eat meat or enough food, I miss
my father so much. You know, when I stand in the kitchen, and I fry pork,
I miss my brothers just like that because in Vietnam not enough food, no
chicken, no pork. One time in Vietnam I bought a little pork, and after I
fried it, they wanted to eat too much. I didn't give my youngest brother much
to eat, and he stole my pork, and I miss him very much, and now if I eat
pork, I miss him. Yes.

My father was a farmer in a quiet place. My father grows the rice very
much, and peanuts and tomatoes. Many, many potatoes. And corn. My father
is poor now, but my grandfather was a rich man. He had machines to grow
rice. After the war began, the machines burned, and we moved, and that
house burned, too. Again. And we moved to three places. You know when
the soldiers were fighting, we moved to the other place; many, many places
I don't remember. Seven years old, move two or three months, and come back,
come back, and fighting again, and move again. It's a lot of trouble.

My grandfather was in the army. He had farms, many farms. He was a
rich man, my father's father. My mother's father is in Vietnam, too, but now
very old. When I was 11 years old, he was a principal [*municipal leader*]. You

know, my mother could speak French very well. After my mother bore my youngest brother, one month, she died. I took care of my brother. I miss him very much. When he started to speak in Vietnamese, he called me mother. And you know when after my mother died, I was 12 years old, and the Communists tried to fight with the army near my house. And my house is many floors, very high, made of cement, and you can live in a hole under the floor, and army came and after fighting in my house, they fire it because Communists were under my floor.

You know my neighbor cheat me, when I was 20, asked me to go to study the nursing. I like nurse very much. She said if I study nurse, give her money, 100,000. So my father gave 100,000 to her. She took me to Saigon. But you know in Saigon, some people are very bad, so I had a lot of trouble. She took me to be a prostitute for three days, and I didn't know how, so she didn't sell me. Then she took me to go to the army! I didn't know, I say, "Oh!" And then I cried, and the man who was the major asked me, "Why do you cry?" I answer, "She cheated me," so he brought me to the place where my husband was working. So he saw me cry, he asked me why I cry. I told him about me, and he said he saw me honest and he scared some people cheat me again. And after one year he said he loved me.

After I study at the school of army, I work in the radio about one year, and I tend the tape and recorder. When the Communist party came, in May 1975, Communists catch my husband, catch me, too. And I was supposed to go to study Communist, but that night I bore my baby. And they didn't catch my husband and didn't catch me because I bore my baby. Because he stayed home and took care of me because I don't have a mother. Then he came to my parents' house and went to the farm working. And he worked with my father. I was very happy that time. My father liked my husband very much.

His family were well-to-do urban Chinese who opposed his marriage and only gave in when he threatened to kill himself otherwise. For a time both of them worked in a ball-point pen factory and they lived in Cholon, the Chinese area of Saigon, with his family, who largely ignored her, except to call her a "cow" because she didn't speak Chinese. When the Communists took over the government, young men were sent to "re-education camps," doing forced hard labor in jungle areas, where many died. Be Thi and her husband escaped this by going to live with her father and working with him on his farm, and for the first time, the marriage was advantageous to his family.

And at that time I am very happy. My mother-in-law understand me, and she look at me, and she love me more. I never quarreled with my sister-in-law or my brother-in-law or her, so my neighbor saw me very nice, so they told my mother-in-law, so she look at me and said when I lived with my father she would come to visit me. When I lived with her, she didn't like me. She said when she was sick, nobody take care. And you know when I lived with her one time she was sick, and I bring medicine, and I bring rice and food for her. I think she thought of that, and she missed me.

His family arranged for their escape by boat to Indonesia, and she was forced to decide between staying with her father and brothers or going with her husband and his family, who were willing to include her in the escaping group only if she promised to pay back the $4,000 in gold that her passage cost them. It took her three months to decide to go with them, and they left soon after the birth of the second child, another daughter. Her father wanted to keep the older daughter, and again, she was torn between pleasing him and keeping her child.

My father didn't want me to follow my husband. I think he knew a little about my husband's mother, and he said all of my husband's relatives are Chinese, and he worry only me Vietnamese. He worried; he said I must stay in Vietnam with him. So I think I love my husband, I love my father, so I think if I stay in Vietnam, my children didn't have a father and they feel a lot of trouble, and I think all my life I will love my husband, and I decided to go with my husband. And my father agreed with me, and he said I should leave my daughter to stay with him because he loves her very much, and my husband didn't want my daughter to stay, and I am, too. I love my daughter very much; I didn't want her to stay.

The boat trip to Indonesia was agonizing—seven days without food, boarded by Malaysian pirates, terrorized. Then in Indonesia, they were hungry, ill, and despondent. They had fevers and diarrhea, and one of their little girls nearly died. To earn money, her husband worked in a vegetable garden and also carried hundred-pound bags of rice on the docks. One bag fell and injured him, and he still suffers pain in his chest and back from the injury. In addition to the sufferings of deprivation and hunger that the refugees had in common, she had to endure the tyranny of her mother-in-law, who regularly reminded her of the expense of her passage. There were distributions of food for the infants and children: liquid milk and powdered milk; the liquid milk was more desirable. One day, trying to please her, Be Thi offered her mother-in-law some of the precious milk ration, but she refused to drink it, because Be Thi had touched it.

You know when I left Vietnam, I lived in Indonesia; my husband with me we felt terrible. You know, Malaysia robbed all of my money, and we didn't have money for the life, and my husband grew vegetables and sold in the market to earn money. But my mother-in-law quarreled with my husband every day. I was crying that time. I saw she liked milk water; I give to her; I leave milk powder for my children. She said she doesn't like me; she doesn't drink. I was crying; my husband said, "Why?" She said because I put my hand. I never quarreled. She told me wrong; I still don't quarrel. I think if I quarrel with my mother-in-law, my neighbors will laugh and will say that I am bad. My brother-in-law is very nice. I think in my heart when he gets married, I will help him, because he is very nice. But my sister-in-law, when we lived with my mother-in-law, she said the Vietnamese speak like a cow. I think my parents are Vietnamese, my friends' parents are Vietnamese, so I was angry when she said that and decided don't learn Chinese. So my husband speaks Chiu Chow, and speak Guangzhou, and now I want to learn Guangzhou. They just speak Chiu Chow, but Chiu Chow doesn't spend here.[4]

When they first arrived in America, they lived with an "uncle"— a friend or perhaps relative. After a short while, they were established in their own apartment and almost immediately were victims of crime.

Somebody came and took some money and some apples. I only had three dollars. That was the money I borrowed from my husband's uncle. I borrowed 20 dollars, and I spent 17, only had three dollars. And the robber took three dollars, and I didn't have more. And so I didn't have money to go to my husband's uncle. So he drove the car and came to our house, and he asked why we didn't go to see him, and my husband told him our house was robbed and we didn't have enough money to go to his house. And he lent me 40 dollars. Police came to my house, and police said, "Why five people sleep in the house didn't hear the robber come?" My husband, my children, my father-in-law and me, why didn't hear robber come? So my house was robbed on Saturday, and Monday the black man neighbor returned to me the paper from my husband's wallet. He said he found my husband's paper at his yard. And he said my husband must go to police department to report. And so then they robbed again while we were at the police department. They removed the cassette, they cut the electric in the car, and when we got home we saw the car was opened, and my husband call police again.

Police ask me, "Do you think the neighbor is the robber?" I think he is the robber, but I dare not tell the police. So, you know, I had not told about my neighbor, because he had a gun. I go to school in the morning, and in the afternoon I saw he had a gun, and he shot many, many times. I was scared. He shot in the sky. I scared, and I called my husband, and my husband asked me to take my children and leave the house. So when I go out I saw him, and he said, "Would you like to drink wine?" I said, "I don't know; I never drink wine." He said, "What would you like? Do you like cookie?" I said, "I don't like cookies." He said, "Do you like orange juice?" I said I didn't like apple juice, too. He said, "Please, tomorrow go with me." I said, "I'm sorry, I don't have time to go with you."

So my husband was scared. He said to hurry and move to the other place. So my mother-in-law hear her landlord has a house, so my husband asked her landlord. Now I live at one landlord with my mother-in-law. He is Chinese, but my house is not cheap. The other landlord was Chinese, too. When I moved, he didn't return the deposit to me. So you know when I live here, $250 every month, and I deposit one month $500. So when I fix the car, I spend about more than $1,000 for the car and the house. Very big money. I sold the car, for $300, no key. My friend helped me to pull the car to the garage, and he knows how to fix the car. He fixed it for me. Now we have another car.

I sold the car, $300, and my husband borrowed money to buy another car. And this car cost $900. Now we have two keys. And our neighbors now are Chinese; they are very kind. But when I live in Third Avenue, you know, one family was very kind — I think she is from Michigan. She come here, and she was acquainted with me, and I love her very much. She is very kind. Only is black. I think when I come here, many black people don't like Chinese. One time my husband with me go to the bank at East 14th Street; a couple of black people said "Chinese are dogs," and said it many, many times, and my husband and me don't quarrel, and hurry, hurry walk out. I dare not talk. You know now I still am scared of black people. You know on the bus, they smoke, and sometimes dancing in the bus, and sometimes turn on the music on the bus. My husband went to work in San Francisco, and he was robbed one time on the bus. When he was going to get off the bus then the black people reached in his pocket, and he kicked, and the driver asked my husband, "What!" And my husband said the man robbed his pocket, and he hurried to call the police, and the black man ran away. He tried, but he didn't get my husband's wallet.

Be Thi's parents-in-law are divorced; however, their sons paid for them both to escape from Vietnam, and they are now in America. For six months the father-in-law lived with Be Thi and took care of the children while she went to school, but she was nervous about this arrangement, and explains why:

He didn't like me. He didn't like Vietnamese. He said I am Vietnamese; he said why don't I learn Chinese, but I dare not tell him I didn't learn Chinese. He said Vietnamese usually steal something; Vietnamese bad people. He said he hated my husband because my husband is scared of me.

The father accused her of putting soap in his food, but her husband wouldn't believe it and stood up for her. She said she really loves her husband because he knows who is older and who is younger. This must be a way of saying that he is aware of the proper courtesies and observes the correct ways of behavior toward people of all ages. She struggles with the cultural differences she encounters, between Vietnamese and Chinese, between American and Asian, and white and black. She always tries to be fair and unprejudiced.

You know, Vietnamese, some people very bad, very bad. I am Vietnamese; I hate some Vietnamese, too. Mr. Tran in our school, he's not good. He had a little money; he said he had a lot of money, had a big house, had a lot of American goods, I deny that. No! He didn't have those things. He said he had a house one thousand dollars, and he said he will open a business, in upstairs sewing and in downstairs sell cosmetics, but I doubt it. I am Vietnamese, but many Vietnamese are like that. I think Chinese or Vietnamese, some people very bad, too. My mother-in-law says Vietnamese are not good. But now she doesn't hate me. Now, she says I go to school, my husband goes to work, and she never hates me. When my husband earns money, I ask my husband to give her 50 or 300 or 100—she very happy. She rents the films. She has a TV at home, and she rents Chinese programs, and she stays home and hears them. About one month, about $150. Sometimes she plays cards. And my husband said I stay home alone a lot, and he bought the machine to put the film inside the TV. We pay every month. Now if they have Chinese program, every night he took the film, and he watches too late, 12 o'clock, Chinese programs.

You know when I lived with my mother-in-law, I saw many men go to market, buy something, and go home and cook. I saw new for me; I asked my husband why, and he said Chinese men go to market and buy something and cook. The wife not work hard. You know, my husband, too, he cooks, and sometimes he washes clothes. And Vietnamese aren't like that; only women go to market, wash clothes, cook. The men never cook, never wash clothes. And if the man goes to the market, he only eats; he doesn't buy something and go home with it. The Vietnamese money, the women take care, but the Chinese, most men take care. But in Vietnamese only women.

Vietnamese, I am Vietnamese, but some people are very bad. When in the midnight the children were crying, the father didn't pick them up; they put them for the wife, and they never take care of the children at night. If they hear the baby crying, they were angry. Only the Chinese, if the baby at midnight is crying, they get up, they take care of the children, pick them up, and give something for them. I think that is the main difference between Chinese and Vietnamese. My husband is very kind. If at midnight my children are crying, he gets up, and he picks them up. I think if I bear a boy, he will be very happy. He will work hard, and he don't feel tired. You know, I pray every night I will bear a boy. I pray every night.

After the tape ran out, she says that she worries very much about her husband's health, and she begs him to stop smoking, but he won't. He is happy because all of his family is here, father, mother, brothers and sisters. She says, "I am the only one who is alone. I have nobody here. I worry about my family in Vietnam." She wipes the tears from her face when she says that every time she cooks pork, she misses her brother. She prays every night, and she dreams every night of her home and her father. Her husband dreams, too, of Vietnam, but not as much as she does. Her husband would like to have another baby, a boy, but she is very afraid. She had difficult labor, babies are expensive, and they don't have enough money. She says, "You know the Chinese all want boys," and her mother-in-law was very angry because both of the children are girls. He promises her that if she will have a boy then she can have her tubes tied. She tells me that I am very lucky because I have a good husband and only four children, and my husband is still happy with me. She says that Chinese and Vietnamese men are very bad; they drink too much, and gamble too much, and take mistresses, and she worries about her husband, although he loves her very much, and she hopes he will always love her. But she is afraid that if she doesn't bear the son that he wants, he might lose interest in her.

Her third pregnancy was hard on her, especially because her mother-in-law constantly warned her that if the child was not a boy, her husband would leave her. She was desperate with worry that she would be abandoned, and I regularly assured her that she would be taken care of, and the baby, too, even if it is a girl.

MARCH 16, 1982

I went to Merritt Hospital to visit Be Thi, who called yesterday to say her baby had been born Sunday evening after 10 hours of labor. It was a third girl. All I saw was a little round head and black hair. According to Be Thi, she looks like her father. He is resigned—says if God sends him another girl, he has to accept it. The mother-in-law went home from the hospital and told everyone that the baby is a boy. An aunt came today and was surprised to learn it's only a girl. Be Thi has gained weight and looks lovely but very sad. She said of the baby, "When I see her, I love her, but I'm afraid." The father insists she bottle-feed so that she can soon get a job and leave the baby in the care of the grandmother. Be Thi is afraid she won't care for her well. Be Thi hasn't heard from her father or brothers in eight months and is worried that they have died. Tomorrow, she goes home. Her husband took two days off from work to care for the three- and five-year-old girls. He says she can wait seven years to try again for a boy. The doctor is very nice and told her that when she comes for her checkup he will tell her about a diaphragm.

JULY 1983

Be Thi called recently and begged for help to find a house-cleaning job. She has had to drop her typing class because she didn't think she could get a job anyhow, and she couldn't continue to pay the 10 dollars per day her friend charges for babysitting. After all, the grandmother had refused to help with babysitting because all the children are girls. The husband is working at a relative's sewing factory and makes less than $500 a month. A few weeks ago, they didn't have money for milk for the baby and had to borrow from a friend in Berkeley. Her husband's own family don't help them. They are now receiving food stamps and are in the WIC program [food supplements for women, infants and children]. Her husband still smokes heavily. Her father-in-law has moved in with them but doesn't give them any money to help with expenses. He also will not speak to her, but makes oblique remarks to other people about how terrible the Vietnamese people are. She tries to speak to him and tries to cook food he will like, but he won't eat

*with them. She said since she has no father, she wants him to be like a father to
her. "I know who is older and who is younger," she said.*

SEPTEMBER 1983

*Be Thi is working for four American women, doing housework. She is happy
because she now earns about 36 dollars per day. She received a letter from her
father, and on the next day, a letter from her youngest brother, the one who was
a month old when her mother died.*

SPRING, 1984

*Be Thi now has steady housekeeping work and no longer gets welfare, food
stamps, or WIC assistance. But her rent has been raised, and if she is sick, or her
employers go out of town, her income stops. She asked to be paid her bus fare,
which amounts to $1.50 a day, and her employers all refused.[5] She works for
several neighbors who are friends and hold together on wages and benefits. One
whose husband was a partner in one of San Francisco's most prestigious law firms
said she couldn't afford to pay more because he is retired now, and Be Thi is need-
lessly worried that they may be having a hard time. Her employers have put her
on the Social Security rolls but have not given her any raise to compensate for the
fairly sizeable loss in take-home pay, at a time when all other costs are going up.
She asked for a raise, and says one employer told her, "That's your problem," and
added, "You know, you can't get any job that's better than this, because you don't
speak English well enough." She cried when she was told this. Nevertheless, she is
forgiving and generous. One employer had a large family dinner on a Sunday,
the day before her husband was entering the hospital for hip surgery. Be Thi
worked that day to help her and refused pay for it because she felt sorry about his
surgery.*

SUMMER 1984

*Be Thi tells me she has a brother in Vietnam who married since she left and
who already has two or three children. She also has a female relative who has
eight children. She has written to each of them saying what she has learned in
America about family planning.*

NOVEMBER 25, 1984

*Be Thi had the day off on Thanksgiving, until five o'clock, when she went
to work for one of the American women. It was a beautiful sunny day, so she
washed her family's clothes, by hand, in the bathtub. Her husband had one shirt
that he liked especially; it was his best one. She washed that, and also his best
pants and other clothes. The clothes were stolen from the line, and she is sure they
were stolen by their neighbors, other Vietnamese. She says, "I dare not tell the
police, because then they would be angry and do something worse."*

They have a two-bedroom apartment and rent one bedroom to a Vietnamese couple in return for babysitting service. This has been an improvement; the father-in-law has gone, and she likes this couple. They can't move to a better neighborhood for two reasons — there is no place better that they can afford; and the babysitter insists on living within walking distance of the gamblers' special buses that go to Reno each weekend and come back in the middle of the night. She is gambling her welfare money and claims she comes out well ahead every week.

JANUARY 1985

Be Thi is concerned about her husband and his job. He has worked for a long time in a sewing factory, first as a buttonhole maker, and now as foreman. There are only seven employees, some of whom are part owners. Their landlord, who is Chinese and, according to Be Thi, very nice and good to them, is also one of the owners. Her husband, however, is unhappy as a foreman and wants to quit. This morning he planned to talk with the landlord, and perhaps he won't finish the day. He is responsible for making the employees work, and one difficulty is that they all talk and won't listen to him. One of the employees is an undocumented alien from China and has a borrowed social security number. He isn't a good worker and won't listen to instruction, but has the protection of his aunt, who is one of the investors and also an employee. If her husband quits this job, getting another could well depend on whether or not this contretemps damages his network.

FEBRUARY 16, 1985

Be Thi came today. She was going to Chinatown to buy some medicine that she claims helps her to sleep and eat better. She says she has no appetite, and she is alarmingly thin. She wants to work all the time, because if she doesn't work, she begins to worry. She talked about her suicide attempt of two years ago. She says her husband now gives her his paycheck and no longer gambles, although he gives money to his brother, who goes to Hong Kong to gamble, which angers her. He still smokes heavily. Her husband sometimes "talks very loud" to her, and this makes her unhappy. However, he must be awfully weary; he picks up the garment workers early in the morning in the company car and delivers them again in the evening, and usually doesn't get home until after 10 o'clock, 6 days a week. It wouldn't be surprising if he felt like shouting at someone. Together they make two thousand dollars a month and no longer get any public assistance, food stamps, Medi-Cal, WIC, or welfare. They don't have a car but can sometimes borrow one for shopping.

She worries that they have no medical insurance. Her husband's boss tells them that if they have insurance they will still have to pay 20 percent of their medical costs, and that if they need medical care or hospitalization and have such low income, they would only have to pay 20 percent anyway, so they are ahead without insurance. Her younger brother, the one she raised from infancy, is living in the forest to avoid military service and writes that he desperately needs clothes — jean pants and jean jacket. He says if she really loves him, she will send them to him. But she is reluctant to do this because she thinks he wouldn't receive them, and it would just waste her money. What she hopes to do is to find someone here in the refugee community to whom she can give money for assistance, and in exchange their relatives in Vietnam will give money to her father and brother. She says there are a lot of people in Vietnam now who are making a lot of money and are willing to do this, in exchange for help given to their relatives here. But they only want to do it in hundred-dollar increments, it seems, and she doesn't have that much money yet. Her husband pays for rent and utilities; the other expenses of the household are all her responsibility. One of her employers has cut back to one day every other week, and she can't find anyone who will hire her for the alternate days, so this is a loss of about a hundred dollars a month.

LATE FEBRUARY 1985

Our class was invited to visit a sewing factory. The proprietess is related, either directly or by marriage, to a number of the students. Two of them, cousins, are grandchildren of her father by his first wife. Her husband is the uncle of Be Thi's husband. The women and a few men who work there all appeared to be happy to have visitors. I recognized several of them as former students. The factory is upstairs, well lit and fairly spacious. The sewing machines appear to be well maintained, whirring quietly, and the workers keep a steady, but not frantic, pace. From an anteroom comes the smell of sesame oil and rice steaming.

MARCH 2, 1985

Be Thi's babysitter left this morning at five for Reno to gamble. She is still on welfare, but she sent a hundred dollars last month to Vietnam, and was angry because whoever she sent it to was cut short on the exchange and didn't get as much as she expected.

MAY 23, 1985

I talked with Be Thi a few days ago on the phone; everything is going well for them. The girls are all well, the older two liking school, and the youngest now talking. Her husband's sewing factory has moved to a new location just a block or so from their house, so he walks to work, and he is making good money. He works late at night but comes home for supper. On Sundays they go shopping and sometimes visit friends. She was really very happy. But a few days later, it was another story. A Chinese from North Vietnam had come to the factory, with a gun barely concealed under his shirt, and demanded five hundred dollars. Her husband told him he didn't have cash there, and neither did any of the workers. The man is a member of a gang called the Black Tigers, and she says they are Viet

Cong who are on welfare and have nothing to do but sit around all day, smoking and playing cards, and working a protection racket. They have been going to grocery stores, restaurants, and sewing factories. Her husband stalled the man for two hours, offering him a job if he needed money. The man's pitch was partly that he needed money for his wife and children, and that he should be given the money for that reason. However, he wasn't interested in a job. Finally he agreed to leave, but said he would return the following Thursday, and then if he didn't get the money, he would smash the machines or shoot someone. Be Thi's husband conferred with his landlord, who is also the owner of the factory. He is a Chinese who has lived here for 20 years or more, owns a lot of houses and apartments, and has invested a hundred thousand dollars in equipment for this factory. They agreed that it was foolish to call the police to catch this one man, because if they let the gang go at large, they would just retaliate. So this time they will try to pay just three hundred dollars and threaten to call the police if there is a next time.

A few days later, Be Thi had a letter she had written to send to the police, telling all they know about this man — his name, where he lives and where he hangs out, and who some of the other gang members are. I called my contact at the OPD, with her permission, to alert him that the letter was coming. She was rightly fearful of being identified, but had sublime confidence in the American justice system; I hope we can maintain that. But she asked, "I wonder why does the United States let the Viet Cong and these bad people come here? Why don't they send them back to Vietnam?"

September 18, 1985

I returned last week from our trip to Scandinavia, and it's hard not to be mawkish about returning to America. It was epitomized by my trip to the bank: there were four tellers — Julie, blond, born in Finland; the others were a black, an Asian, and one who looked Pakistani or perhaps Afghan. The black and the Asian were born here. I rejoice in this variety. Trying to see our country through foreign eyes, I can see much that would not be appealing — the chaotic aspects of our society, the waste, the frivolity and ostentation that are so evident; I notice how dirty our streets are, in contrast to those we saw on our trip.

My class this term has an enrollment of 43, all Chinese of one sort or another, one from Brazil, and others speaking a variety of Chinese dialects. They seem to be more advanced and clever than other classes I've had. All write well. After the first class, one young woman stayed to tell me that she "very liked" my teaching and "very enjoyed" the class.

Be Thi called to welcome me home. She is well and happy — she had a week of vacation and went to Tahoe and Monterey with her family and fellow employees of her husband. In two months she will be free of debt to her brother-in-law. She has gained a few pounds, and so has her husband. He now weighs 123 pounds. But tragedy has struck again in the garment business. Her brother-in-law had a small factory that was threatened several times by Chinese from North Vietnam, and about two months ago they came, robbed all the employees of money and jewelry, beat the brother-in-law badly, poured paint on two thousand dollars worth of garments, and damaged machines as well. They warned him not to tell the police. I think, however, that he did, because in order to collect insurance, he had to. But because his driver's license, which they took, had her address on it, they have had to move for safety. They now live in a few rooms above the garment factory where her husband works, which belongs to the man who was their landlord. He has been extremely good and helpful to them, took them to Tahoe for vacation, pays her husband well, and is trying to find better housing for them. Her babysitter moved with them, and she says they are very crowded. Be Thi doesn't tell anyone where she works but says she works in a bakery, to protect her American employer from getting involved in this garment business racket.

JANUARY 6, 1985

Be Thi came on a recent Saturday, bringing a beautiful flower arrangement. She was happy because they were invited to a wedding that evening. She is still struggling over her employment. One employer no longer wants her every Tuesday, and others employ her on a haphazard basis. Some of her employers say they will give her a raise sometime, but it is all indefinite. One brought her something from France, and another a sweater from England. She no longer gets subsidized school lunches for her children, because she has given her Social Security number to her employers and is paying tax. She has to pay over three dollars per day for their breakfast and lunch at school.

More significantly, she has finally repaid the four thousand dollars that she borrowed from the brother-in-law to pay for her escape from Vietnam, but now he wants her to pay him more. At that time, gold was four hundred dollars an ounce, and he had to give 10 ounces for her escape. Gold is now selling for a higher price in Vietnam, although it is lower here, and by some specious reasoning, he is trying to convince her that she should pay him for 10 ounces of gold at the current Vietnam price. My husband told her she should tell him to give her the four thousand dollars back, and she can buy 10 ounces of gold for 3,200 dollars, give it to him, and keep the 800 dollars difference.

SEPTEMBER 2003

I drove to see the shop that Be Thi and her husband have bought. In the same block are a rundown supermarket, a small bank, and a restaurant that closes at 3 P.M. Across the street are a well-known fish and seafood market, now with new owners; a tattoo parlor; and a nail parlor. Next to the shop is a bar, with a narrow doorway and no windows. Some rough-looking men are hanging around the door. Be Thi tells me they are very nice and help to protect the shop in the evening. The shop has a little Buddhist plaque over the door and signs in various languages posted in the windows. The shelves are nearly bare: racks of snack food in cellophane bags, Chinese cookies, some canned goods, soft drinks. The coolers along one wall are filled with soft drinks, beer, and some liquor. There are cigarettes as well. The money maker seems to be the corner where one can play Super Lotto. A table and chairs are set up there. The wall is plastered with winning lottery tickets. An assistant is working at the cashier's counter, where there is a sno-cone or slurpy machine. Customers come and go, buying a pack of cigarettes, a newspaper, a can of soda.

Prominent on the floor at the back of the shop is an altar where a happy Buddha statuette holds a cigarette in his hand, and in front of him are a small cup of coffee with a spoon, several little cups of water, a small container of sand with burned incense sticks, a bowl of mangos, and a lucky bamboo plant. Behind him is a red plaque with gold letters, in Chinese; this, she says, is to bring good luck, so many people will come. Above eye level, on the top shelf of this rack, are several containers with green plants.

Be Thi looks very pretty today — hair pulled back with a tortoise shell barette, long bangs over her forehead. She wears some make-up and still has beautiful teeth. She wears diamond stud earrings, a jade ring, several gold bangle bracelets, and a heavy gold chain around her neck. She wears a flowered sleeveless jumpsuit, has put on a little weight, and looks healthy. She takes me by the hand and shows me around the shop. In the office area in the back of the shop, her husband is talking on the phone to her father in Vietnam, and his face lights up when he sees me. In the storage room at the very back is a much more elaborate altar, with three small statues, two of familiar Buddhas, and the third [Hindu?] with what looks like an elephant trunk and several arms. She thinks he is from Thailand. This is evidently left by the former owner. More mangos, water, incense. She says they bring flowers twice a month, and she prays here every day for good luck. Be Thi's own religion is Cao Dai, whose saints include Confucius, Jesus Christ, and Victor Hugo.

Some time ago, she says, there was a murder in the store, so it wasn't a lucky place. The neighborhood looks as though this could be a commonplace occurrence, but she thinks they are bringing good luck to it now. They can't make any money from Chinese customers, but only from blacks. She says it's good to be next to the supermarket, because people come in who don't want to wait in line there.

Be Thi as always talks volubly, sometimes contradicting herself, alternating joy and sorrow. The oldest daughter lives at home, has a good job in an office, and is planning a wedding next year. The second daughter has been married and is divorced; she lives in a house owned by her sister's boyfriend, in order to help him by paying rent. Her four-year-old son lives part time with her, part time with his father, sometimes with Be Thi and her husband; for two years when he was out of work, he took care of the child. The youngest daughter has a good job with Pacific Bell and saves her money. Now she wants to buy a ticket for her grandfather, Be Thi's father, to come from Vietnam to visit. He came once before and stayed for three months and enjoyed it but got bored with nothing to do. One of Be Thi's employers paid for his ticket to come; Be Thi went to Vietnam to bring him. Now he is older and not well, but they want to bring him here for one last visit with the family.

Be Thi has gone three times to Vietnam to visit. The first time, she had been away for 15 years and didn't know whether her father was still alive or not because no one had told her. Everything was so changed that she didn't even know how to get to his home. Her brother still runs the farm but can't make any money because it is so expensive to get the rice to market, and then he has to sell it right away, and not wait for the better price later. He also grows fruit but can't sell it for enough to make any money. It is difficult if not impossible to make money now in Vietnam, she says, but a few minutes later she is telling me that it is easy to make money there by speculation and investment. When she was there, her father told her of a piece of property for sale and advised her to buy it, for 2,500 dollars. After they returned home, they gathered 15 investors in a scheme and were able to buy it. Each one paid 200 dollars a month for 15 months. At the end of 15 months there was 2,500 dollars to buy the property.[6] Since then, the government has put in a new highway, with paving, streetlights, and flowers in the median, and the property is valued at 50,000 dollars. Someone from Australia has offered to buy it, but she wants to build an apartment block, perhaps for 100,000 dollars, and derive income from the rent.

When they called her father today, they learned that his nephew had just died and was to be buried at what will be nine o'clock this evening. She will want to pray then. The nephew was only 42. She thinks he died so young because life there is so hard.

She came here in 1980 and began her first housekeeping job over 20 years ago. That employer's husband, before he died, exacted a promise from Be Thi to continue to work for his housebound widow, and she has kept this promise while also working at the store seven days a week. In recompense, she will receive a bequest when the widow dies. She still works for two or three other women who have been good to her, paying for plane fare to Vietnam; they call her "honey" and tell her they love her.

Be Thi's sister-in-law, now widowed, lives with the mother-in-law, who yells at her every day and says she hurts all over. The doctor says she won't live much longer, but she wants them to send to China for a worm that costs a thousand dollars for just one worm and will make her better if she eats it. She also wants the bird sputum — what bird's nest soup is made of — which also costs a thousand dollars, and the daughter-in-law, who makes $6.50 per hour at a sewing factory and has two small children of her own, feels obliged to buy it for the old lady because she yells at her so much. She also wants Be Thi's husband to take his mother to Reno to gamble, but he has said he is too busy now.

Be Thi reiterates how lucky she is, how grateful she is for her housekeeping jobs. She says when she started, they only had two dollars. She is happy and bubbly but gradually begins to lose her fizz, and the tears come. She wonders about going back to Vietnam when she retires. She says with real conviction, "But I am so lucky to be here." The subject of my writing a book came up naturally; another of her employers had told her that she should write a book about her experiences. So when I tell her that I want to write the book for her, her eyes brighten and she claps her hands with delight. When she tells her husband that I want to put their life in a book, he, too, is pleased. He is tall and terribly thin, charming and polite; his English is careful and very clear. He thanks me very graciously for coming. As I am leaving, Be Thi bursts into tears; he smiles kindly and says, "She is happy. She is always like this."

In 2004, on September 16, Be Thi agreed to another tape-recorded interview. She still works as a housekeeper for several of the same women; the store is open seven days a week, and she and her daughters work there evenings and on weekends.

For Linda's wedding, we closed one day, Sunday, and the customers complained about it. Because most of the customers, they come every day. They are so nice. They come for lotto. They love it so much. The track, on 200 dollars we make about 12 dollars. But the lotto, 3 percent. But if a jackpot, then just ½ percent. But it's okay. We don't sell much canned food, because most of Chinese don't go over there; they buy in Chinatown. So we just sell beer, wine, water, and some soft drinks, like that, and some chips. Bread, but not much. Because some people don't like to go to supermarket, get in a long line; they just like to go over there and get it and go.

Before, in the morning, from nine to one o'clock my husband was alone. And after the day he was robbed, we have one man stay there with him in the morning just to stay by the door, so always two now. And evening, is difficult, so after work I have to be there, so more people, is better. In the evening, I be there, and the kids be there, too, three or four is better. Because you know it is dark at six o'clock or seven o'clock, and we worry about that. We were robbed in the daytime, yes, and then almost seven o'clock, evening. I worked at Mrs. D's, and I called my husband, and nobody picked up the phone, and I said, "Oh, something is wrong." And then I worry about it, and I call back, and then the guy work there, he said, "We were robbed, and we are waiting for the police to come. Oh! This the first time. And I went home, and the police were there; two weeks later came back, the same man. He robbed about 14 stores in Oakland. Each store, he go one time first. And then he came back the second time. And then he came back a third time. Our store, he came the first time, and then the other store, he came the second time already, and the police let us know on Wednesday night. And they said, "He will be back in your store, and you have to be careful. Because each store, he come twice. And then we are scared, too. So the whole family stayed evening at the store. And then Thursday night, he got caught, and we were so happy! He robbed the store near his house, and the Vietnamese girl knew his face, and she followed him to his house, and then she called the police. And the police got in his house, found some guns in there. So he is in jail now, but we don't know when he will get out.

We bought the store in March, 2003. More than a year ago. And we were robbed two times, [whispers] black people. And then at home, when we go home, we worry about Chinese. Because you know, we never know. Mexicans have gangs, too; Vietnamese have gangs, too, Chinese have gangs, too. And so at home we have to watch. Lucky, our store is near the bank. So we put money in the bank every day. It is difficult. I think we will be paying at least two more years. But, well, we keep praying every day. Work is still okay, and I have enough money to pay. Sometimes it's hard; the business sometimes go up, sometimes go down, and we never know.

My husband was working for a sewing factory a long time ago, and then after that, when the government sent some work to Mexico, and then at that time he cannot make money anymore. And then we close, and then he worked for the design of clothes, about two years; they closed out business, too. And then he had no job for three years. And he stayed home; he feel awful. Yes, he was laid off one year before Tina had the baby. After that, he worked a little bit, and then they closed down, and he stayed at home and took care of the grandson. And after three years, he said, "Oh, no, I want to work because it's so sad. Boring at home." So he went to the store we bought and bought the newspaper every day. And then he saw the sign to hire people at the weekend, and he said, "Okay, I'll just come to work on the weekend, and get some money, Saturday and Sunday, seven hours a day." That helped a lot, you know. And then he worked just about a year, and then the owner said he wanted to sell the store. And he got home, and he said, "Oh, he wants to sell the store, so how will we do when I have no job!" And I said, "Oh my God." He is so happy to work, you know, and he worries that at his age and he has no skill; it's difficult to get a job.

We feel sad, and I sat down, and I said, "Oh, I wish I had money to buy the store." And suddenly the phone rang! The phone ring is the lady, is also a friend too. And then we talk to her about it, and she said, "Oh, I will help you." And I said, "How?" She said, "You should refinance your house, and buy it." I said, "Oh, I didn't think about that." And she said, "Okay, I can help you if you really want to buy it." And she did. But we didn't think about refinancing the house, you know; we want to pay off. So after that, when she talked to me, I said, "Okay, let me think about that." And I talked to my husband, and talked to the kids. The kids say, "Dad is old, and I think it's rather buy the store for him to work than he go somewhere else." So I said, "Okay, I call her back the next day; we want to do that." And she helped us buy the store. That's why we pay higher on the house now. The store, we rent, that's $2,300 a month. We just own the store, but the property, we don't own. I wish—I told my husband some day if we have money and they sell it, we will buy it and fix it up. That business area is good. But I don't think they will sell it. The owner is Chinese, too. They worked in the sewing shop with my husband before.

My children help, too, on weekends. Monday, because just one man helps my husband, they stay home and help. But weekends, Saturday, we really need them. They have to go to the wholesale store and get the stock. And then Sunday lots of the time me and my husband there, and let them rest, and sometimes they are not busy and they come on Sunday. But sometimes they have their own things to do. But you know, the kids work seven days a week, too.

Linda is expecting her first baby. She and her husband live together with us. He works in Novato, sound engineer, a good job, but the problem is, far, far away. He's Japanese. His mom is in Japan; his dad is here. He was born in Los Angeles.

Tina rents a room not far away. She doesn't like to live together. She says, "Mom, I want to be free!" Okay, so she wants to move out, so that's okay. Not far away, and her kid, some days stay with us, some days stay with her, and some days stay with daddy. He's Vietnamese. So that's why the boy stays us with most of the time; we love him so much. Tina worked for Pacific Bell seven years, so she has a good job there. She loves it so much. She didn't finish college. She's the smart one in the house; you know that.

Jeanie lives at home. She has a boyfriend, but not married yet. She says, "Mom, I want to work, and I want to save money to buy a house." And she says, "When I buy the house, I say, goodbye, Mommy." She is—she is quiet, so different from her sisters. She always thinks—I don't know how to call it, but she organizes her life, so good; she always thinks something in the future. She says, "Mom, I am thinking that I want to buy a house." She finished college.

I started to work 21 years ago. Do you remember the first time, it was so difficult? I worked for Mrs. C. And then six other ladies. Look like yesterday, but such a long time—I can't believe it. Mr. C., before he died, he said, "Honey, how many years?" And I said, well, 20 years. And he said, "Oh, my God, look like yesterday." And then before he died, he said, Honey, if I die first, you stay there and take care of mom and take care of the house. I know when we are gone, everybody needs you, but *please, please,* don't go. Wait for the house to sell, and then leave." I promised that, so I have to stay. Also Mrs. D. and Mrs. P. say, please don't leave them. So I love them so much. My job is like my family. They all love me, and I love them, too. That means a lot, you know.

Mrs. D. wants me to go over there to take care of the house. She lives at Tahoe, but back and forth. She loves to be there very much. He died just five days after Mr. C. That was terrible. Mr. C. died on the third, and Mr. D. on the eighth! Difficult. Both of them were so nice, too. They all do pay Social Security now. At first I didn't want to. But after that, Mr. C. said, "Honey, you have to do it. When you are old, you won't have money." And he talked with Mr. P. and the people I work for. He is so special man, too. I'm lucky I got in there. Do you remember I didn't want to work, but after that, she was so nice; she taught me how to cook and brought food home for the kids, and she bought some clothes for me.

We have insurance now. When we bought the store, we have health insurance now. But when my husband was laid off, we have no insurance. We just got it back last year. It is so scary when you have no health insurance. But the time I didn't have health insurance, Mrs. D. was so nice. For teeth or something, she said, "Just go to the doctor, and we pay for you." So they are wonderful. Last Monday she called me from Tahoe. I worked for Mrs. P., and she said, "Honey, you came to this country; you grow up in Vietnam, and a lot of things you have to learn. And if you don't know anything, you have to talk to us, because we care about you; we worry about you." The first time we bought the store, Mr. D. was so sick, but he worry about all the paper we have to sign, and he said to bring to him, and he have to see it, but you know, he was so short of breath, so I dare not to bring to him, so we have a lawyer. So I told him, "Don't worry; everything will be okay," but he said, "Honey, not 150 dollars, 150,000 dollars — you have to know that. So you have to be careful." They were so nice.

We don't have enough money. We paid 135,000, but we had to remodel everything. Dirty. The store, seven years didn't clean. The ceiling, the health department came out and said we had to do — I don't know how to call in English — but rough ceiling, we have to do that. The floor is broken, so that's why the total, the whole thing, is $150,000. So we still owe the owner $35,000. So until April 2005, no more. So we cannot wait. So we keep going. I told my husband, "How is it, work seven days a week?" He said, "Oh, I like it." I know it's work hard, but he need a job.

My mother-in-law lived with the younger son until she died. She died last year, 76 years old. She smoked, you know. And went to Reno. Oh, she loved it so much! She wants to, so we have to give her money, one hundred dollars, something like that. And she went over there to Cache Creek [*casino*]. When she was sick, my husband and his brother brought her one time before she was gone. She went over there almost every week! One time she wanted my husband to go to Reno with her, and I was so upset. I talked to her and said, "You know, you cannot bring my husband over there every week." And I know she was mad at me, but I don't care, let her mad, because my family, and then my husband understand, and he didn't go, and then when the doctor told her that she just lived for six months, and then my husband and his brother, both of them brought her there, so that's okay, before she is gone, she liked it, so just a few times. And she did win money. She lucky, I guess. She didn't give any money back to us. Oh, no. Just for her to make her happy. The last time that she was sick, her hands were shaking. My brother-in-law called my husband, "How about that we all go together with her one time," so I did, went with the three sisters-in-law and three sons together, seven of us; we went the last time to Thunder Valley [*casino*], and the whole family want her to be happy. Her hands shake; she couldn't open her purse to get money. She had fun, but she didn't play much. Slot machine. She loved it so much. Because you know, in Vietnam culture, the kids work and give money to their parents, so she's thinking over here we have to do that, too. But that's okay, we give her, but have to save money because gambling never get it back, never.

My father is still alive in Vietnam, and the doctor said he will live until the end of the year. You know, on Linda's wedding, I didn't think my dad came, but Jeanie, the week before she got a job at Pacific Bell, she said, "Mom, when Linda's wedding, will you bring grandpa here?" And I said, "Oh," because my dad cannot speak English, you know, and then he have to be here. Mrs. M. helped me to pay the ticket; he came here three years before that. And then I went home, pick him up, and brought him home. But this time, if I go home, because we have a lot of work, we have the store, and I cannot leave. But she said, "You have to think about your dad." We want him to be here to see all of us. And then I think, she is so nice, she talk about that. But I said no. And then two weeks later she said, "Mom, what did you think? You have to think about your dad, how long he live. And our family cannot go home to see him. Why don't you bring him here? I pay the ticket for Grandpa."

The second time she told me, and I cried, and I didn't think she thought about that. And okay, so I called my dad and my dad said, "No, I don't want to come." And after that I called him the second time in two weeks, and I said, "Dad, because you be family, about 11 people come here, so the kids say they need you." So then he said, "Okay, so I will go." He came three weeks. And then after the wedding I brought him home. I went to Vietnam with him, just 10 days. And then I came back home. After that, he was sick. Now I think in Vietnam the doctor poor doctor, you know. I sent a letter to my brother; I said, "You have to bring dad to another doctor to make sure, see what's happening in his brain and his body." So I just sent $200 for them to bring my dad to the doctor.

Send money to Vietnam, have the agency, sell ticket; we just tell them the address and give them money. One hundred dollars are four dollars, some-times three dollars. Just about one day, and they brought the money to them. And it gets there. So right now he spends just about 70 cents per day for the medicine. So 70 cents for us is okay but in Vietnam, my brother cannot make money to give him 70 cents a day. But he took this medicine, herb medicine; it doesn't hurt anymore, so I'm so happy about that.

My father live in Tay Ninh, about one hundred kilometers from Saigon. Our family grow up in the farm. I love there, but I feel, you know, I am lucky in here. Because work in the farm is so difficult. Not much money at all. Like this time, I call my brother, said the drought over there is so hot, and rice and peanuts cannot sell because no good. So he said, "Sister, you have money; can you help me?" And I say, "Ok, when I win lottery, I can help you."

I help my father; that means a lot. I said I love all of my brothers so much because when my mom died, I am the oldest; I am 12, and the 10 and the 7 and the 4 and the 5-month-old boy. I had to take care of the baby. And when he began to talk, he called me mommy.

And each time I come home, he cry a lot when I left. He cry a lot, and he said — you know what he said? Because I told him, in this country when we get old it is difficult. Nobody take care of you; the kids have to work. He said, "No! You have to come home, and I will take care of you because you took care of me before." He is so nice. I am the big sister, look like mother, and I cooked and washed for them. When I left, it is so hard. My dad would cry every day. And missed Linda, because she was three years old in Vietnam.

The first time I came home, 15 years, my brother said, "The time you left at home, not enough rice to eat, not enough money," and they had to move near Cambodia and work there to make money, but so difficult. So they cooked rice soup every day to eat because not enough rice, you know. And they didn't know where we were, and after that, about six months, they got a letter from Indonesia that we are still alive, and they were so happy. We think about the time we left Vietnam, so difficult.

Oh, I am lucky. We are so lucky. I told Linda and Tina, "We are so lucky we are here." When they were young, they went to Vietnam. I think Linda was 12 when we went home. And then do you remember that when we left, my mother-in-law didn't want my husband to bring us here? And I was pregnant with Tina, and then she said, "No," have to leave me there, and my husband come here alone. After that, my husband said, "No, if we go, we go together; if we die, die together." Otherwise he stay in Vietnam. And she scared; she let me and Linda and Tina go, too. But I didn't know about that until we came here. And after that, my husband told me when we came here, and then I told Linda and Jeanie and Tina, "We are lucky that your dad said that the whole family; so that's why we would come here."

Otherwise, if we stay in Vietnam, "Linda, how are you thinking! Maybe you got married already, and then we work so hard, maybe have no teeth, you know have difficult life over there." And then Jeanie said, "Oh, maybe you don't have me, too; oh, lucky!" So they know about that. That time my dad said that he miss us a lot, too, but I told him, I say, "Well, my mom died when I was young — is difficult for me. Then I have to go with my husband, because I don't want to the kids to have no father." That time I was 26 years old. I said, "I'm sorry." That I say, rather for me I don't see my dad than my kids, because they are so young. Tina that time just was one month old, then three months when we left Vietnam.

We left Vietnam in June 30, 1979, then were in Malaysia for three days, and the navy in Malaysia pushed us back to the sea. And we found a way to go Indonesia and live in that island — flies looked like a beehive! Flies a lot. When we eat we have to stay in the net. That time a lot of people die again, because dirty. And drink water, came down from the mountain to the sea, and people have diarrhea and die every day. And then people buried in the hill. Oh!

And now I was thinking about that. If somebody pay me a million dollars to do that again, I would say, "No! No way!" But we don't know why that time we did; it was so scary. Six hundred people on that small boat! It was so heavy, and then people have to throw away clothes and food. Seven days. I sit like this for seven days [*huddled, with arms around knees*]. Seven days. Thank God, a lot of people throw up, but I didn't. Only me. And I sat down there, and a boy, he was sick and had diarrhea, and oh God! When we got in Malaysia, I couldn't walk, because I had seasick.

And I remember one Vietnamese couple had three daughters. He had no clothes because all the clothes was throw away in the sea, and the three daughters cry a lot; they had no food. And I had some dry meat. You know, when we left Vietnam, we cooked meat and dried it so well, and then we can eat on the boat, and then I gave it to them. Because just about three or five or six years old, you know, were hungry. And I give to them to eat. And then when we went to Malaysia, he came to me and said, "Thanks a lot; you saved the kids, were hungry and no food, and you were so nice and gave it to them. I said, well, we have to love each other, because that time if the boat were broken, we all died.

My husband and I speak to each other in Vietnamese. I want to learn Chinese, but when I married my husband, his sisters and family didn't love me at all; I didn't want to learn Chinese. I learned some Cantonese right now, but his dialect, Chiu Chow, no. In Thailand, they use it, you know. And I love it because I want to learn Chinese customs and culture. But his sister didn't talk to me, and they yell at me, and I said, "Oh no, I don't want to learn it." Because if I learn it, I know I will feel bad, so just let them talk, and I don't care. So he has to speak Vietnamese. He learned it from me. We lived with his mother about six months, and we moved back and lived with my dad until the day we left. So it's better.

Oh yes, I learned Chinese now, but not very much. My girls speak Vietnamese. They learned Chinese a little bit, Cantonese, but not my husband's dialect. And most of the time they speak English at home. And Jeanie's boy friend is Vietnamese, so she learned much Vietnamese right now, but before, I said, "Jeanie, get in the refrigerator and get" — I speak Vietnamese — "*You-lao*" — that means cucumber. She said, "Mom! Please, English! I didn't know *you-lao*."

So Linda and Tina and Jeanie, they all do well now, so that's good, and I'm so happy. Oh, lucky we are here. In this country, we don't care, boy or girl, right? So I said, "Oh thank God I'm here." You know, boy or girl just the name, but Chinese don't think about that. When Jeanie arrived, my mother-in-law said, "Girl again!" Oh, I was crying. She know that I worry, and she told my sister-in-law that I worry that she didn't love me and that's why I was crying. And I thought, well, maybe I try one more time for the boy. But I told my husband, we work so hard — no, boy or girl the same; we don't want any more. But later she learned, and also she changed a little bit. She liked the girls, but not very much. But the kids are good. Linda said, "Mom, even she is crazy, but she is my grandma." Linda said, "Mom, think about it. She left China when she was three years old, and her mom remarried again, and she lived

Be Thi with granddaughter Miya (2), and grandsons Kai (5) and Christian (12) at Monterey Bay Aquarium, 2010.

with half-sisters who didn't get along well together, and then she got married, and didn't get along well with her husband, and the kids in the family terrible, because the father and mother didn't get along well, fighting every day. So Mom, forget about that." So I'm so happy that the kids understand how hard I work, and they love me a lot.

The little boy will be six in November. He's in first grade now. And he said, "Grandma, can you bring me to school tomorrow?" And I said, "No, Grandma has to go to work." But we love to have him in the house. Everybody loves him a lot. Linda and Jeanie, if he's not home one day, they all miss him a lot and run to Tina and brought him home. When his dad left, he worried that he didn't know where did he go. He came to me and said, "Grandma, Paul not home any more." He called his dad by name; he calls his mother by name, too. Paul not home; can you let me stay with you? And I said, "Of course you have to stay with us. We love you. Stay here, honey." And he was so happy. He worried. And now he went to school, he has to pay lunch every day. And the first week his mom gave money to him. I don't like that, because if he carry money in his pocket, I worry that other kids hit him. And I went to school last Tuesday, and I paid the whole month, and then he got in line, he had no money in his pocket. He worried, and I was outside, and he said, "Grandma, I didn't have money; how do I pay for my lunch?" And I said, "Grandma paid your lunch already, so you don't have to worry." So he almost cried, because he doesn't have money. He's a very good boy. Doing everything, he be careful, you know. And he worry. I don't know how to call it. He is nervous inside. And last night he asked me again, he said, "Grandma, do I have to pay for lunch?" And I said, "Grandma will always pay; you don't have to put money in your pocket." It is so dangerous to put the money in his pocket. So I just told the school, rather we do the whole month. So we did. The teacher wrote down the name and everything.

So later, you want to write a book for all the students. Oh, good! I cannot wait to read it. Oh, God! And I am so happy to be here, too, and talk to you. If we have more time, we will talk more about what happened in my life. You know, I told them about the book that you told me, and they said, "Mom, if your life would be in a movie, a lot of people will cry, I know!" And she said, "You had a difficult life, and difficult time. And work in the sewing shop so difficult!" Jeanie was four years old, stand up in the chair, and bagging! Jeanie did, so fast to help. They stayed there helping until 10 P.M. Linda, Tina, and Jeanie, at the sewing shop, worked so hard! I remember, I never forget, Jeanie, four years old, stand up on a chair and do it [*pulling down the plastic bag*]! Working, bagging, because the blouses have to put in the bag. And then you know the law over here, the kids cannot work, but after the people gone, they help. Because we must work.

OCTOBER 13, 2005

Be Thi came by to see me on her way to work this morning. She told me anecdotes that I hadn't heard before, but which obviously made a big impression on her, to be recalled so many years later. When she first began to do housework, she cleaned upstairs one day and downstairs the next. On the day when she was to clean downstairs, her employer went out for a while, and when she returned, she went upstairs, then came down and inquired whether Be Thi had gone upstairs while she was out. Be Thi said no. But the woman had found the toilet cover up, and she claimed she always left it down, so she said she knew someone had been upstairs. Be Thi was so frightened by this that the hair on her arms stood up; she assumed that an intruder had come in an open window. Seeing how upset Be Thi was, the woman said, "I trust you, and maybe I left the cover up." Then Be Thi realized that she had been suspected of prowling upstairs. Another time, she had stayed late in the evening to help with a dinner party, and at the end of the party she overheard the host ask his wife if they should let Be Thi have some of the food, and the wife said no, so she went home without having eaten anything. Be Thi has overcome many slights, and now she says that she is lucky to work for people who love her. Her crowning accomplishment: before her mother-in-law died, she admitted that Be Thi has been a good wife.

Be Thi, her husband, children, and grandchildren went to Vietnam in 2009 for a final visit before her husband died of cancer

Left: Be Thi with a ceramic figurine, 2005. **Right:** Be Thi at her husband's second funeral, Tay Ninh, Vietnam, 2010.

on February 5, 2010. A second funeral was held for him at Be Thi's brother's home in Tay Ninh, Vietnam, six months later, in July 2010.

AUGUST 17, 2009, AN E-MAIL MESSAGE FROM BE THI'S DAUGHTER, UPON RETURNING FROM VIETNAM

We mainly stayed in my grandfather's village (Tay Ninh) which is about a two-hour drive from Saigon. My father had a lot of people care for him while we were there. He spent most days laying on a hammock watching everyone from my grandfather's porch. He saw and talked to a lot of friends he had known for many years who came to the village when they heard he was back. He was never bored since there was always about 10 people around him. Dinners were eaten on the floor but my father sat in his wheelchair nearby so he was still a part of it.

Now that he is back, he says what he misses most are the people always around him. It was an amazing trip for the entire family. I took my four-year old and one-year old along. I was so afraid of having them in a village but they did just fine. The first day there my son caught a frog, went fishing, took a nap on a hammock, rode on a scooter, saw newborn piglets, had fresh sugar cane juice, and chased chickens! My husband, who is Japanese and does not speak Vietnamese, managed to get along just fine with our family there. In the end he fell in love with them and they love him. The memories will last a lifetime.

Be Thi at her daughter's wedding, May 2009; the wedding was moved up a year early to accommodate Be Thi's husband who was terminally ill.

Just His Two Hands

"When he came, he just had his two hands, nothing else." Kim is speaking of her father, whose life, like hers, has been a cycle of migration, loss, and unremitting work, swinging from wealth to deprivation, and back to prosperity. She speaks in a straightforward, matter-of-fact tone, sometimes wiping away tears without changing expression. Some of her story is repeated in three different versions. In

the first tape-recorded interview, in 1981, when she is 34 years old and newly arrived in America, her English was limited, she was less at ease, and there was no weeping. Twenty-two years later, I took notes on an informal conversation held in her bakery/restaurant. We knew each other better then, sat close to each other at a small table, and she wept freely as she recalled in vivid detail the escape from Vietnam, especially thinking that her baby had drowned, and then finding him alone and crying on the beach.

The second tape-recorded interview took place in my home in September 2004, with her husband present. He interjected only once, to say, "Since my kids go to school, every year they don't have vacation. They stay and work hard, too, do something. Until now, don't have vacation." Kim adds, with tears running down her face, "We work hard; then my kids have a good future. That's the one thing let me to leave the country." She is not always tearful; she laughs at herself for losing her car in the parking lot, and for sentimentally keeping the first chair they were given here.

Kim recalls that as a 16-year-old in a wealthy family, she visited Hong Kong with her mother and scorned it as a dirty city. Fourteen years later, the Communists confiscated their home and business, and she had to sell her jewelry to try to keep her mother from starvation. When they left Vietnam in the night, her young son shored up his own courage and hushed his little brother's cries. They sat for three days in the boat, so crowded she was unable to move even to urinate. Arriving in Malaysia, they barely escaped drowning. In the refugee camp, she had to choose whether her duty lay first with her father or her children, and she stayed behind to care for her father when her husband took the little boys with him to America. Once reunited as a family in Oakland, with no furniture, they sat to eat around a newspaper on the floor. Years later, when they owned a bakery and worked there 18 hours a day, the children did their homework in the car riding to work before dawn, and returning home late at night. In the end, the children are university graduates and homeowners, and she regrets only that she cannot arrange their marriages according to Chinese custom. Her daughter, born here, complains that she is too strict and scolds her for working so hard; the sons, in their late 20s, telephone her twice a day, morning and evening. She is retired now, and at last she can rest.

SEPTEMBER, 1980

Kim is a sturdy Chinese Vietnamese woman who was a beginner last year, went to an intermediate class in the summer, and now tested for my class. I am her first teacher who does not speak Chinese. After a couple of days, she insisted on going back to the lower-level class. At 10:30 she was back, apologized for troubling me, and asked to return to my class! She writes very well, concentrates completely, with a slightly worried frown, and will soon be a top student. She isn't afraid to talk or ask questions. She told one of the Chinese teachers that it is hard for her to live here, because in Vietnam she had many servants and didn't have to do housework. She had a chauffeur, car, big house, and cook. When they escaped, they had to sell everything they owned, and also gave gold to some friends who needed it to escape. Now that they are here, those "friends" don't remember the loan and won't repay them.

On moon festival day,[7] she brought me four homemade mooncakes, nicely wrapped in plastic and then in a Chinese newspaper, tied with a string. A mooncake is a work of art, about four inches square and a couple of inches high, a glazed pastry casing embossed with intricate designs, auspicious symbols I suppose, sometimes highlighted in red. It encloses a hard-boiled egg yolk that is surrounded by a sweet filling, lotus or bean paste, or a fruit mixture similar to Christmas fruit cake; when sliced, the egg yolk looks like a full moon. At the stores they cost more than two dollars each, probably an hour's wage for many of the students.

I tape-recorded an interview with Kim in 1981, when she had been in America for a year and a half. She says her parents and older brother were born in Guangdong [Province], China. Her father must have been born at about the time of China's first modern revolution, when Sun-Yat Sen led the overthrow of the Qing dynasty. She calls him a farmer; probably he was a landowner. Around 1941, "because China became Communist, then my parents left China, came to Vietnam." At that time he would have been around 30 years old. They lived in the Cholon district, or Chinatown, of Saigon, where her father built up a business dyeing and selling textiles. They prospered and traveled for holidays to resort areas in Vietnam and also to Hong Kong. The family home was a four-story building, typical of that district, with the business on the ground floor, and the family living in the upper stories. Some of the six Chinese servants lived in the house. There were also two warehouses. The mother worked as cashier in the sales room.

Kim, whose name means "golden," was born in 1947, the fourth of seven children. She attended 12 years of school, studying both Chinese and French. She says she has forgotten all the French, but she remembers the alphabet and has very good penmanship. Although she lived in Vietnam, her social contacts were entirely Chinese. After graduating from high school, she learned to speak Vietnamese while helping her father as a sales clerk. This is what she recorded then, in 1981, after living for a year and a half in America, recalling her former life in a well-to-do family:

My older brother was born in China. His English is very good. He can speak many, many languages. My brother studied French in Dalat. Sometimes I must go there with my mother and visit him. Very nice. We went to Vung Tau, Bien Hoa, Ca Mau, Bac Lieu, many places. Sometimes we went to take vacation, sometimes to visit relatives. We went by car. By train must take very long time. I went to Hong Kong for vacation with my mother when I was just 16 years old. Very big buildings, but not very clean like here. They were very dirty. Many, many people in the roads. I don't like Hong Kong. I like here more. Cleaner than Hong Kong.

Before I got married, I worked for my father. I was sales clerk. I sell the cloth. My father had two businesses, one to dye and one to sell the cloth. I was a sales clerk for three years. After that, I got married. I went to school; I finished high school. I studied for 12 years. I just studied Chinese and very few Vietnamese. I know how to speak Vietnamese, but in school I just studied Chinese. I learned Vietnamese from the business. I was a sales clerk, and some customers come, and I talk with them, and then I learned more. I think it's not difficult.

Her courtship and marriage followed Chinese customs.

First time, my mother-in-law and father-in-law go to my house and take my parents and me, go to a restaurant and eat something and talk, and introduce. My father knew my husband before me. My father knew him very well, because in business. My father say he is a very good person; then I listen to my father. One week, my husband came to my house two or three times and took me outside to a movie or to the park, everywhere. The first time, my younger brother went with me, and after that we go just alone. Wedding, just the Chinese custom. To the restaurant, and fill out the marriage form. Many, many people came. Just one day, morning until night. And after 12 days, we must go back to my parents' house to visit my parents. Then my parents visit all the relatives to the restaurant and eat again. That's the Chinese custom. My husband must send me meat, oranges, and many kinds I don't know how to say in English. Then my parents must give me some jewelry and money. The Chinese custom, when the daughters get married, they must leave home and go to the husband's home.

My husband's parents have a business, flour to make cakes. I worked with my husband; I sold flour. My house is four floors, like my parents' house. Downstairs is a store, and live upstairs. First floor, put the goods. Second floor, my father- and mother-in-law. My mother-in-law is very nice. Third floor, my husband and me, and his sister and brother-in-law. Because my husband just have one sister, so she stayed there because just a few people.[8] This floor had three rooms. The house in Vietnam not like the house in America. The house is very long, maybe thirty meters long. Then you can make many, many rooms. There is a hall, and bedroom, bedroom, bedroom. The hall is at one side. One bedroom for me and my husband, one for my sister and her husband, and one for her children. The floors are of tile. Toilet the same as here. Electric lights, refrigerator, air conditioning, too, because Vietnam is very hot. Have a driver to drive the car. My husband knows how, but he had a driver to drive. In Vietnam, most businessman like that.

April 30, 1975, the country taken by Communists. Then they take all my business. In Saigon, there was no war, just in the far away. But then the Communists took all my business, and took my saving account, took all the money, took all the goods, many, many, and let our family go outside the house, and took our house. At that time my little boy was in my stomach. My little boy was born in 1976, after the Communists. In 1977 they lived in my house maybe three weeks, then they told us to go out of the house. Communist soldiers, four, they just wear the Communist uniform. They came in the morning. They just said they would live in my house for a few days. After three weeks they made us go outside, and they took the house. They slept upstairs. When we go outside, they watch you — did you take something outside? They watch all the time. When you want to go outside, they will ask you, "Where you going? Go for what?" If you say you go for shopping, to buy some food, they let you go. If you don't have a reason, you cannot go. We had to leave all our furniture. All at home, just leave alone.

We went to the relative's house, a very small house, relatives of my husband, in Saigon. I go to a flower factory, to make some flowers at that time. My husband, too, go there and make the flowers. The flowers are sent to — I don't know the name — to Russia; the flowers go to Russia, many, many flowers. It was the government factory. After the Communists, all the factories and stores belong to the government. I knew how to make the flowers before I got married. If you don't work with the government, you must do many, many hard work. If you work with the government, then you can work in the factory. They pay just 30 dollars one month.

She began to sell her jewelry for food, as the health of the family deteriorated.

After 1975 we decided to leave Vietnam, but we must wait a long time. Then in 1978 we can leave Vietnam. Tried more than one time. The first time I don't make sure, and then I'm afraid; I don't go. If you don't sure you go, you may be caught and put in jail, again. After the Communists took us out, my father-in-law and mother-in-law died because they were very sick, very unhappy, then die. My mother-in-law died, just 14 days my father-in-law died, a short time. They took my father's business, too, and then they went to live in the warehouse. My mother died, too, because my mother was very sick and very unhappy.

My father left Vietnam with my family. We think, we think a long time, but we cannot go until 1978, October. That time, the Communists let the Chinese go, but you must give them gold. When I leave the house, I take gold with me in the body. I sewed in my little boys' clothes. If no, you cannot take out. I just can get a little. And give the government; then we go. Now I don't have any gold.

The Communists, after seizing the homes and businesses of the Chinese merchants, accepted gold bribes to allow them to leave. The gold was in the form of small wafers about the size of a business card; each trade exacted its commission. The escapees had to pay either to buy a boat or to buy passage on a boat. They bribed officials for exit permits, and then they could be stopped by someone whom they hadn't bribed, or by the same official again, exacting a further payment. Once they reached the high seas, in addition to the marine dangers, there were pirates. Kim's extended family left in seven different groups, hoping to ensure that at least some would survive. They knew someone who had a boat, and they paid in advance for the passage. Twice when they arrived at the meeting place in the night, prepared for the hazardous escape, they found that the boat had already left, and that their money — several thousand dollars for each passenger — was simply stolen.

You give the gold, and then they tell you when and where you come. Then you come. I left Vietnam October 11, 1978. At night, 8 P.M. Very dark; that time very dark. Then you come to the boat.[9] I remember that night, my little boy is very sleepy. He said, "Mother, I want to go home to sleep. I don't want to stay here." He cried. And the big son, he said, "No home, the Communists took our home. If you go home, you don't have home to come." Then we cried.

We left from Vung Tau, went to Malaysia. We had food and water, but we cannot eat. We throw up. My boat is very lucky, but very dangerous, because at that time the sea has very strong air. Storm, very dangerous. Then my husband saw the two fish, very big, very big. After the storm, the two fish go away. I don't know why. Nine people went. My husband, me, and two sons; my father; my younger brother and his wife, and two children. Now I have two sisters who live in Vietnam. One brother lives here with my family in Oakland. One brother in Los Angeles, one brother in Hong Kong, one sister in Australia, and two sisters still in Vietnam. We left at seven times. Because go by boat is very dangerous. If you go one time, maybe you will all die. We go seven times. Because you leave, the government take your home.

When at last they succeeded in leaving in a small crowded boat, they could carry only a small bag of personal possessions, which included her precious book of patterns for silk flowers. She arrived here, confident that she would be able to make money, only to learn that to buy the supplies to make the flowers costs far more than the selling price for imported ones. She gives me two red lilies with green leaves and yellow stamens in a white milk glass goblet filled with white sand. They look almost real. She took a baking course at the community college and learned to bake cakes and pies, which she decorates with great skill. She also makes delicious and attractive Chinese and Vietnamese dishes such as pot-stickers, spring rolls, and mooncakes; unfortunately there is a limited market for them. She tried to work as a domestic cook, but she had to pay a babysitter, and it was impractical. So far, none of her abundant skills are needed in the world she now inhabits.

Before I came to America, I don't know anything. I just hear America, and many soldiers in Vietnam to help Vietnam. I think they are very kind; they help our country. If no the American help Vietnam, maybe Vietnam will become Communist sooner than 1975. I stayed there in Malaysia 14 months. We just know America is a big country in the world. I don't know where to go, and I know America is a very nice place to come. I came by airplane to San Francisco. My brother and my sister-in-law came first. We lived with them, and now we are neighbors. When I go to school, I leave my sons with my father, in my sister-in-law's house.

Now my brother works at Granny Goose, but just on call. And I work at Granny Goose, on call, too, but my brother work a longer time than me. I came to the United States December 28, 1979, after Christmas. When I came to America, I don't know English, even thank you and excuse me. I began in Mrs. Soo-Hoo's class. I knew the ABC's, the same as French, just the pronunciation is different, and the grammar is almost the same. After I came to Oakland one week, I went to Mrs. Soo-Hoo's class. At that time, I am very scared. I can't understand what you explain. I went back and talked to Mrs. Soo-Hoo. "I can't understand; I want to stay in your class." She said, "No, you must stay in Mrs. Lee Swent's class. She is very nice. If you work hard, you can learn more. If you work easy, you cannot learn English." Then I stay.

She remembers the exact date, March 23, 1981, when she entered a CETA (Comprehensive Employment Training Act) job training class to study baking. Her husband is also in job training.

Now, I just study on my English. After that, I hope I can find a job. Then we can live here and very happy, because the United States is very nice. My English is poor; I think maybe I can just do factory work. My husband's English is poor, too; I think maybe the same. I don't think we can have a business again. I have many friends in Los Angeles; they told me to go to Los Angeles. I think I don't have enough money to move. If you move, you must have money to pay the rent for two months. Then I don't move.

My father is 71 years old. The Chinese people, 71 is very old. My father is not very strong, because he worked hard in Vietnam. When he came to Vietnam from China, he just had his two hands, nothing else. Then he must work very hard. And now he is not very healthy. He wants to learn English, but he can't. He doesn't know how to play cards. He just talks. When some friends come to my house to visit, then my father is very happy to talk with them. When nobody comes to the house, then my father just stays alone, very sad. We go to school or go to work, nobody home, just my little boy with my father. After school, my nieces and nephews go to work.

Here is very big country. Many buildings, very good. In Vietnam no such kind of building. The roads is very big. Many, many is very surprise for me. Very interesting for me. Here, I don't know where I can go for religion. In my house, I just do in my house. Cannot do the same in Vietnam. In Vietnam you can go one place and pray, very beautiful. We go there one month, two times. I don't know, and I don't have enough money to go there, maybe must spend money. I don't try to go.

MAY, 1985

Kim called; she and her husband have bought a bakery in Marin County, north of San Francisco. He has quit his job in a restaurant, and they both work in the bakery, 18 hours a day. She completed the baking course at Laney College and one day brought me a beautiful custard pie, perfectly decorated with whipped cream. They have left their children here with relatives and come back on Sunday to visit them. They have a room or apartment in San Rafael where they stay during the week. There are several bakeries now in Chinatown, all doing a land-office business in cakes. Kim told me to tell my friends that she makes good birthday and wedding cakes. Unfortunately, the artisan bakeries that do well among my friends sell bran muffins and whole wheat bread.

JULY 13, 1985

I visited Kim at the bakery. It's near the freeway, in a light industrial area, a block from a fast-food drive-in. The location is good, and the facility looks excellent. The building is new, light and attractive, and the bakery looks large and clean. She seemed thrilled to see me and introduced me proudly to her husband, a nice-looking man, very well-mannered. The two little boys were also there. They have a complete menu of Chinese dishes to take out, as well as a cooler with soft drinks, and several tables so people can eat there. A refrigerator case is stocked with apple pan dowdy, cream puffs, eclairs, wrapped squares of carrot cake, and several beautifully decorated layer cakes, all made there, as well as burritos, corn dogs, and filled rolls which she buys from someone else. Against the other wall are two glass cases of croissants, turnovers, sticky rolls, shortbread squares, brownies, coffee cakes, Danish pastries, and cookies. All of this they make themselves, most of it every day. Except for the croissants, everything is thick with frosting and/or fruit pastes. The bran muffins are covered with syrup and chopped nuts. On the counter was a big vase of silk flowers, a reminder that this was what Kim had expected to be her marketable skill here.

I had coffee, a cherry turnover, and a bran muffin. She gave me a fistful of their cards to give to my friends, as well as a list of their Chinese take-out foods, which are very inexpensive. They have Mongolian beef, kung pau chicken, and mu-shu pork as well as egg rolls, won ton, fried rice, and chow mien. If their health lasts, I think they can make a good business. For the moment, they are certainly exploiting themselves to the limit.

EIGHTEEN YEARS LATER, JULY 12, 2003

I visited Kim at the bakery. Her husband Henry is very friendly. The kitchen is large, immaculate, very orderly. He cooks me a big serving of prawns with *veggies over rice, served in a carry-out box, enough to serve four people. It is Saturday, so business is slow. She wears diamond stud earrings, she says given to her by her mother. Also jade bangle bracelets, and two diamond rings. She explained the lottery system: they have had several winners over $40,000, one of $71,000; they missed by one number a huge prize of many millions.*

I ask about interviewing her again, and she is willing. Today she talked very freely. When she occasionally mopped her eyes I knew she was weeping, but otherwise, there was no change in her expression or tone of voice. This time, she tells in more detail about their escape from Vietnam. Clearly, the recollection of arriving in Malaysia was almost unbearably painful, and she never recounted it for either tape recording.

These are notes from this conversation: They left Vietnam in a 20-foot [20-meter?] boat with 300 people crammed in. It was so crowded she couldn't move for three days. Baby on lap, toddler at side. Toilet? Says she didn't go. Because they were friends of the captain, they paid extra to sit in the cabin. Very terrible. She indicates rocking motion. Malaysia refused to let them land, but the boat was already broken, so it just ran aground, then tipped over. All the children were thrown out in the sea and passed by hand to shore. Kim was the last to leave the boat. She pushed her father out the window into the water; then she left. She found the older boy, but thought the little one had drowned; then she found him off by himself, sitting in the sand and crying. She weeps at the recollection. They stayed a year on the island. There was no water. They dug a well in the sand, water seeped into the hole, and people spent all day in line filling cups, very slowly, to get enough to drink. The Red Cross gave food, but it was sometimes bad, never much. She gave most to her father.

Her first teacher told her to speak Chinese at home so her children would learn it. She agrees that this was good advice, because her Chinese is better than her English. Her older son graduated from UC–Berkeley and works for a computer company in Sunnyvale. Her younger son graduated from UC–Irvine and works for a bank. Both sons telephone her every morning and evening. Her daughter, now 19, is an undergraduate at UC–Berkeley, lives with three girl friends, and comes home on weekends.

She is concerned about finding a husband for her daughter. "I can't get used to American customs. Girl have boyfriend, break up, get another boyfriend. I tell her it's not good. In Chinese custom, children stay close to parents. Here they all go away. I can't get used to it." She weeps again. Daughter says she is too strict, as if she lived in China 50 years ago. She also scolds her mother for working too hard and never taking a vacation.

They now live in the East Bay, but the children went to schools in town where the bakery is. The children rode to the bakery at 5 A.M., helped there, then went to school, helped again in the bakery, and then did homework in the car. She no longer bakes cakes except to order. Chain grocery stores have taken that business. They bake their own bread and rolls. Lunch business is also down now. Several times she spoke of the economic situation. Workers now bring lunch from home or go to Wendy's to buy a burger for a dollar. Several people, obviously steady customers, came in to buy a drink or a lottery ticket. One came for a takeout order. Few people work in that industrial area on Saturday.

NOVEMBER 11, 2003

It was a holiday for many people, but I knew Kim's bakery would be open. I called her at 9 A.M. and she was happy to talk. Many times she said, "You call me any time, just to talk. I'm happy to talk with you." She is too busy now to meet on a weekend because two of her children have bought houses and are moving; mortgage rates are low, only 5 percent, and it's a good time to buy a house. I said, "They are doing very well," and she said, "No, they work very hard." Twice more she said, "They work very hard."

At Christmas time they will close the bakery for a week and go to Calgary to visit her sister-in-law, now a grandmother. After the holidays she will have time and wants to talk with me, although she says she is getting old now and doesn't remember everything. On September 10, 2004, she and her husband come to my house for the interview. Now she uses his last name as hers, conforming to American custom. She brings me a live jade plant in a pretty Chinese ceramic pot. I display the gift that I have kept from 23 years ago: red silk lilies in a milk

glass goblet, and she is pleased. We recall that at the time of the earlier interview, she was working on call at the potato chip factory, and her husband worked at a restaurant in Orinda.

At first I was working on call. Just pack the chips in the bag and watch the machine. On call means any shift, nobody show up, then they call you, and you go right away. I take the bus. I take care of the children by my husband. When I go at graveyard shift, I had to go to work until 12 o'clock, and one day when I go home, my two boys were asleep close by the door. When I open the door, I saw two kids asleep there.

Kim with silk flowers made by her, circa 2000. Then I just waked them up to go to bed, and they cried; they said, "Mom, you don't want to go to work; nobody at home; we were so scared." Then I quit the job. One is born 1974, one is 1976, so at that time, 1980, they were four or five years old, very little.

My husband found a job right away. He went to school in the morning, and then after that he went to work. So when he got home, about 11 or 12 o'clock, so he was very tired. Because we don't have a car, so he took the bus and then changed to BART.

When I first come, after three days, I go to school, and at this time I don't speak any English, so my older brother write me two papers. One paper is tell the driver to tell me to get off in Chinatown. Then another paper is to show the driver when I get to my house, tell me to get off. Then when I get there, I just show the paper, and they will tell me. Then you were my English teacher. Then after I finish your class, then I go to Laney College. Because my English still not too good, I just take cooking and baking. That's why I only learn how to work; I don't need to talk a lot of English. I go to Laney four years. Two years for baking, and two years for American cooking. In the morning, and after school I go to work in the afternoon at Granny Goose. Then after Granny Goose, because work on call is very hard for me, and the children, I quit that job and go work in the restaurant like a waitress.

My father died in 1988, eight years after we come to America. He is buried in Colma, near San Francisco. My older sister goes to the temple all the time, so she knows how to do everything for the ceremony. My older brother, my younger brother, and me, and my two older sisters are here now. My two older sisters came after me. Because the children came here earlier, and when they become citizens, then their parents come. I have one younger sister, but she went to Australia. If I could, I prefer to go to take a look in Vietnam because it's been a long time, and my mother was buried over there, and I want to go there and take a look, too.

Laughing occasionally, she tells about buying the bakery.

I read in the Chinese newspaper, and I call the agent, and then they showed me, and then I didn't have enough money. Then I had to borrow the money from all my relatives, to put together, and then I go buy the bakery. Henry and I together. He got to quit the job, so we got to go there, so we moved over there, and do the business over there. Then we had a very hard time. Just we were self-employed. At that time, we have the kids, can help us. So at three, four o'clock we got to go there, and then we work until seven, eight o'clock at night. So we work very hard to make a living. My daughter was born in 1983. We got the bakery in 1985. I paid my sister-in-law to take care my daughter; then she can take care my father, too. She doesn't need to go to work, so she can take care my father. So I bring my daughter, go to my brother's house, and I leave my daughter over there the whole week, so I pick her up from Friday night, so I keep her with me on the weekend, until Sunday night, I got to take her go back to my older brother's house.

In the beginning, my husband drive; I never drive. My husband taught me, tell me a little bit, because in Vietnam I already know to drive. We have a car. I learned to drive here when my younger daughter went to school, to kindergarten. The first day of her school is my first day I drive my car. I was so nervous, and I even forgot where I put my car. Because so nervous, after I take her go to school, then I couldn't find my car. I go around, around; finally I find my car.

We paid about 20,000. At this time I still don't have the money. Borrow a few thousand, few thousand, from all the relatives. Then I add the Chinese fast food. It was near the post office. Henry did the cooking and baking. I take care of the front. I make the cookies and make the bread, and then he bake it. All my kids, they help. At first, I let them stay home in the morning until about six o'clock; then I go pick them up, and go to the bakery, eat breakfast and help about two hours, and go to school. They work very hard. Before they go to school, they help until about eight o'clock; then I take them go to school. So after school they come back to the bakery; they help me out, clean the floor, clean tables, clean everywhere. After that, they do their home-work.

I sick, but I still got to go to work; I cannot close the door. Very hard. When you sick, you got to go to work. The children were so healthy, maybe sometimes just a little bit flu, something like that. They are healthy. The government took care, with Medi-Cal. So after I born my daughter and we get the business, we don't have anymore. Right now I don't have insurance. So expensive. We buy some Chinese medicine. Dentist, can't go. Too expensive.

We bought the house in 1989. Because when both parents work in the same city, your kids can go to that city. In the morning they went and go home at night the same, and do the homework in the bakery, and sometimes they even do the homework in the car. Because they don't have too much time to do it. Sunday is the only day off for me. Sunday I got to go visit my father.

Kim is concerned that she cannot find spouses for her children in the traditional way, and as she speaks of this, again she wipes away tears.

I don't know how to do it. I don't know how, because in the bakery, is no Chinese, and I don't know how to do it. That's the hard part for me. It's really hard. When you go to work all the time, so everybody moves, so you don't know how to contact Chinese friends. You see, about 20 years, now I don't know how to find all my friends. Only my family, still keep in touch. Neighbors, they not Chinese, but very nice. Talking and very friendly. Is good. When you buy a house, you only need very little payment. All you need is to work hard and pay the mortgage. They try very hard.

My husband's sister left Vietnam a few months after, also in a boat. We met them in Malaysia. Because the kids all in Canada, so they go there. Because my brother here, I got to bring my father here. That's the Chinese way. They came here a couple of times, and I went two times to Calgary to visit them. My daughter goes every year to visit them. They were very good to the nephews. Because my daughter doesn't have a sister, so my sister's daughter is just like her sister. They are very close. Cousins. They get along very well. They are a lot older than my daughter. His sister is retired now. Before, she did the clean up, and his brother-in-law worked in a factory. We talk by telephone once a week. My sons gave the cell phone to me. For the mother, they give. Because before, I don't have the cell phone, and one time my car broke down under the freeway. So I couldn't find a phone box to call, and the police came, and I had to borrow a phone to call, so after that my kids decided to make me the cell phone.

Now she reflects on the early days here as a refugee, and earlier memories return. Again, she weeps, especially recalling the difficult time in Malaysia when the family had to be separated, but she quickly regains composure and even laughs at some of their early difficulties.

I cannot speak English; I know nothing in here. Everything is so strange. Very hard. I was thinking, we work hard, then my kids have a good future. That's the one thing let me to leave the country. I talk to my children. That's why they work hard, too. They study hard.

In Malaysia, I stayed with my father, because we need Henry to come here to do the paperwork so my father can come. So at that time, my family can go together, but I go talk to the Red Cross, to say, "No, I got to stay because my father is sick, and my father is so old. I cannot leave my father here and my family go." At first they don't let me do that, because they say, your kids are so young. Only three, four years old, so they need the mother, go with. Then I say, "No, if like that, the whole family stay here. If you want my husband to go do the paperwork, then I stay here with my father until the paper is signed, and then I go with my father. Because the kids need the mother, is true, but when they go, they still have the father to take care. If I go, my father has nobody there to take care, so my father needs me, too. That's why I don't go. If you don't let my father go, then Henry has to go first." He came first to do the paperwork. My nephew came earlier and met him and the boys. Then I go with my father. Three months later I came right here, from Kuala Lumpur. Lived next door to my brother and my father. The older boy went to school, and the younger boy stayed with my father; he cannot go to school yet. He is too young.

When we come, we don't have the chair, the table, nothing. Even when we eat, we just put the newspaper on the floor and just sit down on the floor and eat. Then they bring me some chairs, some table; the people donate, and they bring. The chair and table are old; the people donated to the church and they bring to me. At least I had a chair and table to eat. At first, I had to sit on the floor, with a newspaper. I still have some old chair from that time, right now.

You have to go apply for the lottery, and they send the people, come to your store and look; then they decide to let you sell it or not. Every week we have to pay. In the beginning, not too much money. But after we sell some winning tickets, then the people come more. If they win, they are so happy, and I was so happy for my customers, too. But sometimes I just say, "Okay, don't buy too much. If you are lucky, you win, but if you're not lucky, even if you buy a lot, you don't win, so it's no way to spend too much money. Just buy a couple of dollars, is fine." I don't like to gamble! I don't have time, and I don't like it.

Money is not everything, though. On that boat in Vietnam, that was a big gamble. I got to risk everything. But we almost died. Very terrible. Before I left Vietnam, every twice a month, the first day and the 15th, they go to the temple. Come here, I don't see any temple in San Rafael, and we don't have time; we go to work every day. In my house, yes, I have an altar. Used to work, work, work, too much work, and now, too much time. I don't know now what can I do. I watch on television, some news, Chinese movie, American movie.

SEPTEMBER 30, 2004

Kim and Henry took me in their new red minivan for lunch at the Flower Lounge. I gave her the transcript and duplicate tapes of her interview, as well as the pictures I had taken, and she was delighted. She signed the agreement form without reading it; afterwards, she asked me to explain "transcribe, edit, and publish." She is pleased to have her story told. In the car on the way to the restaurant, she spoke of her daughter's plans to take a year off after she graduates next spring from UC–Berkeley. She wants to support herself and work for a year before deciding what field she will study in graduate school. Her parents don't like this and want her to stay in school. I assured Kim that what we call a "gap year" is a good idea and will help her in the long run. I told her of my daughter's similar experience, and Kim said, "Then we should tell her that we will let her do what she wants? That is the American way."

We had a delicious lunch, way too much food. I explained that in America when we say "No more, thank you," we really mean it, and they shouldn't pile more food on our plates, as is the Chinese custom. I tried to get Henry to talk, but he was happy just sitting there smiling proudly at his wife's accomplishment. He works all day in their garden; he has planted fruit trees, flowers. He never did this kind of work before, but he enjoys it now. They also have lots of bird feeders and birds. He knows several languages in addition to English: Vietnamese, Man-

darin, Cantonese, Chiu-chownese, Fukienese. Their sons have bought two houses in Contra Costa County: one with four bedrooms, one with six. Their plan is to rent them out and buy others in a rapidly growing suburb. I asked Kim whether she ever goes to a Buddhist temple, and she laughed. No, she doesn't think that matters; just "don't do anything bad."

JUNE 22, 2005

A telephone message: Hi, Mrs. Lee Swent. I am Kim. I call to tell you I move. You can reach my cell phone. I am Kim. Thank you. Bye.

I called her back. She has put her house on the market and is in a new house one block from her son's house. She is enjoying relaxing; moving was a lot of work. In two weeks she, her husband, and the daughter who just graduated from UC–Berkeley will go to Hawaii for a week to relax. They also plan a European tour before she begins to work. Kim is excited; for 25 years, she says, she worked hard and didn't go anywhere except to Canada to visit the sister-in-law. Now she is happy to relax and travel.

OCTOBER 26, 2006

I had a long phone conversation with Kim. She has just returned from a trip with friends from China, to show them sights in the Southwest, which were also new for Kim. They visited Yosemite, Las Vegas, Grand Canyon, and Hoover Dam. They stayed in Las Vegas at night, saw some good shows, and then toured from there by day. She emphasized that they did not do any gambling. Her daughter

Kim with her granddaughter and her husband, 2006.

has an office job in Oakland, and in less than a year she has been promoted to office manager "because she works very hard." She lives at home, gets up at five, and takes the bus and BART to work, so now they are hunting for a place to live that will be more convenient for her. Last year, one son paid his sister's expenses for a trip to Europe as a graduation present. Both sons together paid for Kim and Henry to go, too, and the three visited nine or ten countries, England and the Continent, for a month. They got very tired, because every day they rode the bus for nine or ten hours and looked around.

The event that she is most excited about took place early this year, when she, Henry, and the daughter flew to Texas or Florida, where they met his sister and her children from Calgary, and they all took a two-week cruise, visiting some islands. The ship was beautiful, there was a lot of very good food, and the ship sailed at night while they slept. Every morning they woke up in a different place, went ashore and looked around, and then went back to the ship for dinner and the night. They didn't get tired, as they did on the tour in France. There were many retired people on the ship; they say it is much cheaper and nicer than going to a retirement home. She strongly recommends it for me.

I remember once taking an ESL class on a short boat tour of the Port of Oakland, and how it affected the refugees from Vietnam. Some turned back at the dock, unable to conquer their fear. Others boarded but stayed inside the cabin and were afraid to look out. Another time at the Oakland museum one student was so upset by a marine painting that she couldn't bear to look at it. Kim is a strong woman whose present success has overcome, if not erased, the awful memories of her earlier sea voyage.

No Comb

Hong, 19 years old, recently arrived in the United States in 1981, told of her escape from Vietnam by land, through Cambodia to Thailand. Her grandparents were born in China, and both her parents were born in Saigon. She identifies herself as Chinese, born in Vietnam. In her family, they speak the Cantonese dialect; her father also knows the Chinese language commonly called "Mandarin." She is the third of six girls; the only brother is now nine years old. Her oldest sister, a nurse, left Vietnam by boat two days after the Communist takeover and went first to Taiwan, then to France; four years ago she moved with her husband and child to Paraguay. She came from there to visit Hong in the refugee camp in Thailand. The second sister was a cashier in an office; she led the group of escapees that included her husband and little girl, Hong, a younger sister, and the brother. Two girls stayed behind with the parents. The father had a prosperous construction business and as a capitalist was consequently in danger from the Communists.

Nevertheless, the father opposed the attempt to escape; one can imagine the agony of the mother who made the arrangements in secret, in defiance of her husband, putting at risk the lives of daughters and the only son.

Hong explains that they left Vietnam empty-handed; she did not take even a comb. This, for a teenage girl, was especially significant. They were concealed in a truck where bags of rice were piled around nine people, including two very young children. The trip took ten hours, without food, water, or toilet, and for the last five hours, their lives were in peril and they had to remain silent. After spending a few days somewhere in Cambodia, they walked to Thailand, disguised by darkening their skin and wearing sarongs. This was an arduous and dangerous journey of two weeks. In her own words:

My mother is a housewife. I helped to cook; I cook a little. Morning and afternoon I went to Vietnamese school, and in the evening, I went to Chinese school. I learned to read and write Vietnamese and Chinese. My mother can read and write Chinese; Vietnamese can speak, not write. My father can read and write Chinese and Vietnamese. My father had a car, and he drove the car himself. He was the president of his business. My old sister is a nurse. My second sister went to school, and then she took a job in a company office. I'm the third sister. The sister next to me, young sister, is still in Thailand. My two young sisters help my mother.

In 1975 [*when the Communists took over*], we were very afraid, my family very afraid. My father sold the TV and the car and his motorbike, because he was afraid of the Communists. He stopped his business; he stopped working; he stayed in the house. After 1975, the school was the same, but I don't want to go to school because very sad because my father not working. My father is very sad. My old sister went to Taiwan by boat two days after the Communists came. My sister who is here got married after the Communists came, and had her baby, and lived in a different house. Then she and her family, and I and my young sister and my little brother, left Saigon together.

I don't take a boat; I went by walking. My mother took the gold to somebody, and then he took me to go. She paid the gold for three daughters and one son. The brother-in-law paid for himself. I left in January; my mother told me December 24. My mother want me to go, but my father didn't want. Because he said, if you go, you will die. I didn't say goodbye to my father. He didn't know I was leaving. I said goodbye to my mother. She cried, and I cried. We went from my house to the truck station. The truck brings rice to Cambodia. We left my house at nine o'clock in the evening. I took very little, and in Cambodia I threw them away. I don't have any papers, a little money. My sister brought a little gold, but in Thailand bought food. My sister carried the gold; I don't have. I had nothing. Shirt and pants. No comb.

I walked to the truck station, not far. My mother had already paid the truck driver. We were under the bags of rice; the rice was not on us because they made the way. From nine o'clock we were under the rice, and at 4 A.M. the truck began to go. From 4 A.M. until 2 P.M. we came to Cambodia. The worst time was when we should pass the soldier, when they should check the truck. We stayed under the rice. A very hard time. The baby was very smart. She just had two years and a half. When we are under the rice, she says, "Mommy, we go home," and I say, "No, don't talk too loud; be quiet because there is some soldier on top, and if you talk they will catch us," so she just kept quiet until we passed the soldier station. At 2 P.M. we got out and another man I don't know took us to his house.

And then I washed, and they gave us food to eat. I was living in Cambodia about a half month, and then I went to Thailand. I took a truck again, and this time we were not under the rice. Then we had bicycles to run in the mountains. Very hard. We walk on the sand, in the woods. Many trees, and on the sand you go down and go up; very hard. About two weeks we come to Thailand. There were policemen, but I take the shirt same as the Cambodia people, put the towel on my head, and then take the sarong, same as the Cambodia people. Because that man in Cambodia take me to get the clothes. Because if the police see you, look white, you die. But the police didn't see me because I look very black.

Hong spent 10 months in a refugee camp in Thailand. Her sister came from Paraguay and somehow arranged for her transfer to another refugee camp in Indonesia. Hong was seasick for the entire five-day boat trip to go there. After eight months in that refugee camp, where she studied English, she flew to America, arriving just after her 19th birthday.

A special to the New York Times, *March 18, 1985, by Barbara Crossette, from Songkhla, Thailand:*
"Ten Years after the Vietnam War ended the 'boat people' are still coming. About 1,500 a month flee Vietnam by sea, according to United Nations figures. Another 2,000 leave monthly by air as legal emigrants under the Orderly Departure program. Hundreds try to escape overland across Cambodia to Thailand. Those who come by boat ... are no longer the rich and well-connected.... Yet nearly all of them have high hopes of a new life in the United States."

Huang Celebrates New Year with His Sister

In February 1983, Huang was absent for a week during the time of Tet, the Vietnamese lunar new year, and when he returned to class, he was eager to tell us that he went to what sounds like "Newark" to visit his sister. Since Newark,

California, is less than 20 miles away, we assumed that is where he went. No, no, he went to New York City. With the help of other students, he told the story. His sister lives in New York City and he wanted to — indeed, according to his culture, he must — visit her and wish her a happy new year. He learned that Highway 80 goes from Oakland to New York. So on a nice February day, he and two friends set out, in their shirt sleeves, or perhaps with light jackets. Taking turns, they drove and drove, and in a few days, they were in New York. They called the sister, found her apartment, had a happy time and a good dinner, and then they piled into the car and drove back to Oakland. Yes, it was a long drive, but the road was good, and the weather was fine.

He has no recollection of any mountains or big rivers; when he drove, he kept his eyes on the road, and when not driving, he slept. He doesn't realize how lucky he was not to be caught in a blizzard. He has no idea that he has driven over five thousand miles, across a continent and back. The important thing is that he had a very good time observing Tet as he was supposed to.

6

Newcomers from Cambodia

Our Mind Is Not at Peace

This man and his wife, ethnic Chinese refugees from Cambodia, requested having an interpreter for their interview in March 1983 because their English is limited, and they wanted to be sure the story was told correctly. They didn't want their names used, because they still feel endangered, but aside from these reservations, they were eager to have their story known. He does most of the talking; she bursts in to tell of her ordeal and the heroic efforts to save their children. They had gold and knew several languages; their intelligence, courage, and luck helped them to survive unimaginable horrors as they went from affluence to virtual slavery. It is generally accepted that out of a population of seven million in 1975, three million Cambodians died or were killed by the Khmer Rouge. This is the translation by a bilingual friend:

I am 43, my wife is 42. I was born in Cambodia. My father was born in China, came to Cambodia when he was young, to avoid the eight-year war against Japan. My mother's father came from China; my mother's mother was born in Cambodia. My wife's family is the same. We all speak Chiu Chow dialect of Cantonese, and in school we learned Mandarin. We also speak Cambodian and some Vietnamese. The Cambodian people contempted [*sic*] the Chinese because we were in business and had more money so we could hire good lawyers, and we always won in lawsuits.

I was born in a small town, and I had an older sister and two younger sisters. When my mother died, my father married again, and I have two stepsisters. My job was to bring water from the well, in two barrels hanging on a shoulder pole. Sometimes we had to take a bath in the river. We had a large kitchen and also a yard. We cooked in the yard, because of the sunlight, and so the smoke could escape easily. We burned coal; there was no gas or electric stove. This was our house in the country. When we lived in Pnom Penh, we had a kitchen.

I had to leave the village and go to Pnom Penh, the capitol, for middle school. I studied until 18 years old. My wife and I both attended school for nine years. My wife grew up in a city called Ji Jing in Chinese, Kla-Jeh in

Cambodian. In her house there was tap water. We attended the same Chinese high school in Pnom Penh, but we did not meet each other. We were introduced by a friend of my father, and when we liked each other, we could be engaged. Our generation is the first to have the choice.

After high school, I worked for someone for three years and saved enough money to go into business for myself. I sold watch parts that were imported from Hong Kong, sometimes by licensed importers and sometimes by smugglers. I traveled around the country and sold to dealers and repairers. I could keep up with inflation and support my family by working 10 days a month. My house in Pnom Penh was built of cement, like a box, with two levels. In the lower level, the front part is the shop. The middle is the regular living quarters, and the back is the kitchen. The upper level is for the children. The house is divided by plywood for rich people, and by cloth curtains for poor people. My house had plywood. The floor was tile, and the roof was red tile. The children were born in a hospital. A maid did the cooking and shopping. When the third boy was born, a nanny took care of him in her home.

Before 1970 was the Sihanouk government. Before 1970 there wasn't any riot or war, and we had a good life. I had three children and a wife; I only had to work 10 days a month, and we had enough. March 18, 1970, was the end of Sihanouk, and there was the Lon Nol government. We had more freedom, and we could still have our business. The prices went up every day, and some people could not pay the rent, but we had enough money. Then the Khmer Rouge came from the countryside and invaded Pnom Penh. At first, all the people thought peace was in sight. We welcomed them and cooked for them and celebrated. After they were full, they chased us out of the city. These people were not educated; they did not have shoes on their feet. When they saw the motorcycles, they got hold of them and drove around crazily and hurt people.

Then on April 17, 1975, they came in small groups, two or three of them, dressed in black, carrying guns. They knocked, door to door, and told us that U.S. airplanes were going to bomb the city, and everybody had to leave, just for 24 hours, and then we could come back. And they told us to leave right away, and if you refused, they would kill you. We believed them. The oldest boy was 10 years old, the second was seven, and the youngest was 17 months old. When I went to pick him up at the nanny's house, he cried, so she said to leave him with her. I thought it would just be for three days, so we left him, and then we didn't see him for four years. Not until the "second revolution"[1] when we were in Vietnam; we heard about him from my cousin. My cousin told me to come back and pick him up. We went back for him then.

When we were ready to leave Pnom Penh, my wife wanted to bring along some necessary things like toothbrushes. I told her not to; instead we took a lot of Cambodian paper money with us, but when we left the city, it was no good. People threw away the money on the road. With all the money you had you could not even buy an egg. In 1975, all the government, and hospitals, stopped. They chased us away from the capitol, and no one was left there. We drove our car at first, but on the first day we came to a bridge that was bombed, and we had to leave the car and walk. They wanted to kill anyone who worked for the government, or who had an education, and the Chinese people. If you came to a village, if they were friendly to Chinese, it was okay, but some of them killed every Chinese.

On the road we saw people who "dropped off" their mothers because there was not enough food to go around. Some people had to discard their own mother, because there was no food. There were people who thought with money you could buy anything. They starved to death because they could not get food. Especially the Chinese suffered, because most of them were businessmen, not very strong, and they did not know how to catch fish. They only had paper money, and it was useless, so they starved to death. We were fortunate; when we left Pnom Penh I put two bags of rice in the car. We had no salt; we could get some salt from the Khmer Rouge. After we threw away the car, we had some gold, and two bags of rice, and we carried it and gave it to Chinese on the way. We only carried a small bag with us. A lot of people died, and a lot of people killed themselves, and whole families killed themselves because they could not take it anymore. Along the road there were so many corpses. Even in the bright sun above our heads we had to walk. Sometimes we stopped to cook some lunch, and the Khmer Rouge came before the food was ready and chased us away. After 20 days, we came to a small town near my home town, and we had to mix with the Cambodians, and we couldn't go anywhere; even to go to the bathroom, they watched us. We couldn't go to my parents or even to look for our little child. We lived in the country town for nine months, in a shelter made of mud mixed with dry weeds. We had a mosquito net for a wall, and we lived with Cambodian people and had to eat the same kind of Cambodian food, like rotten fish, and rice and salt. I was very sick with a fever, but I had some gold, so I got some medicine.

I told the government I was a worker, because if I said I was a businessman, they would knock on the door and tell you to go to see someone, and then you disappeared. We never thought of killing ourselves because we had to find our other child, and we thought it would soon be over. I had to go into the jungle to collect leaves for buildings, and to cover the roofs. A lot of people died in the jungle, of fever; they just dropped dead, like flies, when they were working there. Our religion is tao, and we prayed.

After nine months, they said we could leave, and so we went to where my parents lived, seven or ten miles away. And they ordered us to build little houses in the jungle, and then they chased us out and made us live in those little houses. And they made the women work in fields like farmers. The children were put into groups. The old women took care of the little ones, and the children were separate, and the teenagers were separate, and couldn't live with the parents. We were called "new people," people from Pnom Penh. They disliked us most. We were sent for the worst jobs. During these three years and eight months I was gone for more than a year.

Once I was sent away for six months to build a dam, and my wife thought I had died. There was no postal service, and it was too far to have some friend pass some word to her. She thought I was dead. There were two million workers building the dam, and they worked from four or five o'clock in the morning until 11:30 A.M. Then they served us congee [*rice porridge*]. From noon we worked until 5:30 P.M. Then from 7 P.M. to 10 P.M. These six months we had only congee, very dilute congee. The ingredients of the congee was just several rice kernels. We had milk, ten cans of milk for 25 workers. We mostly drank water. Sometimes we ate wild berries. Sleeping accommodation was just an open space. At noon time we were sometimes so exhausted that we had to lie down, sun or rain, under a small mosquito net. We ate wild plants and roots that we could find, and we had to sleep on the ground. There was a lot of dead water and so many flies that if you tried to talk, they flew into your mouth. For instance, if you and I were talking at this moment, mosquitoes were flying into our mouths. But the project was a failure, because there were no engineers or technical personnel. When the flood came, all the construction was washed away because there was no engineering calculation. The dam was just a pile of dirt.

Even my father, 60 years old, was sent away to work, and young children, even little ones, had to carry the human and animal waste. We lived like this for two years; they called us "new people," and we were not in touch with our families. Then we moved to another small city. My parents were sent away to another town, and after a few months they said they were free to leave, so they went back to their town, but their house was gone. Then they came to a place near us, and after a few months, the army told us we had to leave that place because there was no food, so 10,000 people just lined up and left. My father carried a lot of things, and along the road he felt very tired, so he dropped out of the line and threw away some of the things and just put the gold and precious things in his pocket and went back into the line. His relative saw him leave the line and thought he had escaped, and he'd better escape, too, so he took his family and left the line. He went back to the town where my parents had their house that was destroyed, and somehow he finally escaped, and I met him here in the United States, and he told me that he knew that there were 10,000 people in that town who just disappeared, and afterward, they [*the government*] gave away their clothes, so they know they were all killed, so I know that my father and stepmother were killed, and my stepsisters. My older sister is now in Vietnam, and I don't know what happened to my two younger sisters.

My wife's parents were very lucky. The town where they stayed had a good leader, so there was enough food, and no one was killed. We weren't lucky, because we had to live with other people and couldn't cook our own food. We had to go and wait in line to get food that was already cooked. The place where we lived did not have enough food. Three cans of milk for 40 people, and the congee was very dilute. We often fed on potato leaves. Otherwise our stomachs were too hungry. We ate congee and salt for 27 days each month. We had wild vegetables for three days. We were not allowed to cook ourselves. Meals were served by the government. They rang the bell at mealtimes. We took our bowls to the center for food.

In 1979, the Vietnamese invaded Cambodia, and the Cambodian government collapsed, and we moved in with my wife's parents, and it was a better time. We had gold and could get some food. And the Cambodians saw us and were jealous, and that's when we decided to leave Cambodia. After the government changed, security wasn't so tight, so we left at midnight, and went to another small town, altogether 16 people, including my wife's parents, her brother and sister, and my wife and I and our two sons. We used our gold and bought a cart and oxen and buffalo, and left for Vietnam. At the border we threw away everything but gold, and split into groups. I was lucky because I could speak some Vietnamese words, and I gave some gold to the guard and said if you take me to Saigon, I'll give you more gold, so I could cross the border.

My wife wasn't lucky. She had 60 ounces of gold, and the Vietnamese soldier found my wife's gold and took it away and put her and our two sons in jail for 56 days, and then they were sent back to Cambodia and had to live in the jungle again. So it was a really bad time, and with no gold, she went from door to door to beg for food to feed the two sons. She moved from place to place and finally came to the Vietnamese border and told someone, and when I got the news, I used some gold to pay somebody to bring her and the boys to Saigon.

When we left Pnom Penh, I had almost one hundred ounces of gold, and diamonds and other precious things. In Saigon, we could buy a house with three ounces of gold, and more than 10 people lived there. We had friends, and thus we managed to have a living within a short time. I had a business to make bicycle tires, and my wife hired teachers for the children. But it wasn't very peaceful in Vietnam. The Vietnamese government wanted all the Cambodian refugees to stay together in one place. But they would come for them in the night, so we didn't sleep at home. We also gave gold to the police, and we would sleep with Chinese people who had lived in Vietnam for a long time. Every night we would stay with other people in their house. At five or six o'clock when it was getting dark we left home and went to our Vietnamese friends' houses. We came back to our house at dawn. We did this every night. We found no peace.

At that moment, my cousin in Pnom Penh sent word to me about my son, and my wife went back to Pnom Penh to fetch him. She went by car from Saigon to the Cambodian border, and then she hired someone to row a small boat, a sampan, up the river to Pnom Penh. And when he saw her, the child didn't know her and didn't want to leave the nanny, so she had to take the nanny and the nanny's two children, and all of them left Cambodia and went back to Saigon. Probably the nanny was good to our son. We knew the whole family. They could have disposed of him. A lot of people got rid of their own parents and children because there wasn't enough food. He was fortunate. He was protected all those years. They never told the boy the truth; he thought he was the nanny's son. One month after their safe return, we formed three groups and were ready to leave Vietnam. There were 16 of us.

Then when we decided to escape again, we had to go through Cambodia to get to Thailand. We could do this because we spoke the language. We took a car to the border and then went to Pnom Penh by boat. We stayed there for 20 days and said we were just visiting friends. We had to pay seven ounces of gold per person to get a guide to go to the Thai border. It's about three hundred miles, and first we hid in a truck with bags of salt. Then we paid for someone to take us on bicycles for a long way. At the border, it was dark, and also there is a big river, and Cambodian troops detained us until we paid them more gold so we could escape. The river was 15 miles across, and deep, up to my chest. I carried the littlest boy on my shoulder. I didn't have shoes, so the skin came off my feet, and they were bleeding. We couldn't cross in a group, just as single persons, and halfway we were caught by Lao people who are fighting the government; they had lipstick on their face and ornaments all over their bodies. They are robbers who attack women and kill men. They were going to shoot our son, and we could not say that he was our son, or they would shoot us, too. And if they knew we are a family, they would know that we were trying to escape from Cambodia. So my wife just said to him, "I know this boy very well, and I know that he is good." And we gave them some more gold, and they let him go. The gold was rolled in small rolls, and we hid it in our body [*in the rectum or vagina*]. We said that we wanted to go to this area to find a new life, not to cross to Thailand.

And our second son was separated from us, and when we got to the border, we couldn't find him. And many Vietnamese people, because they couldn't speak Cambodian, were raped and killed, but we were lucky because we told those people that we were all from the same place, and it is no good to hurt each other. So we lived. And my wife told the policeman to broadcast if any strange children, to come to the police station, and she will pay one ounce of gold for her child. And he was just about to broadcast, and she saw her son, and that's how she found him. And they kept us overnight in that police station, and they raped the Vietnamese women, and some of them they killed.

And this was because they could go to the Red Cross and ask for six bags of rice for each person, each head. So that's why they kept us for the night. And we were lucky because we could speak Cambodian, and then at the Red Cross, we could speak Vietnamese, and so they let us leave Cambodia and go to the refugee camp in Thailand because only Vietnamese could leave Cambodia, so we could cross the border to Thailand.

My cousin wasn't lucky. He wanted to leave with us, but the guide cut us off because too many people, so the guide would come back for the second trip, so he got on the second trip, only 10 days apart, but now he is still in Thailand. The reason is, he didn't speak Vietnamese language, so he had to go through a lot of trouble, and then he got into a Red Cross who took Cambodian refugees, and now he is still in Thailand.

In Thailand, we moved around in four camps. Everybody had to do this. We were there for six months. Then we were in the Philippines for six months. We were very lucky. My older sister wasn't that lucky. Her family came along with us to Vietnam, but they were rounded up the first night that they were in Saigon. And her husband died in the detention camp, and now they are still in the Vietnamese detention camp.

My wife's brother lives in Michigan, and he sponsored us. We went to Michigan first. Her father lives here, in Oakland. We live about half an hour away by foot, not too far. We were lucky; we had a lot of gold. A lot of people just starved to death. Some people, if you made friends with some Cambodians, then they would protect you and look after you a little and share their food with you. And some people actually ate their own children, and they would take the internal organs out and use them for food. It was very hard to buy shoes.

We are really thinking of the good for the children; they can have a better education here. For us it's much harder, because we don't have the language. And also, because we were in business, we don't have any skill to find a job. I could survive in South Asia because I can talk all the languages there, but now in the United States I don't have the language. We are still not at peace; our mind is not at peace yet, because if one day the government support is taken away, we just cannot know how we can survive. And we do worry about this recording, and want to be sure that our names and addresses aren't disclosed, because there could be Cambodian Reds around here.

7

THE LAND OF THE FREE

They came with such high hopes. They found a land of abundance, and so they planted vegetables in the median strip, in vacant lots, in the parking strip in front of the house. They put out snares for the pigeons and squirrels in the park. They went to the waterfront and cast out a net or a line. In the park they found newly sprouted mushrooms that they harvested for a stir-fry dinner. They opened a restaurant in the living room so friends could drop by and have a bowl of noodles, and in the kitchen they set up a beauty parlor/barber shop to offer haircuts and manicures. Why, if this is the land of freedom, should they need to buy licenses and permits? To their surprise, they are hassled by the police, shunned by the neighbors, even arrested; in the case of the mushrooms, they go to the hospital and die.

They come to class flushed and exhilarated, with letters proclaiming in bold type: "Congratulations! You can win three million dollars!!!" They could not understand the message in fine print.

Before her surgery, Kai meets with the gentle and compassionate doctor who lists all the possible bad outcomes: paralysis, choking, loss of sight, incontinence. She probably knows the conditional words "might" and "may" and "could," but she is terribly frightened. In the end, none of these things happen, and she was alarmed for nothing.

The young man says that in Vietnam he was a "businessman"; each morning he bought a pack of cigarettes, and during the day he sold them singly, earning enough to survive. Sometimes he also sold bicycle parts. He expects to be equally enterprising here, selling the occasional hubcap found in a gutter, or reselling candy bars or cigarettes. He learns that he has to have a license, a registered place of business, and pay taxes on his profits. His sister, who survived in Vietnam by selling "something like cookies" in the street, cannot do that here without inspection, registration, and license. The "freedom land" for which they risked so much is not entirely free.

The dream can become a nightmare. Dr. Ma was an ear, nose, throat doctor in northern China; his wife was trained in acupuncture, a traditional Chinese medical procedure. During the Cultural Revolution, they were forced to work as peasants in "the countryside" and were separated for years while their two young sons were taken care of by someone else. In 1976, he was drafted to work again as a doctor after the disastrous Tangshan earthquake, when it is estimated that nearly a million people were killed. It was another traumatic experience for him. Now in Oakland, Dr. Ma works nights as a hospital orderly. The older son enrolled at the university and was an honor student in the pre-medicine course, working evenings at a filling station by the freeway. One Saturday night, evidently he resisted a robbery. The killer probably drove off the freeway, shot and killed the boy, stole 35 dollars from the cash register, and sped off again. There were no witnesses, and there is no prosecution, no possible recompense. The bereaved parents continue to attend English class, to place their hopes on a better life for their younger son.

CHAPTER NOTES

Foreword

1. Following the Boxer Rebellion, 1898–1901, the Qing Empire was fined war reparations. The Theodore Roosevelt administration used the Boxer indemnity funds to create a scholarship program for Chinese students to study in the U.S. that has been called "the most important scheme for educating Chinese students in America and arguably the most consequential and successful in the entire foreign-study movement of twentieth century China" (Wikipedia).

Preface

1. The Qing Dynasty ruled China from 1644 until an uprising in Wuchang on 10 October 1911 led to establishment of the Republic of China.

2. From *The Christian Science Monitor*, January 3, 1983, an article by Sara Terry, staff correspondent, Los Angeles, "The Changing Face of California." "The United States is experiencing a wave of immigration described by demographers as one of the largest and most significant in the country's history. And California is riding its crest.... During the last decade, according to the 1980 census ... Asians increased ... to make up approximately six percent of Californians.... We must now think of California as a border for the Pacific-Asia region."

3. On 7 May 1954 the French garrison at Dien Bien Phu fell to the forces of Ho Chi Minh, ending French colonialism in Indochina. The Geneva Accord later that year mandated the partition of Vietnam into Communist north and non–Communist south, pending national elections scheduled for 1956. They never took place, leading after 1959 to hostilities known as the second Indochinese War. An estimated 900,000 refugees fled from north to south Vietnam.

Chapter 1

I Come from China by Swimming

1. During the first years of the People's Republic of China, everyone was required to wear a blue cotton uniform.

2. Traditional Chinese writing, or calligraphy, is done with a brush, and the rules for holding the brush were very strict; these men had obviously been privileged and classically educated. Younger men, and women generally, did not have this training.

To Take Care the Old Man

3. Confucius (Kung Fu Tzu) was born on September 28, in 551 B.C. in what is now Shandong Province, China. Confucius's family, the Kongs, has the longest recorded still extant pedigree in the world today. The father-to-son family tree, now in its 83rd generation, has been recorded since the death of Confucius. According to the Confucius Genealogy Compilation Committee, he has two million known and registered descendants, and there are an estimated three million in all. Of these, several tens of thousands live outside of China. His teachings emphasized the need to respect superiors and elders, and the concept that "what you do not wish for yourself, do not do to others" (Wikipedia).

4. An economic and social plan that resulted in a famine and possibly more than 20 million deaths (Wikipedia).

5. The Communist party tried to do away with religion, calling it "superstition." Traditional Buddhism uses writing on paper as aids to prayer, and customary rituals use paper money, translated as "spirit money." Attempts to outlaw these long-standing customs were not always successful.

6. On 1 October 1949, referred to as the "liberation," the [Communist] People's Republic of China [PRC] was established. The government of the Republic of China [ROC] then moved to the island of Taiwan.

I Am a Person

7. These are the marks of a well-educated man, at a time when the vast majority was illiterate.

8. Lee Chung says that the village of Lung Du has 40,000 inhabitants. This may be an overestimate.

9. The Chinese generally don't consider "native intelligence" as important as effort; if a student works hard enough, he will get good grades.

10. It was unusual for a woman to be literate. The books he reads are the established canon of classic education, analogous to Shakespeare and Chaucer in English, another indication of high status.

11. This was the period when great numbers of young people called "Red Guards," wearing red armbands and waving little red books of quotations from Chairman Mao, were given free railway passes and roamed the country.

12. He learned the alphabet, as opposed to Chinese characters.

13. Richard was technically a refugee, not an immigrant. Richard's immigration status progressed from a refugee with a white card to a resident immigrant with a green card, and then a naturalized U.S. citizen, able to sponsor his siblings and mother as immigrants. His godfather, like many others from the Guangdong area, came to the United States during the Chinese exclusion period when immigration from China

was restricted to merchants, diplomats, ministers, students, tourists, and those claiming derivative U.S. citizenship. He returned once to visit his home village, establishing the relationship that later supported Richard. The obligations were reciprocal: to help the newcomer to become established, and in turn to care for the godfather in his old age. It is not unusual for such a "sojourner" father to have children born five or ten years apart, according to his visits home. It is necessary to have a son to take care of you in your old age; hence the custom of giving a male infant to someone who has no sons.

14. The main ethnic groups of southern China.

Seldom Flower

15. The second wife is a topic to approach gingerly; in some levels and at some periods in Asian society, a prosperous man would of course have more than one wife. The contemporary Asian refugees are sensitive on this point; they know that Americans feel varying degrees of dismay or disapproval at the idea. Ruth's mother warned her of the misery of the second wife. The Vietnamese captain (pages 58–60) protects his half sister, the child of his father's other liaison, and takes responsibility for her son. Luu (pages 151–152) seems to feel that her "half-mothers" are interchangeable. Phuong (page 156) may not be the only wife, although she never explicitly says so.

16. Chinese families traditionally maintain ties to an ancestral village, especially for birth and burial.

17. The Opium Wars, also known as the Anglo-Chinese Wars, were the climax of trade disputes and diplomatic difficulties between China under the Qing Dynasty and the British Empire after China sought to restrict British opium traffickers. It consisted of the First Opium War from 1839 to 1842 and the Second Opium War from 1856 to 1860. Open warfare between Britain and China broke out in 1839. Further disputes over the treatment of British merchants in Chinese ports resulted in the Second Opium War. China was defeated in both wars, leaving its government having to tolerate the opium trade. Britain forced the Chinese government into signing the Treaty of Nanking and the Treaty of Tianjin, also known as the Unequal Treaties, which included provisions for the opening of additional ports to unrestricted foreign trade, for fixed tariffs; for the recognition of both countries as equal in correspondence; and for the cession of Hong Kong to Britain (Wikipedia).

18. Whampoa Military Academy was established in 1924 as the "Chinese West Point."

19. Hong Kong fell to the Japanese forces on 25 December 1941 after 18 days of fierce fighting.

I Don't Mind Hard If I'm Happy

20. Teachers are not supposed to receive gifts, but it was impossible to obey this injunction. Gifts, refused in the classroom, were handed to us in the street, left on the hood of our parked car, or brought to our home.

Double Glory

21. One of Mao Zedong's early poems, "Yellow Crane Tower," tells of Wuhan's two mountains, Tortoise and Snake, now linked by a famous bridge. *Mao Tse-Tung Poems*, p. 3.

Chapter 2

1. Stanley Karnow, *Vietnam, History*, pp. 110–111: "Though national personality is difficult to define, two important elements formed Vietnam's character.... Rice cultivation ... requires cooperative labor. Vietnamese communities thus developed a strong collective spirit.... Their country's frequent wars also infused in the Vietnamese a readiness to defend themselves.... Their commitment to nationhood had been forged long before."

Chapter 3

1. British Broadcasting Company dispatch, 30 April 1975 [1 May in the U.S.] "The capitulation of the South Vietnamese government came just four hours after the last frenzied evacuation of Americans from the city. President Ford ... ordered United States ships to remain indefinitely off the Vietnamese coast to pick up refugees."

The Man Who Escaped Twice

2. The "white market" is an officially tolerated free enterprise system of sidewalk stalls, where one can purchase everything from Japanese TV sets to American toothpaste. Mr. D. said that his family had asked him not to send packages anymore because it made it hard for them. Perhaps receiving a package from abroad makes them vulnerable to other pressures.

From the *Christian Science Monitor* of Thursday, April 21, 1983, an article called "Ho Chih Minh City," by Edward Girardet, special correspondent of the CSM, writing from Ho Chih Minh City, Vietnam:

> At present, two important mainstays of the Vietnamese economy are the "care" packages — some 500,000 arrived in 1982 — and hard currency transfers from relatives living in the United States, France, and other third asylum countries. For many southerners, the monthly packages, which contain anything from nylon stockings to bicycles that can be sold at high prices on the "white market," have become a principal means of survival.... The recipient [of a parcel from abroad] knows that he can probably sell the goods, particularly the medicines, on the white market, for as much as ten times their worth.

Miss Tran

3. The refugees from Vietnam commonly brought their wealth in the form of diamonds or gold, thin rectangular wafers about three inches by two inches, in a wallet, sewn into clothing, or in extreme cases, molded into suppositories and hidden in rectum or vagina.

Wartime Bride

4. Tet offensive, January 1968 — Stanley Karnow, *Vietnam*, pp. 536–37: "The Communists struck at seaside enclaves.... They displayed unprecedented brutality, slaughtering minor government functionaries and other innocuous figures as well as harmless foreign doctors, schoolteachers and missionaries. Nowhere was the battle fiercer than in Hue, which Communist units held for twenty-five days, committing ghastly atrocities."

A Tale of Two Keys

5. Mr. Tran speaks of observing the anniversary of the parents' death. He uses the word "celebrate," just as some Americans call a memorial service a "celebration of life." In Mr. Tran's tradition, a photograph of the parent is placed on the home altar, together with round fruits, such as oranges, to symbolize the continuity of being. The lack of a photograph is keenly felt; many refugees feel guilty now because they cannot properly observe a parent's death.

6. "According to the Geneva agreement, the movement of civilians between the North and South was scheduled to cease on 19 May 1955.... Since the preceding August, 74 United States Navy and 39 MSTS ships had evacuated 310,848 passengers from North Vietnam, all but 17,846 of them civilians.... In combination with the effective ten-month operations of the French, about 800,000 people had been carried to freedom." Hooper et al., p. 298

Chapter 4

I Don't Think Our Generation
Would Belong Anywhere

1. Dzung helped with translation of "My Master's Robe," published by Parallax Press, 2002.

2. The Vietnamese "national poem" is the epic story of a young woman who triumphs over many vicissitudes.This is how it ends: *The Song of Kieu, Epilogue [XXV]*

> This we have learned: with Heaven rest all things;
> Heaven appoints each human to a place.
> If doomed to roll in dust, we'll roll in dust;
> We'll sit on high when destined for high seats.
> Does Heaven ever favor anyone,
> Bestowing both rare talent and good luck?
> In talent take no overweening pride,
> For talent and disaster form a pair.
> Our karma we must carry as our lot —
> Let's stop decrying Heaven's whims and quirks.
> Inside ourselves there lies the root of good:
> The heart outweighs all talents on this earth.
> — Nguyen Du, *The Tale of Kieu*, translated by Huynh Sanh Thong

From "*A Manual for Indochinese Refugee Education, 1976–1977,*" prepared by the staff of The National Indochinese Clearinghouse, Center for Applied Linguistics, for Department of Health, Education, and Welfare, United States Repatriate and Refugee

Assistance Staff, p. 117: "*Kim can Kieu*, the long poem which is the recognized centerpiece of Vietnamese literature and which is said by experts on Vietnamese literature to portray the very soul of the Vietnamese people, is, in fact, the story of a beautiful young woman, buffeted by the vicissitudes of life, lamenting her hapless fate ... feeling sorry for oneself, indulging in self-pity, moping in one form or another — something most Americans are inclined to resist — is frequently given in to by the Vietnamese. 'Tui phan' or 'lamenting one's fate' is the term they have for it."

(Author's note: I feel that these narrators, far from "moping," have expressed a calm acceptance of one's fate without self-pity.)

Now, Anywhere Is My Country

3. He learned the "Roman" alphabet, as opposed to the Chinese characters.

4. "In April [1955], USNS *Marine Adder* (AP-193) and *Marine Serpent* (AP-202) sailed on an eight-day cycle." Hooper et al., p. 298

5. From BBC News, 21 April 1975, "The President of South Vietnam has been forced to resign.... In a TV and radio address, outgoing President Nguyen Van Thieu said his forces had failed to stop the advance of the Vietcong."

6. A tael is a unit of weight used in Asia, usually about 38 grams.

7. Robert Strange McNamara served as Secretary of Defense under Presidents Kennedy and Johnson, from 1961 to 1968. Several books were written about him and the Vietnam War. In 1995, he published with co-author Brian VanDeMark *In Retrospect: The Tragedy and Lessons of Vietnam*.

I Don't Want to See Sad Again

8. "Sewing factory," "sweat shop," "piece work": these terms have pejorative connotations; "flex-time," "on-site child care," and "merit pay" are more acceptable words for the same practices that mutually benefit workers and employers. The sewing factories in Chinatown are crowded, but for the Chinese that is not a bad thing. My students are puzzled that Americans like to eat in a quiet restaurant; they expect a good one to be popular, and hence noisy and crowded. Possibly they are more likely to feel uneasy working in a cubicle than in the sewing factory, and working indoors, sheltered from the weather and operating an electric-powered machine, is not a pitiable condition, compared to working in a rice field. The workers come to the factory when possible and are not penalized for leaving to go to school or to another job. Most of the factories provide at least steamed rice and vegetables for lunch. As I walk to school on a garbage collection day, I observe many oil, soy sauce, and pickled vegetable containers in the trash piles outside the sewing factories, evidence that a good deal of cooking and eating goes on in the factory. I filch some of the brown ceramic ones to use as flower holders. "Piece work" as a system of payment provides a safety net that is both productive and not demeaning. A fast worker earns more, and the slow worker still earns something. For those who have a machine at home, sometimes provided by the factory owner, sewing at home, paid by the piece, is an important source of extra income. Men, women, and children cooperate, working in minutes or hours as they can. The social role of the sewing factory is important. Mothers can bring infants until they are toddlers. Information is exchanged: a sale on children's shoes at Sears,

a shipment of star fruit at Tin's market, the questions asked on the citizenship test, how to get a driver's license, and, no doubt, a realistic evaluation of the ESL teachers at the Chinese Community Center.

Chapter 5

You Can Go Anywhere, You Can Speak Any Word

1. Perhaps Palau Bidong refugee camp.

Luu Gets a Job

2. The mooncake, three or four inches in diameter, encloses a hard-boiled egg yolk so that a slice shows a golden circle like a full moon.

Grandma, We Listen to You

3. Felix Rohatyn, who was born in Austria, whose family fled from the Holocaust, and who eventually rose to become a top financier in New York and U.S. Ambassador to France, is quoted (*New Yorker* magazine, January 24, 1983): "A theory of wealth which is that of a refugee. The only things that count, basically, are things you can put in a toothpaste tube or carry in your head."

We Have to Love Each Other

4. This dialect of Chinese is not useful here; the Cantonese [Guangzhou] dialect is more commonly spoken.

5. Some of her employers compensated in other ways, by paying for plane fare to Vietnam more than once, and by giving her free legal and financial advice.

6. The math doesn't add up here, but the narrative is exactly as Be Thi related the story.

Just His Two Hands

7. From the website http://www.moonfestival.org/ of the San Francisco Chinatown Merchants Association: Celebrated in Asia for more than 1,000 years, the Moon Festival marks a time to reflect upon the bounty of the summer harvest, the fullness of the moon, and the myth of the moon Goddess, Chang O (or Chang E). The Moon Festival is a distinctly and authentically Asian holiday, which has been likened to a sort of "Chinese Thanksgiving." It is among the most popular holidays in Asia, ranking alongside the celebration of the lunar New Year in cultural significance.

From *Wikipedia*: The Mid-Autumn Festival, also known as the Moon Festival ... is a popular harvest festival celebrated by Chinese and Vietnamese people, dating back over 3,000 years ... also sometimes referred to as the Lantern Festival or Mooncake Festival. The Mid-Autumn Festival is held on the 15th day of the eighth month in the Chinese calendar, which is in September or early October in the Gregorian calendar. It is a date that parallels the autumnal equinox of the solar calendar, when the moon is at its fullest and roundest. The traditional food of this festival is the mooncake, of which there are many different varieties.

8. According to Chinese custom, the sister should live with her husband's family; in this case, because she was the only daughter in a small family, an exception was made, and she could remain in her parents' home.

9. From a report to the Subcommittee on Immigration, Refugees, and International Law; Committee on the Judiciary, House of Representatives, April 11, 1990:

The Orderly Departure Program (ODP) was established under a 1979 Memorandum of Understanding between the United Nations High Commissioner for Refugees and the government of Vietnam to provide a safe and legal means for people to leave Vietnam rather than clandestinely by boat. The agreement provides for the departure of immigrants and refugees for family reunion and humanitarian reasons. In addition to serving as an orderly, predictable means for those wishing to depart the country, it also serves to relieve the flow of refugees into first asylum countries and to save the Vietnamese government the embarrassment of the uncontrolled illegal exodus of thousands of its citizens.

Chapter 6

Our Mind Is Not at Peace

1. On 7 January 1979, the Vietnamese captured the city of Pnom Penh, and the dictator Pol Pot was deposed. During this brief lull, some Cambodians went back to retrieve possessions or, like this narrator, to rescue family members. It is generally accepted that 50 percent of the estimated 425,000 Chinese living in Cambodia in 1975 perished under Pol Pot's regime.

The Khmer Rouge exterminated as many as two million Cambodians — a quarter of the population. Most, herded into forced marches to slave-labor projects, perished from famine and disease, mistreatment and exhaustion, and the atrocities included cases of cannibalism. Thousands, branded parasitical intellectuals merely because they spoke a foreign language or wore spectacles, were systematically liquidated.... The Vietnamese invaded Cambodia in late 1978, drove the Khmer Rouge out of Phnompenh, created a surrogate regime and halted the genocide (from Stanley Karnow, *Vietnam, A History*, pp. 57–58).

BIBLIOGRAPHY

Of the many relevant books available,
these are some I found most helpful.— E.H.S.

Bauer, Wolfgang, and Herbert Franke, eds. *The Golden Casket*. London: Allen & Unwin, 1965.

Bloodworth, Dennis. *Chinese Looking Glass*. New York: Farrar, Straus and Giroux, 1967.

Buttinger, Joseph. *The Smaller Dragon, a Political History of Viet Nam*. New York: Praeger, 1958.

Cargill, Mary Terrell, and Jade Quang Huynh. *Voices of Vietnamese Boat People*. Jefferson, NC: McFarland, 2000.

Chang, Iris. *The Chinese in America: A Narrative History*. New York: Viking Penguin, 2003.

Chinese America, History & Perspectives, published annually from 1987. The Journal of the Chinese Historical Society of America.

Dinh, Linh. *Night, Again: Contemporary Fiction from Vietnam*. New York: Seven Stories Press, 1996.

Du, Nguyen. *The Tale of Kieu*. Translated by Huynh Sanh Thong. New York: Random House, 1973.

Elegant, Robert. *The Center of the World*. New York: Funk & Wagnalls, 1968.

Fadiman, Ann. *The Spirit Catches You and You Fall Down*. New York: Farrar, Straus and Giroux, 1997.

Fitzgerald, Frances. *Fire in the Lake: The Vietnamese and the Americans in Vietnam*. Boston: Little, Brown, 1972.

Freeman, James. *Hearts of Sorrow*. Stanford: Stanford University Press, 1989.

Hanh, Thich Nhat. *Being Peace*. Berkeley, CA: Parallax Press, 1987.

_____. *The Miracle of Mindfulness*. Boston: Beacon Press, 1990.

_____. *My Master's Robe*. Berkeley, CA: Parallax Press, 2002.

_____. *Peace Is Every Step*. New York: Bantam Books, 1991.

_____. *Present Moment, Wonderful Moment*. Berkeley, CA: Parallax Press, 1990.

Hooper, Edwin Bickford, Dean C. Allard, and Oscar P. Fitzgerald. *The United States Navy and the Vietnam Conflict, Volume 1, The Setting of the Stage to 1959*. Naval History Division, Department of the Navy, Washington, D.C., 1976.

Karnow, Stanley. *Vietnam, a History*. New York: Viking Press, 1983.

Kristof, Nicholas, and Sheryl WuDunn. *Thunder from the East*. New York: Knopf, 2000.

Lam, Andrew. *Perfume Dreams.* Berkeley, CA: Heyday Books, 2005.

Langguth, A.J. *Our Vietnam: The War, 1954–1975.* New York: Simon & Schuster, 2000.

Latourette, Kenneth Scott. *A History of Modern China.* London: Penguin Books, 1954.

McCunn, Ruthanne Lum. *God of Luck.* New York: Soho Press, 2007.

_____. *Sole Survivor.* San Francisco, CA: Design Enterprises of S.F., 1985.

Myrdal, Jan. *Report from a Chinese Village.* New York: Pantheon Books, 1965.

New York Times. *Report from Red China.* New York: Avon Books, 1972.

Parkinson, C. Northcote. *East and West.* Boston: Houghton Mifflin, 1963.

Pham, Andrew X. *Catfish and Mandala.* New York: Farrar, Straus and Giroux, 2000.

Rutledge, Paul James. *The Vietnamese Experience in America.* Bloomington: Indiana University Press, 1992.

Schurmann, Franz, and Orville Schell, eds. *China Readings 2: Republican China.* Harmondsworth: Pelican, 1968.

Sidel, Ruth. *Families of Fengsheng.* Middlesex, England: Penguin Books, 1974.

Snepp, Frank. *Decent Interval.* New York: Random House, 1977.

Snow, Edgar. *The Long Revolution.* New York: Random House, 1972.

Spence, Jonathan D. *The Death of Woman Wang.* New York: Viking Press, 1978.

_____. *The Gate of Heavenly Peace.* New York: Viking Press, 1981.

_____. *The Search for Modern China.* New York: W.W. Norton, 1990.

Takaki, Ronald. *Strangers from a Different Shore: A History of Asian Americans.* Boston: Little, Brown, 1989.

Tenhula, John. *Voices from Southeast Asia: The Refugee Experience in the United States.* New York: Holmes & Meier, 1991.

Trigg, Louisa Hagner. *The Real Dragon.* Santa Barbara, CA: Fithian Press, 2001.

Wong, Jade Snow. *Fifth Chinese Daughter.* New York: Harper, 1950.

Yang, C.K. *Chinese Communist Society: The Family and the Village.* Cambridge, MA: M.I.T. Press, 1959.

Yung, Judy. *Unbound Feet: A Social History of Chinese Women in San Francisco.* Berkeley: University of California Press, 1995.

_____. *Unbound Voices: A Documentary History of Chinese Women in San Francisco.* Berkeley: University of California Press, 1999.

INDEX